TEACHING AND LEARNING ARGUMENT

Also available from Cassell:

James Britton: *Literature in its Place*
Cedric Cullingford: *The Nature of Learning*
Donald Gallo: *Authors' Insights: Turning Teenagers into Readers and Writers*
Linda Hall: *Poetry for Light*
Julie Jensen: *Stories to Grow On: Demonstrations of Language Learning*
John Osmond: *The Reality of Dyslexia*
Andrew Stables: *An Approach to English*
Judith Schwartz: *Encouraging Early Literacy*
Rosemary Stevenson & Joy Palmer: *Learning: Principles, Processes and Practices*
Morag Styles, Eve Bearne & Victor Watson: *After Alice*
Sarah Tann: *Developing Language in the Primary Classroom*
Stephen Tchudi & Susan Tchudi: *The English-Language Arts Handbook*
Constance Weaver: *Understanding Whole Language*

Teaching and Learning Argument

Richard Andrews

CASSELL

Cassell
Wellington House
125 Strand
London WC2R 0BB

387 Park Avenue South
New York
NY 10016–8810

British Library Cataloguing-in-Publication Data
A catalogue record for this book is available from the British Library

Library of Congress Cataloging-in-Publication Data
Andrews, Richard. 1953–
    Teaching and Learning Argument/Richard Andrews
        p.   cm. – (Cassell education)
    Includes index.
    ISBN 0-304-33279-8 (hardback). – ISBN 0-304-33281-X (pbk.)
    1. English language – Rhetoric – Study and teaching. 2. Persuasion (Rhetoric) – Study and teaching. I. Title. II. Series.
PE1404.A53   1995
808.53 – dc20

94-41443
CIP

ISBN 0-304-33279-8 (hardback)
       0-304-33281-X (paperback)

Typeset by Action Typesetting Limited, Gloucester
Printed and bound in Great Britain by Redwood Books, Trowbridge, Wiltshire

Contents

For
John Ferris

Actions regulated by norms, expressive self-presentations, and also evaluative expressions, supplement constative speech acts in constituting a communicative practice which, against the background of a lifeworld [are] oriented to achieving, sustaining and renewing consensus – and indeed a consensus that rests on the intersubjective recognition of criticizable validity claims. The rationality inherent in this practice is seen in the fact that a communicatively achieved agreement must be based *in the end* on reasons . . . . Thus the rationality proper to the communicative practice of everyday life points to the practice of argumentation as a court of appeal that makes it possible to continue communicative action with other means when disagreements can no longer be repaired with everyday routines and yet are not to be settled by the direct or strategic use of force. For this reason I believe that the concept or communicative rationality . . . can be adequately explicated only in terms of a theory of argumentation.

(Habermas, *The Theory of Communicative Action*)

In virtue of their criticizability, rational expressions also admit of improvement; we can correct failed attempts if we can successfully identify our mistakes . . . . Argumentation plays an important role in learning processes as well. Thus we call a person rational who, in the cognitive-instrumental sphere, expresses reasonable opinions and acts efficiently; but this rationality remains accidental if it is not coupled with the ability to learn from mistakes, from the refutation of hypotheses and from the failure of interventions.

(ibid.)

Acknowledgements

A book on argument cannot be the product of a single voice: by definition, it is the result of a concert of voices. I wish to acknowledge these voices, as they play an important role in the making of the book and in the forming of my own voice(s) on the subject.

My first debt is to those colleagues with whom I have worked on questions of argument over the last five or six years: Patrick Costello, whose knowledge of the field of critical thinking and grounding in primary school practice have opened up a new dimension of argument to me; Stephen Clarke, whose longstanding support and friendship, coupled with critical integrity and energy, have been a constant source of inspiration; and especially Sally Mitchell, with whom I worked closely on the Leverhulme research project on argument between 1991 and 1994. Her contribution to this book is enormous, both in material that she has provided, and in the unassuming intellectual clarity and grace with which she has approached research and collaboration.

A wider circle of colleagues and friends has also contributed to the thinking behind the book: these include Robert Protherough, Judith Atkinson and other members of the Leverhulme project steering committee not already mentioned – Jerry Booth, Patsy Stoneman, Martin Brooks, Alan McClelland and Paul Drew. Peter Medway and Aviva Freedman in Ottawa have been models to try to emulate as well as generous with their friendship and criticism; Deborah Berrill, Mark Reid, George Myerson, Carol Fox, Howard Gibson, Tony Adams, Gunther Kress, Roslyn Arnold, Ian Reid, John Sinker, Ian Bentley, Keith Rose, Ilana Snyder, Ken Watson, Pam Gilbert, Claire Woods, Bob Shafer, David Homer, John Dixon, Janet White, Robert Fisher, Joan Moretti, Henry Hagins and others have contributed through sheer interest in the project.

I also wish to thank those teachers and students who have worked with me on the three projects that inform this book, and the postgraduate students whose questions and promptings have made me go back to my material and ideas and think again. In particular, I would like to mention Ruth Vincent, Nick McGuinn, Jean Hill and Lesley Tucker of Beverley High School; Barry Roger and Tony Marsh of Beverley Grammar School; and Lesley Hughes, David Hope, Steve Gardham and Brian Cox of Longcroft School, Beverley, for their help in conducting the initial doctoral study; and the Year 8 students at those schools in 1988–89, especially Philippe Close, Simon Cusworth, Katy

Steel and Emma Walters, whose insights into the practice of writing narrative and argument taught me a great deal and whose humour and intelligence was so engaging.

The teachers and students involved in the two major research projects are too numerous to mention, but each played a part in shaping the outcomes of the work on argument. Some are mentioned in the text of the book itself, and I am particularly grateful to Jan Sarjeant, Gloria Reid, John Adamson, Deborah Burnett, Pauline Foster, Pam Rose, Deborah Dalton, Margot McAlindon, Heather Grayson, Margaret Morris, Kevin Fitzsimmons, Jane Lodge, Alastair Michie, Lynda Dennett and Les Smith for permission to include accounts of their work. Spellings of children's work have been regularized throughout the book.

Over the seven years during which the thinking and practice behind this book have taken place, I have been supported by various funding bodies and wish to record my thanks to them for backing what must have seemed at the time a very dark horse: the English Schools Foundation and Island School in Hong Kong; the University of Hull Research Committee; the Standing Conference on Studies in Education; the Esmée Fairbairn Charitable Trust; and the Leverhulme Trust.

During the projects, work has appeared in a number of journals, and I gratefully acknowledge the following: *Language Matters, The Times Educational Supplement, English in Education, The English and Media Magazine, Educational Review,* the *Cambridge Journal of Education* (UK), *English Journal* (USA), *Typereader, Literacy Learning: Secondary Thoughts* and *English in Australia* (Australia).

Thanks are also due to Audrey Rusling for her tireless work in transcribing discussions arising from the research projects and her help in preparing the typescript of this book; to Mark Bobb; and also to Beth Humphries for her excellent copy-editing of the manuscript.

Finally I wish to acknowledge the debt I owe to Dodi Beardshaw who has helped me learn to see argument in a positive light, connected to feeling and working toward consensus and harmony.

All the shortcomings in the book are my own, and I hope that you, the reader, will use them − and any strong points you find − to build your own, better, arguments.

Richard Andrews
Beverley, England, 1994

Chapter 1

Problems

It was rare to find children presented with a task which involved presenting coherent argument, exploring alternative possibilities or drawing conclusions and making judgements. While it is recognized that this is a difficult form of writing for young children, it could have been more regularly encouraged among the older and more able pupils.

(DES, 1978, p. 49)

DEFINITIONS

Say the word 'argument' to most people − especially children − and they will assume you mean 'quarrel', 'row', 'tiff', 'spat' or some such exchange that involves a heated clash of usually opposed views. Indeed, the passion and feeling expressed in such exchanges are very much part of the subject of this book, in which one of my aims is to explore the common ground between the popular notions of argument and the more formal, academic connotations of the term, with a view to building bridges between the two. By building such bridges, I hope to make argument (in the formal sense as used in schools, colleges and universities) more accessible.

An example of an 'everyday' argument occurs in *Sons and Lovers* where Paul and Miriam are picking flowers in a field, with Clara 'a little way off...looking at the cowslips disconsolately'. Paul approaches Clara:

'Why don't you get some?'
'I don't believe in it. They look better growing.'
'But you'd like some?'
'They want to be left.'
'I don't believe they do.'
'I don't want the corpses of flowers about me,' she said.
'That's a stiff, artificial notion,' he said. 'They don't die any quicker in water than on their roots. And besides, they *look* nice in a bowl − they look jolly. And you only call a thing a corpse because it looks corpse-like.'
'Whether it is one or not?' she argued.

'It isn't one to me. A dead flower isn't a corpse of a flower.'
Clara now ignored him.
'And even so – what right have you to pull them?' she asked.
'Because I like them, and want them – and there's plenty of them.'
'And that is sufficient?'
'Yes. Why not? I'm sure they'd smell nice in your room in Nottingham.'
'And I should have the pleasure of watching them die.'
'But then – it does not matter if they do die.'
Whereupon he left her, and went stooping over the clumps of tangled flowers which thickly sprinkled the field like pale, luminous foam-clots.

(Lawrence, 1948, pp. 291–2)

Although this is an example of an everyday argument taken from literature rather than from 'life', it feels like an accurate account of how such real arguments develop.[1] First we can note that 'argument' in its more narrow sense is hardly what is happening here; a better term might be 'quarrel' or 'difference of opinion', though the brevity and typicality of the exchange suggests that the dialogue hardly constitutes a distinct speech genre. The characters are 'argumentative' in the sense of being tetchy with each other, and yet they also exhibit argumentative procedures in a more formal way. 'Why don't you get some?' isn't an invitation to argument unless it is spoken in an accusing, challenging way, but Clara's 'I don't believe in it' is an argumentative ploy in that she takes a position on the question. Paul's 'I don't believe they do [want to be left]' takes up the gauntlet. Clara restates her position, using emotive language to drive home her point: 'I don't want the *corpses* of flowers about me'. Paul counters with an attack on her notion, an assertion that flowers die as quickly on their roots as when cut, a positive assertion that 'they look jolly' anyway, and an accusation that her argument is based on narrow ground. Clara takes him up on the last point, and they quibble on the meaning of the word 'corpse'. After a pause, she tries a different tack: 'what right have you to pull them?' Paul answers with non-reasons – 'I like them, and want them' and then an answer that has nothing to do with 'rights': 'there's plenty of them'. Thereafter, they spar with statements whose intention is more to spite the other than to move on the argument.

What kind of argument is this? Its nature is more to do with scoring points than with the exploration of different positions. Development of individual points is minimal because the intention is to rebuff the other's statements. It gets nowhere, because both positions are entrenched: neither character accepts any of the other's points. There is strong emphasis on the verbal. The only way for it to end is in violence or for one of the characters to walk away, as Paul does at the end. And yet it shows many of the characteristics of argument in more formal situations.[2]

The term 'argument' is derived from the Latin *arguere* meaning 'to show, to make clear, to assert, to prove; to accuse, to blame'. In *that* definition, there seem to be three strands: argument as exposition (to show, to make clear); argument as part of a process of logic (to assert, to prove); and argument as part of a legal process or of dialogue (to accuse, to blame).

The Oxford English Dictionary (*OED*) has seven definitions:

(i)   proof, evidence;
(ii)   (in astronomy and mathematics) the angle, arc or other mathematical quantity from which another required quantity may be deduced, or on which its calculation depends;

(iii)   a statement or fact advanced for the purpose of influencing the mind; a reason urged in support of a proposition;

(iv)   a connected series of statements or reasons intended to establish a postition (and hence to refute the opposite); a process of reasoning; argumentation;

(v)   a statement of reason for and against a proposition; discussion of a question, debate;

(vi)   subject matter of discussion or discourse in speech or writing; theme, subject;

(vii)   the summary or abstract of the subject matter of a book; a syllabus; the contents.

Principal to our investigation are (i), (iii), (iv) and (v). Indeed, these might be seen collectively to describe the *process* of argument, or argumentation. It is *argumentation* − or the process, the *action* of the argument, the means to ends − that is the main focus of this book. 'Argumentation' is separately defined in the *OED* as:

(i)   the action or operation of inferring a conclusion from propositions premised; logical or formal reasoning;

(ii)   interchange of argument, discussion, debate;

(iii)   a sequence or chain of arguments; a process of reasoning.

We can see from a comparison of (iv) above with these definitions that the term 'argument' can be seen to embrace both the product and the process.

The three less central definitions of 'argument' are nevertheless worth considering for the light they shed upon the central meanings of the term. The second, 'the angle, arc or other mathematical quantity from which another required quantity may be deduced', if applied to written argument, suggests that it may proceed by a series of angles and directions rather than by a straightforward number of steps (a metaphor more suited to logic) or by the 'for-and-against' model. That is to say, any particular spoken or written argument could be described in terms of its 'angles': sometimes the argument will run obliquely to previous points, and at other times it will turn 180 degrees or proceed in a straight continuous line for a number of points. One of the metaphors that can be used to describe argumentation is based on angles, points, lines and measurement.

Definitions (vi) and (vii) noted above shed light from a different angle. These are concerned not so much with argument conceived as an arrangement of abstractions, but argument as a subject or theme on the one hand, and argument as list, syllabus or narrative on the other. An example of the latter is the argument that appears at the headings of chapters in eighteenth-century novels. This 'argument' is a summary of a narrative; indeed, a short narrative in itself. It highlights the connection between narrative and argument: one that several writers tried to explore more fully in *Narrative and Argument*,[3] and which I explore further in the present book.

Missing from the *OED* definitions is the more popular notion of what argument is − the definitions we opened this chapter with: a row, a dispute, a 'difference of opinion', a 'ding-dong', a fiery exchange expressed in the understated 'We had words'. Such arguments are driven not so much by reason but by passion and feeling − if it is possible to distinguish reason from feeling so clearly. A related definition to this one is indicated by the Scots phrase, an 'argy-bargy', meaning a bandying of argument or a tedious argument.

As far as a working definition for the book is concerned, argument can be taken to be *a process of argumentation, a connected series of statements intended to establish a position and implying response to another (or more than one) position,* sometimes taking the form of an actual exchange in discussion and debate, and usually presenting itself in speech and/or writing as a sequence or chain of reasoning.

ARGUMENT OR DISCUSSION?

What is the difference between argument and discussion? First, I would say that argument is a mode of discourse rather than a particular genre or form. As a term it sits alongside other broad categories of ways of communicating in speech or writing, like 'narrative', 'lyrical' and 'descriptive'.[4] These categories themselves are not mutually exclusive: a single piece of writing could contain elements of all four modes. Nor are they definitive: you could argue that 'dialogic' or 'dramatic' might take their place alongside 'argument-ative'. The truth is that these terms describe huge areas of types of discourse. Not only are they imprecise on a horizontal level, with much overlap between them; they also stand in uncertain relation to levels above and below them, like 'function' and 'genre'.[5]

Nevertheless, these terms are in use and it is best to try to define them. I have offered a working definition of 'argument' above. Some people feel that 'argument' is not the right term to describe a breadth of types of discourse which includes debate, the essay, advertisements, Socratic dialogues and other persuasive and/or dialogic communic-ations. They prefer the term 'discussion' because of its less adversarial associations, its openness to consensus, its exploratory nature. Interestingly, the term 'discuss' derives from the Latin *discutere* meaning to dash or shake to pieces, to disperse, dispel or drive away. These associations, as well as the sense of examining or investigating (its first recorded use in England in 1340 in this sense) are now obsolete, and the notion of breaking up or driving away is clearly no part of the present sense of what it means to 'discuss'. Nor, for that matter, is the way Chaucer uses it to mean 'to judge', 'to settle or decide', or Shakespeare to mean 'to make known'. We are clear that today 'discuss' means to investigate or examine by argument, to sift the considerations for and against, to debate in an informal way. Discussion, however, is more small-scale, more informal than argument. Most discussions are courteous explorations of issues; when they become acrimonious or polarized, they cease to be discussions and turn into disputes, arguments or rows. Discussion also tends to be limited to spoken exchanges, except in cases where – ritualistically – essay questions invite students to 'discuss' a proposition or question in writing. In that context, 'discuss' means to lay out the arguments and/or take a critical stance towards an issue.

Discussion, then, is not the right term to cover the range of interests in this book because 'discussion' is embraced by 'argument' rather than vice versa. 'Argument' is a term that can include everything from the tentative and mutual exploration of an idea in a harmonious fashion – by an individual, pair or group of people, in speech or writing – to formal debate or acrimonious row or fully-fledged written statements of a position. None of these last three examples of argument can be called 'discussion'.

The terms 'essay' and 'rhetoric' – both closely related to argument but one a specific written form and the other a field of discourse in itself – will be discussed elsewhere in the book: 'essay' in this chapter and in Chapter 6, and 'rhetoric' in Chapter 2 and in the final chapter.

THE PROBLEM(S)

There is little doubt that the learning and teaching of argument in schools is 'in need of research' (Beard, 1984, p. 113). Clarke (1984), Freedman and Pringle (1984), Gorman *et al.* (1988) and others have indicated as much. There is a fairly widespread feeling that students in secondary schools write and speak argument less well than they do other modes (like narrative or 'description'); and also a sense in primary schools that children can argue well at a much younger age than is usually assumed. The various problems with argument are laid out and discussed in the rest of this chapter, and include the difficulty of finding argumentative reading material, difficulties with abstract thinking, problems with models of cognitive development, and problems with structure.

LACK OF 'GIVEN' STRUCTURES

Problems with writing argument are posed by Gorman *et al.* (1988), who found that although the results of a large-scale survey in schools in England and Wales showed that 15-year-olds 'have commands of more types of discourse than the 11 year olds', it appears that 'neither age group is particularly confident in the uses of writing that have to do with the development of hypotheses, speculation or inquiry' (p. 7). In what may be a problem as much brought about by schools as inherent in the type of writing itself, researchers found that difficulty with writing is encountered when the structure is not 'given' − that is to say, when the structure has to be created to suit the subject matter to be communicated. One of the reasons for this difficulty is that argumentative writing often proceeds by set formulae which are not enjoyed by students and which cramp their expressiveness, or there is a struggle to find a 'structure' that will carry the argumentative message − as opposed to narrative where it is *assumed* (wrongly, I think) that the structure is provided by the content and/or is to be found ready-made in experience.

Furthermore, although students were found to have more practice in the writing of '"factual" accounts rather than in using writing as a means of questioning or speculating about a given state of affairs' (ibid., p. 14) − a finding that corroborates that of the earlier Schools Council study (Britton *et al.,* 1975) − students seemed unable to use any classificatory skills as a foundation to writing argument:

> Pupils proceeded to write their descriptions in an additive way rather than by logical selection, producing an unfocused listing of similarities and differences without benefit of an overview.
>
> (Gorman *et al.,* 1988, p. 132)

The perception of something lacking in the argumentative writing of schoolchildren is not new. A 1978 report on primary education in England had suggested that it was 'rare' to find children presented with a writing task which involved coherent argument (DES, 1978), but the perceived difficulties may not, as is often assumed, be cognitive. They may be as much to do with the way the task is presented to the students. The Assessment of Performance Unit (APU)[6] researchers found that the marks for an argumentative writing task set to 11- and 15-year-old students corresponded fairly closely to the spread across all tasks. They concluded from this part of the evidence that 'for neither age group was this the most difficult task, nor the easiest' and that 'this kind of evidence raises a question mark over the idea of a unique association between argumentative writing and notions of complexity and difficulty, however these are defined' (DES, 1978, p. 144). There thus seem to be contradictions in the findings. On the one hand there appears to be a general feeling that students at 11 and 15 find argumentative writing difficult, and on the other, pockets of evidence that this is not necessarily the case. The later section in this chapter on students' views confirms the general picture.

The problems that were identified with the writing of argument were of various kinds:

> At times problems in argumentative structure were caused by the volume of subject matter, but more typical of 'breakdowns' was the sudden appearance of illogically placed information, gaps in knowledge, wildly exaggerated statements, or passages of semi-confusion possibly hinging upon the misuse of a word or phrase.
>
> (ibid., p. 146)

Not surprisingly, 15-year-olds showed themselves more competent in the writing of argumentative prose than 11-year-olds, using forms of journalism, commentary and reportage to argue positions. The 11-year-olds seemed to derive their structures from speech, leading them to 'experiments with graphic presentation ... but also into outbreaks of dramatic dialogue in the midst of standard prose paragraphs' (ibid., p. 148).[7]

With specific regard to narrative and its relation to argumentative writing, the APU report noted the following:

> The use of narrative in our culture as a vehicle for persuasion is a mode of such long standing, and potential sophistication, that it would be a mistake to conclude that young writers are backward because they respond to an argumentative task by producing a story. We do need to ask questions however about the ways in which such questions are conceptualized, and whether the same writers have any capacity to abstract from the narrative frame such key points of the episode as would serve to shape the logical underpinning of the general belief. If neither of these 'revisions' can be undertaken, it may well be that such children are for the moment stuck in one mode of written discourse, unable even to exploit that one for anything other than a recounting function.
>
> (ibid., p. 154)

It is important to point out that this passage suggests that narrative might be a mode for the expression of an argumentative *function*. In this book we are concerned with both the functions of argument and its *modi operandi*.

The overall position of the APU report is to suggest that 'while there are few pupils who are not alert to the use of writing to argue a personal case, most would benefit from a systematic study of the great variety of linguistic techniques which speakers and writers draw upon when taking an authoritative stand on matters of controversial interest' (ibid., p. 158). This is not an uncontroversial position in itself, partly because it seems to raise the spectre of the teaching of different genres to students.

Part of the problem with argumentative writing is the lack of time devoted to it in schools. While the APU report noted that only 8 per cent of the substantial sample of 11-year-old students questioned engaged in this kind of work regularly (the study took place between 1979 and 1983), Medway (1986) found that argument accounted for only 4.8 per cent of 12-year-olds' written work in the 21 English classrooms he studied. Martin (1985) in a study of Years 1–6 in Sydney found only 0.5 per cent of 1,500 scripts engaged with exposition and explanation.[8] In a study related to that by the APU, Gubb (1987) suggested that 'narrative and reflective writing could be regarded as being at opposite ends of a notional scale of writing difficulty' (p. 16).

FROM SPOKEN TO WRITTEN ARGUMENT

A member of the APU research team, writing separately about the problems faced by students composing argument (Gubb, 1987) noted a confusion in students as to whether they should attempt to write a balanced objective account of a case or a hortatory statement in an effort to persuade a reader of the validity of a point of view. Problems also occurred in the transition from spoken to written argument:

> Breakdowns occur in logic, grammar gets forgotten; changes of topic take place with disconcerting abruptness and passionately expressed views are reduced to trite one-line opinions.... Discussion suddenly seems to have little connection with discursive writing.
>
> (p. 163)

The difficulty in moving from spoken to written argument seems largely based on the fact that spoken argument is almost always dialogic and consists of relatively short utterances (depending on the degree of formality). Written argument, on the other hand, is usually monologic. Anyone trying to make the move from spoken to written argument thus faces the problem of how to incorporate two or more voices into a single univocal piece of writing. This problem is addressed in detail in Chapter 3.

Other problems identified by Gubb include the finding of material to support arguments and the discovery of suitable subject matter; the question of the organization of such material; and finding means of expressing the connections in an argument in coherent form. In the four schools used in her study, all the teachers seemed to spend a disproportionate amount of time on the first of these problems (material, subject matter) and to depend on conventional notions of 'for-and-against' structure. Some of the statements made by teachers in this research shed further light on the problems faced, not only by students: 'They can't see the difference between a row and an argument; arguments are a row and they expect to be shouted at and they expect to shout back'; 'to be persuaded is almost to be beaten'; and 'Continuous argument from one point to the next, that's where the problem lies ... so then you've got to give them some sort of guideline' (p. 164).

Gubb concludes that more time should be spent 'on the *how* of discursive writing' (p.182) and that students 'need to understand the form [of argumentative writing] in all its variety, if they are to learn to use it effectively' (ibid.). One of the solutions offered is to provide more written models of argumentative discourse.

LACK OF A RANGE OF MODELS FOR ARGUMENT

The principal North American investigations into the question of difficulties with argumentative composition in schools are those by Freedman and Pringle. In a study based on the narrative and argumentative writing of 500 students in Ontario (1984), they found no obvious contemporary 'grammar' of argumentative structure to help them assess the argument scripts and worked out criteria as follows:

> First, the whole piece of discourse must be unified by either an implicit or (more commonly) an explicitly stated single restricted thesis.... Secondly, the individual points and

illustrations must be integrated within a hierarchic structure so that each proposition is logically linked not only to the preceding and succeeding propositions but also to the central thesis and indeed to every other proposition within the whole text.

(Freedman and Pringle, 1984, p. 74)

They found that grade 7 and 8 students (in the 11 – 13 age range) were more competent at story (98 per cent) than at argument (12.5 per cent) and posited several reasons to account for this imbalance. Referring to Vygotsky (1986, 1978), they suggested that 'in order to produce a unified and logically structured piece of discourse, one must first be able to abstract and conceptualize'. This involves perceiving objective bonds that bind similar objects, analysing similarity in order to determine common elements, formulating what is common in language and verbalizing the concept, being able to apply these formulations and interrelating them with other abstract formulations. They refer to Vygotsky's formulation 'thinking in complexes' (see Chapter 2), where children are able to recognize objective concrete and factual common bonds, but not abstract and logical ones, and suggest that 'this is analogous to the strategy employed by our student writers which we call "focal" in which each of the individual points presented related to the central topic, though none of the points related to each other' (Freedman and Pringle, 1984, p. 80).

In the full report on which the 1984 article is based (Pringle and Freedman, 1985), it was concluded that 'even at grade 12 level a significant number of students were unable to write an argument that satisfied the minimal criteria for a successful argument' (p. ix) and that sudents needed much more help with argumentation. Further observations on the inability of students to revise at the 'macro-level' (i.e. above the level of the sentence) and on the need to counter the 'pervasive model of persuasive discourse, which is the only model available to many students' (ibid.) when they try to write argument reinforce the picture of a mode of discourse within which it is difficult to compose and revise.

Despite the relatively low percentage of students who could successfully compose arguments according to Pringle and Freedman's criteria, the figure marks an improvement on an earlier study (reported in Pringle and Freedman, 1979, 1980) in which the specific topic for argumentative writing was 'Violence on television is a controversial topic with arguments on both sides. Give the basic position of each side before developing your own opinion.' As Pringle and Freedman record:

Writing on this topic, a significantly smaller percentage of the students was able to realize the conventional argumentative structure when rated according to our same crude measure.

(1985, p. 35)

The authors conclude that the change in the nature of the assignment, rather than any difference in teaching strategy, accounts for the improvement in performance between the two projects. In the second study, 'students were only asked to present one side of the issue' (ibid.).

In general, then, Pringle and Freedman found that competence in narrative writing – 'the organization, the sense of form, the control, the psychological decentring and perception' (1979, p. 19) disappeared in the argumentative mode. The argumentative essays were typically 'formless, incoherent, and, above all, awkward' (ibid.), short on ideas, poor in structure and showing no evidence of real revision in their composition.[9] That same problem with the handling of abstractions was also mentioned by Kraft (1975) in the dramatically-titled 'The death of argument'.

ARGUMENT IS NOT READ IN SCHOOLS

Among other studies during the 1980s, Clarke (1984) in an article entitled 'An area of neglect', suggests that part of the problem in gaining competence in argument is that children do not come across models of argumentative discourse in the form of reading.[10] He argues that English lessons in secondary schools had, in the previous twenty years or so, veered away from such texts as Orwell's essays – texts with a political, sometimes polemical dimension – towards texts that were 'literary', personal and intended on the whole to celebrate or explore individual experience. The only examination of persuasive communication was via advertising, an old chestnut of English teaching (like 'similes and metaphors' in poetry teaching) which often seems like a token attempt to look at non-literary language – with a concomitant purpose of keeping such language at bay. Such units on advertising are still often the only attempt in secondary English curricula to address questions of documentary or argumentative language. The formula seems to be 'argument' = 'persuasion' = 'advertising'.[11] In order to remedy this neglect of argumentative reading, Clarke suggests that not only should there be more argumentative texts in class and school libraries, but that the contexts of those texts, the rhetorical situations in which they were composed and received, should become part of the business of English teaching. I will come back to the rhetorical dimension of English and its relation to the development of argument in Chapter 3.

THE ESSAY: A CONVENTIONAL MODEL

As the research into argumentation at sixth-form and higher education levels (discussed fully in Chapter 6) has shown, the essay is both a liberating and problematic form for students who are being led through the various *rites de passage* of the academic world. But it is not only at 16 and beyond that the essay presents an opportunity and a barrier. Much of education in English and other humanities subjects in compulsory schooling uses the essay as a way of testing what students have learnt.

It is worth reflecting for a moment on the definition of the term 'essay'. I have found in my own research and in that of the projects on argument that there is no clear agreement on the meaning of the term; the situation is complicated further when we take different cultural assumptions (for example in North America) into account. The *OED*, again, has several definitions, all of which shed some light on how we interpret the term 'essay'. Its use as a verb points to the first aspect of its usage, which is to do with 'trying' and 'testing'. Linked to this aspect is the definition of the noun as 'a first tentative effort in learning or practice' and also 'a rough essay, a first draft'. It is surprising that with the increase in the status of drafting and revising in English secondary and primary school classrooms since about 1980, the term 'essay' has not taken on more of this aspect of its (French) origin. Rather, the most generally used meaning for 'essay' is the last one recorded in the *OED*: 'a composition of moderate length on any particular subject, *originally implying want of finish, but now said of a composition more or less elaborate in style,* though limited in range' (my italics).

The convention of the essay is best illustrated by the following working notes of a student teacher. In this case, 'essay' is qualified with the adjective 'discursive' to distinguish it from 'imaginative' or 'factual', this giving the term 'essay' an overall role as a written assignment of 'moderate' length as opposed to the more specific 'argumentative essay'. The term 'discursive' is interesting in itself, suggesting not so much the essay as discourse (and perhaps then dialogic and exchange principles at the heart of it) but on the contrary, the essay as a 'loose sally of the mind'. The irony of the supposed freedoms of the essay form are clear in these notes, intended for a class of 14- to 15-year-olds:

Year 10 Discursive Essay

Write an essay of at least 500 words on one of the following topics, making sure you put BOTH sides of the argument.

1. EUTHANASIA
    It is every person's right to chose when to die.
2. LAW AND ORDER
    The British Police should never be armed.
3. NUCLEAR WEAPONS
    Nuclear weapons should only be in the hands of the 'superpowers'.
4. HOMELESSNESS
    It is people's own fault if they are homeless.
5. ABORTION
    Unborn children have an equal right to life.
6. THE ENVIRONMENT
    We can live without the rainforests.

The emphasis on 'both sides of the argument' is, I would suggest, part of the problem. This is the conventional approach to essay-writing and the teaching of argument, and yet it assumes (1) that there are always, and only, two sides to an argument, (2) that these are the topics in which the child is most interested and (3) that 'at least 500 words' will be the right amount for the discussion of these topics. A quick look at the topics offered will convince you that 500 words might only begin to do justice to them.

The instructions for the essay are accompanied by 'Notes for writing a discursive essay':

A spider diagram is a useful way to start. Put your TOPIC in the centre and brainstorm ideas around it.

Divide your ideas into 'for and against'. Put the points 'for' on one side of the page and the points 'against' on the other, e.g.

'For'	'Against'
If police were armed there would be more loss of life	Police need to be armed against violent criminals

Arrange each pair of ideas into a paragraph or use one paragraph for your view and one for the opposing view.

Use any facts and figures you can find, e.g. from books, papers, leaflets, TV programmes and videos, interviews.

In the closing paragraph, sum up what you have said and state your personal views.

Here, the notion that there are two sides to the argument is reinforced by the conventional 'for-and-against' method of planning for a school essay. The idea is taken further, however, in the instruction that 'each pair of ideas' must be arranged into a paragraph or one paragraph used 'for your view and one for the opposing view'. This last instruction is highly prescriptive as far as the writing act is concerned, but also interesting in that it seems to contradict what comes later: 'in the closing paragraph, sum up what you have said and *state your personal views'*. This instruction assumes, then, that the writer is to decide whether he or she is 'for' or 'against' the proposition in the first place, and to convey this position in the writing; but only to state the personal views − as if these are separate from the views underlying the writing of the main body of the essay − at the end.

I am not saying that the model presented here is a disastrous one. Spider diagrams are a useful way to start in brainstorming the ideas that might contribute to a piece of writing on a particular topic. It is also good practice to research such an essay in books, magazines and other sources (though guidance as to the nature of such research would help). But the overall impression is of a model of writing that is not close to the personal lives and convictions of 14- to 15-year-olds, that is highly programmatic (and thus likely to be seen as a ritual rather than as a genuine piece of argument), whose audience is likely to be the teacher (who in turn will read it for assessment purposes) and which assumes that argument is always predicated on an adversarial basis.

WHY ESSAYS?

Why has the essay form come to dominate writing for assessment in the humanities? Womack (1993), in an article entitled 'What are essays for?' calls the essay the 'default genre' for student writing in English after GCSE. A close look at various versions of the National Curriculum in English also reveals that the essay is the form or text-type[12] towards which all writing is tending. It is as if all the other forms of writing are preparatory to the writing of essays. Womack traces the emerging dominance of the essay as we know it as taking place in the late eighteenth century. From its position as one of a range of forms that made up the classical repertoire − forms like the fable, epistle, character and eulogy − it emerged as the sole survivor of the Romantic quest for transparency of expression in the school curriculum. Whereas in the first part of the eighteenth century it was associated with ease of expression, 'looseness' and personal rumination (a tradition that started with Montaigne and Bacon and has continued right through to the present, as in *The Oxford Book of Essays:* Gross, 1991), by the end of that century it had been appropriated as the best form in which to practise the expression of thoughts on a particular topic in schools.

The essay has, as has been expressed elsewhere in this chapter, a contradictory nature. On the one hand it has a central position in schooling because of its generality, its ability to act as a vehicle of expression for a wide variety of topics and subjects, its median length, its openness, its mark of relaxed civility. On the other hand, it is the tool of examination and differentiation, and it plays this latter role very well indeed because of all the forms of writing, it is the most explicit and general. The 'transparency' is manifested in the demands it makes on a writer to lay out, integrate and justify his or her points with clarity. In other words, your mistakes are more readily observable in the essay form and so, from an examiner's point of view, it is easier to differentiate between the performances of a number of students. This is surely the principal reason why the essay is both loved and hated by students: loved, because the writing of it *is what they learn,* and hated because they are being judged in relation to their peers or against certain criteria on the basis of that written product.

It is no coincidence, therefore, that in an assessment-driven curriculum like the English National Curriculum the essay is the form towards which all writing is leading; and that it continues to hold sway in academic examinations at 18 and at undergraduate level. Whether we can also call the doctoral dissertation or thesis an 'essay' is, itself, an academic question: the dissertation is simply an essay writ large. As Womack points out, by that stage in the education stakes the essay *is* the course.

The transparency of the essay — the quality that makes it a form of expression and a tool of assessment at the same time — is a transparency of artifice. Students have to learn that combining their subjectivity with an apparent objectivity is one of the hallmarks of a 'good essay'. The line is a very fine one between being too personal and being too dry and rigid; but treading that line becomes the mark of a good student in the humanities. At times, being competent in the diplomatic and rhetorical skills of essay-writing is as important — if not more so — than knowing your subject. And many students find the argumentative and rhetorical skills required for essay-writing a recurrent — sometimes insurmountable — problem.[13]

THE FIVE-PARAGRAPH ESSAY AND OTHER VARIATIONS

Classical rhetoric, often assumed to be the precursor of notions of the structuring of writing, has no clear guidance on the question of how to put together an argument. In the *Rhetoric,* Aristotle asserts that 'a speech has two parts. It is necessary to state the subject, and then to prove it', but then follows with 'at most the parts are four in number: exordium, statement, proof, epilogue' (1926, III, 13–19). Even the four-part structure might be further subdivided into the so-called 'Arsitotelian six-part oration': exordium, narrative, division, proof, refutation, epilogue. To complicate matters further, the Roman manual of rhetoric, the *Ad Herennium* (possibly by Cicero) advises that 'the most complete and perfect argument . . . is that which is comprised of five parts: the Proposition, the Reason, the proof of the Reason, the Embellishment and the Resumé' (1954, p. 107). This five-part model can in turn be reduced to four or three parts: 'the fullest argument is fivefold, the briefest threefold [without the last two parts] and the mean fourfold, lacking either the Embellishment or the Resumé' (ibid., p. 113). In short, then, we have everything from a two-part model to a six-part model in classic rhetoric, and certainly no orthodoxy to look back to as exemplary. Indeed, the *Ad Herennium* itself furnishes us with the most practical and seemingly modern advice about the composition of argument: 'it is often necessary to employ such changes and transpositions when the cause itself obliges us to modify with art the Arrangement prescribed by the rules of the Art' (ibid., p. 187).

THE NATIONAL CURRICULUM IN ENGLISH AND THE ESSAY

The National Curriculum in English is divided into three main profile components: speaking and listening; reading; and writing. In the original version (DES/WO, 1990), argument is represented largely in the first of these profile components. In this section the 1990 version of the curriculum for English is discussed first, followed by a look at the two later versions.[14]

Speaking and listening

The 1990 Programmes of Study for Key Stage 1 included the following. Planned situations and activities should cover:

> discussion with others; listening to, and giving weight to, the opinions of others; perceiving the relevance of contributions; timing contributions; adjusting and adapting to views expressed
>
> development of speaking and listening skills, both when role-playing and otherwise − when expressing opinions
>
> development, by informal means and in the course of purposeful activities, of pupils' powers of concentration, grasp of turn-taking, ability to gain and hold the attention of their listeners, and ability to voice disagreement courteously with an opposing point of view.
>
> (DES/WO, 1990, p. 23)

All activities should,

> help to develop in pupils' speaking and listening their grasp of sequence, cause and effect, reasoning, sense of consistency, clarity of argument, appreciation of relevance and irrelevance.
>
> (ibid.)

When we come on to Key Stages 2 to 4, the general provisions determined that pupils should be given the opportunity to learn how to:

> express and justify feelings, opinions and viewpoints with increasing sophistication
>
> discuss increasingly complex issues
>
> assess and interpret arguments and opinions with increasing precision and discrimination
>
> ask increasingly precise or detailed questions
>
> respond to increasingly complex instructions and questions
>
> discriminate between fact and opinion and between relevance and irrelevance, and recognise bias
>
> discuss issues in small and large groups, taking account of the views of others, and negotiating a consensus
>
> engage in prediction, speculation and hypothesis in the course of group activity.
>
> (ibid., pp. 24−5)

More specifically, in order to achieve Level 4,

> pupils should be encouraged to express their opinions and to argue a point of view; to be receptive to the contributions of others and make their own contributions effectively.

and in order to achieve Level 5:

> pupils should be helped to make more extended contributions to group or class discussions and to informal or formal presentations. . . . They should be helped to make their questions more probing, and contributions to discussions more reasoned.
>
> (ibid., p. 26)

There is no specific mention of argumentative skills in order to achieve Level 6, but at Level 7:

> the topics for discussion should vary widely and involve the development and probing of argument and evidence. It should also require the presentation of the main issues. Literary texts (including drama scripts), the use of language, responses to the media, pupils' own written work and the use of information technology might furnish many of the materials and topics for discussion for which planned outcomes, *e.g. in written work or presentations* (italics in original) might emerge.
>
> (ibid.)

At Level 8, the 'increased opportunities' for undertaking 'individual, responsible and formal roles' might include,

> some debating activities within a formal structure, opportunities to give talks on a topic of individual interest or expertise.
>
> (ibid., p. 27)

and at Levels 9 and 10, while greater fluency is the general principle, pupils were required to:

> take leading and discerning roles in discussion, to encourage others to make contributions and respond to them with understanding and appreciation . . . to be rigorous in argument and the use of evidence, and to take effective account of audience and context
>
> and should be helped to recognise that speech ranges from intimate or casual spontaneous conversation through discussion, commentary and debate to more formal forms.
>
> (ibid.)

Reading

There is no such extensive reference to argument in the 1990 Programmes of Study which support the Attainment Target for reading at Key Stage 1.

At Key Stage 2, however, pupils were expected to,

> learn how to find information in books and databases, sometimes drawing on more than one source, and how to pursue an independent line of inquiry.
>
> (ibid., p. 31)

and in order to achieve Level 5, pupils:

> should be shown how to distinguish between fact and opinion.
>
> (ibid.)

It was not until Level 7 that the non-literary texts suggested included persuasive writing. Up to that level, 'non-literary' meant largely referential writing. Examples given at Level 7 were advertisements, leader columns from newspapers, and campaign literature from pressure groups.

At Level 8, pupils should be taught how to,

> recognise the author's viewpoint and — where relevant — persuasive or rhetorical techniques in a range of texts

> (ibid., p. 33)

but nowhere else in the Programme of Study for reading was there specific reference to the reading of argumentative texts.

Writing

Again, there was no reference to argument at Key Stage 1 in the Programme of Study for writing, though there was a general requirement that pupils should undertake a range of 'non-chronological' writing.

At Key Stage 2, pupils should,

> read good examples of descriptions, explanations, opinions etc., and be helped to plan and produce these types of writing by being given purposeful opportunities to write their own.

> (ibid., p. 37)

It was not until Key Stages 3 and 4 that pupils should be made aware of a range of functions of writing:

> for communicating meaning to others: reporting, narrating, persuading, arguing ...

> for thinking and learning: recollecting, organising thoughts, reconstructing, reviewing, hypothesizing.

> (ibid., p. 39)

It was at these stages that pupils should have opportunities to write in a range of forms (e.g. pamphlets, book reviews, advertisements), be able to express a point to view in writing, and use writing to facilitate their own thinking and learning. More specifically, in order to achieve Level 8, pupils should:

> be helped to recognise the patterns of organisation of formal expository writing: e.g. the introduction, development and conclusion of the academic essay; the use of illustrations and examples in persuasive writing and of comparison and contrast in argument.

> (ibid., p. 41)

In the general provisions for Key Stage 4, the forms that students should be given the opportunity to write in were extended to include essays and reviews of books, television programmes and films or plays; and the 'wider range of communicative purposes' included,

> expressing a point of view, persuading, comparing and contrasting ideas, arguing for different points of view.

> (ibid.)

It is clear from the above summary of the place of argument in the National Curriculum for English that it was in speaking and listening that the principal work in argument was expected to take place. Argumentation was seen as beginning earlier in speech in that there was no reference to argument in writing or reading at Key Stage 1. The general provisions for Key Stages 2 to 4 provided plenty of opportunity for spoken argument, but little in the way of written or read argument until Key Stage 3. ·

Indeed, it was in the Programme of Study for writing that we find the only reference to 'good examples of descriptions, explanations, opinions etc.' as models to read and follow; in the Programme of Study for reading, there was a requirement for pupils to be shown how to distinguish between fact and opinion.

When it came to Key Stages 3 and 4, the movement in writing seemed to be towards the formal academic essay. There was little scope for alternative forms of argument or inventiveness. It seemed as though the conception of argumentative writing was limited by the chronological/non-chronological distinction referred to earlier. This distinction is an unhelpful one in thinking about language modes such as narrative and argument, and is the subject of a critique by Gibson and Andrews (1993).

In the 1993 proposals there was no mention of argument at Key Stage 1 in the Speaking and Listening profile component – instead the emphasis was on 'narrative' and 'description'. The assumption was that knowledge is received rather than fashioned and argued out, and that pre-packaged thought is conveyed via exposition. At Key Stage 2, however, pupils should be taught to:

> talk to explore, extend, or trace the logic of an idea, discuss to find things out and to share accounts or insights
>
> (DfE/WO, 1993, p. 14.2)

> learn how talk can facilitate the solving of problems e.g. by defining the nature of the difficulty and suggesting alternative solutions
>
> (ibid.)

At Level 4, they were to convey detailed information, narration and personal opinions coherently and when listening and responding contribute a relevant personal viewpoint to an explanation or account. In general, they were to deal positively with opposing points of view and use talk to explore, extend or trace the logic of an idea, discuss to find things out and to share accounts or insights.

As far as Reading is concerned, the proposals emphasized the literary at the expense of a wider range of forms and styles of communication. There was a general provision that, through the study of literature, non-fiction books and other sources of information, pupils should be taught how to identify key points and ideas in a narrative or argument. Pupils should use supporting evidence at Level 5, but the lack of emphasis on reading argument was an obvious lacuna (see Clarke's concerns, p. 9 above). It is as if the world of discourse is divided into two very simple categories: fiction on the one hand – the staple and foundation of English study in this formation and indeed of many English departments in secondary schools; and 'non-fiction' (note the negative definition) which seems to get subsidiary billing. This vast and varied world of non-fiction is often mis-termed 'factual'. Not only is there a 'factual' channel on satellite TV (the rest is 'entertainment' and fiction),[15] but it seems that those who provide categories for kinds of writing produced in schools are also bound by the simplistic division of discourse into 'fictive' ('creative', 'imaginative') and 'factual' or 'information based'. At a time when access to information is at a premium in library provision via CD-ROM and other technology, in 'project' work at primary school level, in the government's determination to promote transmission modes of teaching (rather than interactive, transformational modes of learning) through its curricular and assessment reforms, it is worrying that argument and argumentation are sidelined or categorized as a subsection of 'information',[16] when in theory and practice they sit much more happily in their own domain, blending and mixing with other modes like narrative and description and dialogue to provide a cutting edge for the development and nurturing of thought in connection with feeling.

The study of literature (specifically the literature of a narrowly conceived 'cultural heritage') was paramount as a means by which to develop argument in the National Curriculum proposals. At Level 7, for instance, pupils should 'support their interpretation of a text by selecting apt quotations and evidence (DfE/WO, 1993, p. 42) and work towards the 'lit crit essay'. As my argument in Chapter 6 suggests, students are unlikely to take critical stands in relation to the literature they read at this level, and so will be limited to interpretation rather than criticism of a text. Received opinion — again, not conducive to thought and argument — is likely to be preferred to original exploration of the text in question.

In the 1993 proposals the third Attainment Target, Writing, was 'simplified' to include spelling, grammar and handwriting. There was no reference to argument in Key Stage 1 (though, as Chapters 2 and 4 will show, there is plenty of evidence that children *can* argue in writing, even at the pre-school stage) and at Level 2, the old emphasis on the distinction between factual and imaginative writing. Happily, the distinction between chronological and non-chronological writing was dropped (though not from the sample papers published towards the end of 1993 in preparation for the 1994 Standard Assessment Tests). However, progress was generally characterized by 'increasing control of varied forms and styles of writing, e.g. the story, the descriptive account, poetry, the formal essay, the discursive, the persuasive etc.' (ibid., p. 49)

At Key Stage 2 there was mention of a wider range of purposes for writing and forms such as the pamphlet, book reviews and formal letters are listed. But the conventional view of argument (and it conflation with 'reporting') is maintained. In a report (ibid., p. 59):

> paragraphs should be sequential, coherently outlined arguments for and against. The concluding paragraph should offer an overarching summary and recommendations.

Such essays and reports were supposed to exhibit 'correct negation' and 'passive sentences' as 'appropriate' (ibid.). At Key Stages 3 and 4, too, there was an assumption that there is a fixed diction and grammatical propriety for formal essays. Text-types are assumed to be fixed and teachable, very much along the lines of the theory and practice of a particular group of writers in Australia.[17] Similarly, these text-types are assumed to have standard structures at the discourse level. At Level 7, for instance, pupils were to,

> use the patterns of organization of formal expository writing eg introduction, development, and conclusion in an essay; comparison and contrast in argument.
>
> (ibid., p. 64)

and only at Level 9 were pupils expected to write with flair and imagination as well as control. An example of what might be produced at this level is given. It is a good one, and it is a pity that a version of it is not included earlier in the curriculum:

> A written submission to present the case for the continuing existence of a community centre has to be prepared. It should include an objective review of the situation and the itemising of factors in favour of its retention. Supporting evidence might include interviews, examples of past achievements, a leaflet or brochure, article from the local press etc.
>
> (ibid., p. 67)

Assignments such as this point the way forward for the writing of argument. Despite the fact that the assignment leaves no room for the pupil to develop his/her own views on the future of the fictional community centre, and despite the simulated nature of the assignment (who is the audience?) there is at least the couching of an assignment in functional form rather than prescriptive text-type form ('This is your problem' rather than 'Write an essay...') and an acceptance that the final product − even though it won't be tried out in practice − might include a range of different forms.[18]

ARGUMENT AND THEORIES OF COGNITIVE DEVELOPMENT

There is clearly a connection to be explored between theories of cognitive development and the ability of children and students to argue. The general assumption about children under the age of about 13 is that they cannot argue because they have not developed to the stage of 'formal operations', which means the ability to entertain and operate with abstractions. I will examine this assumption here in the light of discourse theorists who have based their models on the cognitive theories of Piaget, and also look at other theories of cognitive development − principally those of Vygotsky − which support the notion that argument is possible much earlier than most educationalists have assumed.

Milner (1983) sees a connection between developmental stages of writing and Piaget's final three stages of development. Part of the problem with his model is that Milner is uncritical about the sequence of language forms in exactly the same way as the National Curriculum accepts the conventional sequence. These writing modes are arrayed as 'narrative, descriptive, explanative, analytical and artistic' in a set order. Not only is this sequence fixed − *pace* Piaget − but like the worst of Australian genre theory dogma, children are not allowed to move on to the next stage until 'full control' of the mode in question is achieved. That is bound to mean that some children would never get beyond narrative, and thus lead straight into the hands of the APU or Martin (e.g. 1985) position that children must be *taught* non-narrative genres to liberate them from a diet of pure narrative. The false assumption made by Milner is that children cannot create 'artistic' work until they have passed through all the previous four stages. In the face of the huge amount of artistic writing produced in schools by 5- to 7-year-olds (some of it narrative, some poetic, some dialogic, some descriptive, some 'explanative', some analytical − and some a combination, mix or blend of these), such an assumption is untenable.

Another assumption that has informed much educational research in the development of writing has been that of seeing the child as progressively 'decentring'. This notion has been linked to assumptions about narrative and argument, in that narrative is seen as more expressive, more self-centred than argument, which is seen as having to take on other points of view in order to operate satisfactorily. Even Moffett (discussed more fully in Chapter 2), who adopts this notion in the exposition of his model of discourse development, is bound partly by the theory of decentring (though in his later work he sees students moving 'up and down the scale' of the concrete to the abstract and the egocentric to the decentred). At the same time, Moffett perceives that narrative has to take on other points of view via third-person narration, dialogue and so on and that argument infused with personal energy and commitment is as valid as argument driven by requirements of balance and the consideration of other views.

Contradictions such as those outlined above are inevitable if too singular an approach is taken to the anlysis of children's writing within a Piagetian framework. The basic problem is one of reconciling intellectual development with rhetorical and pedagogical sequence. Bruner and Haste (1987) see the search for 'concordances between stages of cognitive development and the mastery of certain linguistic forms' (p. 10) as typical of work on language and thought in the 1970s. What finally discouraged such efforts at correlation was the 'variability introduced by situation and context' (p. 11) and they register a significant change in priorities:

> The emphasis over the last decade has shifted away from concern with syntax and semantics, and with stages of development, towards an understanding of the role of discourse and dialogic processes.
>
> (ibid.)

At the same time there has been a revaluation of the work of Piaget, synthesized in Case (1985) and prompted by critiques of Piaget's formulations. One of these critiques is by Donaldson (1978), who argues for the embedding of reason in real-world problems (pp. 76–85) as much for adults as for children. She cites cases of children who, presented with a disembedded problem, are unable to solve it until the format is changed to one with real-world significance.

Dissatisfactions with, and misrepresentations of, Piagetian theory have coincided with the rise in the prominence of the work of Vygotsky (1986, 1978), discussed in Chapter 2 alongside Applebee's notions of development in narrative competence.

METAPHORS OF ARGUMENT

As Lakoff and Johnson show in their invaluable investigation, *Metaphors We Live By,* the metaphors that are used to talk about a particular field can be very revealing about the way we construct that field and about our attitudes towards it. The principal metaphor for describing argument is that of war and battle:

> We see the person we are arguing with as an opponent. We attack his positions and we defend our own. We gain and lose ground. We plan and use strategies. If we find a position indefensible, we can abandon it and take a new line of attack.
>
> (1980, p. 4)

Other manifestations of this metaphor in the way we see argument are revealed in phrases like 'I destroyed your argument', 'His points were shot down' and in the 'deployment' of evidence or arguments, like the deployment of troops. The significance of this metaphor is that it reveals how we tend to see argument in combative, adversarial terms. Perhaps that is why so many teachers and students are put off.

There are at least two other major metaphors used to map argument, however, each revealing something different about argument and counterbalancing the aggressive/defensive model. These are metaphors of dance and construction. The first of these does not, at present, reveal itself in the language used to describe speech and writing of an argumentative nature, but the 'moves' made in an exchange of views, the 'positions' taken and the 'steps' necessary for a reconciliation or decision are terms which derive from a basic dance metaphor. There is a great deal of scope in thinking of argument in this way, as I demonstrate through practical examples in Chapter 5. The second metaphor – that of construction – is already more integrated into conceptions of argument, as evidenced in phrases like 'Let's build on that point', 'What is the foundation of your argument?' and 'You can't support your argument with sufficient evidence.'

The problem lies in the fact that metaphors of war are predominant and so we tend to see argument in those terms: as adversarial and to do with defeating the other's point of view. Metaphors of dance and construction offer different perspectives and allow us to see argument as also being about moving to new positions through agreement and about building. As Berrill (1991) suggested, the war metaphor seeks to eliminate differences whereas the other two – like classical dialectical argument – seek to explore those differences. I return to the question of metaphors of argument in the final chapter.

STUDENTS' VIEWS

What do students feel about argument as a written mode? What particular problems do they encounter when composing in this mode? In the spring and summer of 1989, as part of doctoral research on the writing of narrative and argument in three comprehensive secondary schools in the north of England, I administered questionnaires to 150 Year 8 pupils about their writing. What they said in response to the question. 'What do you find difficult about writing argument?' confirms many of the problems I have outlined above but the statements and insights of the students themselves shed new light on the question of composing argument.

Many of the difficulties with regard to the writing of argument were expressed in contrast to the ease in working on narrative. Overall 51 per cent of the students said that they found writing narrative easier than writing argument, with 34 per cent preferring argument and 15 per cent either unclear or not answering the question.[19] Typical of views expressed were that:

> stories are much more interesting to me, more fun. And you can explore the world of writing and English much more in stories. There is no limit to what you can do in a story but there is a limit in argument. They're not nearly as fun. (Katy)

Ideas seem to come less readily in composing argument, and it may also be more difficult to express feelings directly or to feel that the imagination can be used. The distance from speech, discussed earlier in this chapter, may present further problems. One student tried to bridge this gap, noting that:

> when I write argument I write it as though I am actually saying it [but it is difficult] because I prefer to express my feelings by talking, not writing. I can put more expression into it when I say it. (Robert)

and another commented, 'I'd rather argue face to face with someone'. The lack of 'someone to argue with' was felt strongly by several students, who found it hard to replace the antagonist in writing or to step into his or her shoes. It was felt that it made the argument 'stronger' to be able to take into account the other point of view, and that 'it is not like a real argument' unless the other voice is represented.

Argument seems to necessitate commitment from these students. They found it hard to argue a case unless they felt strongly about it, and harder still to set out the case for and against a proposition. One student commented:

I have to be in an angry mood to do things like this. I hate having to write a letter of complaint over a packet of crisps so I usually just leave it, but I did enjoy writing about 'Birds should not be allowed on the earth' [his title] because it was a bit comical. (Simon)

Having the choice to find their own topics seemed to have helped this process, but if the problem in narrative was stemming the flow of ideas (once started),[20] the problem in argument was more to do with generating enough ideas to sustain the writing:

I don't know how to develop them when I only have a few opinions. (Peter)

I can't usually find enough points to put down. (John)

One student who admitted a difficulty in finding a topic to write about – or, more accurately, one which prompted him to take a particular stance – added the following somewhat resigned comment,

I suppose with the amount of disgusting things on this planet I should be able to write at least a hundred pages on just one topic. (Ian)

but part of the overall problem was a lack of reading material to provide something to argue against or models of good written argument, as Clarke had suggested in his 1984 article,

You don't come across arguments in books very often. (Peter)

Problems with dearth of content and models inevitably lead to problems with arrangement:

I probably don't know a lot about the subject and find it hard to put it in an order. (Ian)

I don't know which way it sounds best. (Stephen)

An exception to the majority was one student who wrote, 'if you don't mind my saying so, my mind is bursting with ideas' (Paul).

In general in the questionnaires, then, much more was said about the difficulty of generating content for arguments than with narratives. More will be said about the particular problems and discoveries about composing argument later in the book. In the meantime, the final words before a summary is made of the problems facing those who want to write argument can be those of a student who turned out to be one of the most eloquent in expressing his difficulties and triumphs in written argument. Here, he is talking about the problems of moving from a plan to the actual writing of the argument:

I tried to fit the different rail tracks together so that one would lead to the other, which is quite hard to do. (Philippe)

S U M M A R Y

I have tried to set out some of the problems with composing written argument. They can be summarized as follows:

● In writing argument students have to create their own structures to more of an extent than in other modes of discourse.

- At the same time, there are conventional forms within the mode (like the essay) that can prove inaccessible and/or too rigid for writers who want to express their arguments. These forms are often couched in formulaic ways, deriving from structures that are now less appropriate to their functions than they were.
- There are problems in moving from spoken to written forms. Argument in speech almost always involves more than one voice. When these voices have to be distilled to the single voice of conventional argumentative writing, there can be problems of accommodation.
- Argument is not read much in schools or at home; there are consequently few models to act either as subliminal influences on the composition of argument or as direct exemplars of the mode.
- The National Curriculum – in England and Wales at least – reflects conventional and limited notions of the place of argument in the development of writing abilities.
- Uncritical dependence on some of the theories of Piaget regarding cognitive development gave the social dimension of argument a low profile in the middle of the twentieth century. Consequently, it has been assumed that children under the age of about 13 are not able to argue. This assumption has had pervasive effects on curriculum planning.

In the next chapter I shall look at some of the solutions that have been put forward to these problems in the last fifteen years or so, before going on to suggest solutions of my own in the chapters that follow.

NOTES

1 According to Bakhtin (1986, p. 63) the artistic genres are the most conducive to reflecting the individuality of the speaking voice – indeed, that is one of their main goals. For a very different, much more formal argument in literature, see the debate between Drs McNab and Dunstable on the causes of cholera in J. G. Farrell's *The Siege of Krishnapur,* p. 250ff.
2 Douglas Walton (1989) in *Informal Logic* sees quarrels as the 'lowest' form of argument, but I find such a hierarchical approach to the field of argument unhelpful because it offers no bridge between informal and formal argument. However, the general tenor of Walton's book complements the present book in that it stresses the importance of a dialogic approach and also *situates* arguments in contexts rather than seeing argument as an element of decontextualized logic.
3 The general aim of *Narrative and Argument* (Andrews, 1989) was to break down the polarized distinction between narrative and argument, and also to define them as modes of discourse rather than as genres. The key contributions as far as the present chapter is concerned are by Kress, Dixon, Hesse and Medway.
4 For further discussion of the differences between these terms and exposition as a mode of discourse, see my introduction to *Narrative and Argument* (1989) and 'Argument in Schools: the value of a generic approach' (1993). For a full discussion of argument as the lexical representation of grammatical information about a predicate – i.e. argument at sentence and word level – see Grimshaw (1990).
5 See Andrews (1993) and Freedman and Medway (1994) for a discussion of the generic possibilities of argument from a modal perspective and for redefinitions of 'genre'.
6 The Assessment of Performance Unit (APU) was set up in 1975 within the Department of Education and Science (DES) to promote the development of methods of assessing and monitoring the achievement of children at school.
7 Though deriving argument structures from speech might seem at first to be an undesirable

quality in the writing of 11-year-olds, much of this book (especially Chapter 3) is devoted to seeing the influence of spoken forms on written ones in positive light. 'Breaking out into dialogue' in the middle of a prose paragraph might well be a sign of inventiveness in the arrangement and expression of an argument.

8 85 per cent of the scripts in the Martin study were classified as narrative/expressive, and 15 per cent as 'factual'. 'Exposition' – the heading under which argument comes, in the form of hortatory or analytical exposition – is seen as factual. I argue against this classification later in the book.

9 Freedman and Pringle reflected further on the material generated in their early 1980s projects in 'Contexts for developing argument' (1989). They noted that the better argumentative essays in their samples were written on school-related or school-taught topics. Drawing on Vygotsky's distinction between scientific and everyday concepts, they suggested that as scientific concepts were structured hierarchically, they were more conducive to the writing of argument, 'not because such structures are handed over ready-made but because the scientific or content-area teaching both models and elicits the kinds of thinking in order to find such organizing structures' (p. 80). They conclude that 'essays on personal or general topics are inherently more difficult to structure than those focusing on scientific or school-related concepts' (ibid.). There is an interesting mismatch here between this latter suggestion and that of Dixon and Stratta (explored more fully in the next chapter) who suggest that 'school topics' are less accessible to students wanting to write good argument than issues of personal significance. In my own experience in teaching 11- to 18-year olds, the best topics for argument are those which combine personal commitment *and* school-based range, partly because there is scope for real action as a result of the arguments. Further debate on this question needs to take into account the broader notion of 'school writing' as defined and explicated by Sheeran and Barnes (1991).

10 See also Clarke (1993), especially p. 199ff. and pp. 216–222.

11 Today advertising is likely to find itself as just one of the 'non-literary' forms of language studied as part of an English programme influenced by cultural studies.

12 I use the terms 'form' or 'text-type' to describe the essay in line with attitudes in North America (See Swales, 1990; Bazerman, 1988; Freedman and Medway, 1995) towards the term 'genre'. Argument, at a different and more general level, seems to me to be a 'mode' of communication. See previous note and Chapters 2 and 5.

13 There is a well-established literature about the essay in North America. See, as points of departure, Kazin (1961), Lukacs (1978), Klaus (1989) and Anderson (1989).

14 The National Curriculum was implemented in England and Wales in the early 1990s as a result of the 1988 Education Act. It divides schooling into four 'Key Stages', covering ages 4–7, 8–11, 11–14 and 14–16. The National Curriculum for English, originally drawn up by a working group chaired by Professor Brian Cox, consisted of three main 'profile components' – speaking and listening, reading and writing. Each profile component consists of 'Attainment Targets' and in English the first two were the same as the first two profile components. The third, fourth and fifth Attainment Targets – 'Writing', 'Spelling' and 'Handwriting' – came under the umbrella of the third profile component, 'Writing'. Each Attainment Target had ten levels of attainment, described by the 'statements of attainment'. Broadly speaking, students were expected, on average, to attain Level 4 by the time they finish at primary/elementary school, and Level 7 or 8 at the end of compulsory schooling. In the summer of 1992, the Secretary of State called for proposals for a revision and 'simplification' of the National Curriculum for English. These proposals were published in April 1993 (DfE/WO, 1993) and a revised 'slimmed down' curriculum published in 1994 in the wake of the Dearing Report (Dearing, 1994).

15 In a survey of programmes on the four main English TV channels in July 1992, I counted only 3 per cent that could be termed 'argument'. These were, at the time, a popular debating/opinion show called *Kilroy, Prisoner of Conscience,* a five-minute programme in which public figures spoke on behalf of individuals imprisoned for their views, party political broadcasts (also brief), *40 Minutes,* an excellent programme in which members of the public were given the opportunity to make programmes putting forward a particular point of view; and *J'Accuse,* a programme in which arts figures could build an argument against a particular

individual, institution or idea. The other 97 per cent was made up of drama, light entertainment, documentary, sport and other features. There were no distinctively argument-based programmes for children.

16 A typical example of the subsuming of argument under informational modes and genres is to be found in the Key Stage 3 English 1992 pilot paper, 'Factual writing' (Levels 6–10). The brief for the students was as follows:

> You are to write a report to the headteacher of your school about ways of encouraging reading both at home and at school. In writing your report, your should refer to the information in the survey [provided] and include your own ideas.

On the 'task sheet' itself, the word headteacher is changed to 'governors', but confusingly, the sheet is headed 'Developing the Argument'. It is not only unclear as to who the exact audience is (you are likely to know your headteacher better than your governors) but also who 'you' as writer of the report is. Are you a parent, an expert or a 14-year-old? Is the assignment a report or an argument? Does it have persuasive intent? Are we to assume the audience is sympathetic or unsympathetic to the suggestion of 'ways of encouraging' reading at home and at school?

17 The 'genre debate' in Australia is presented in Reid (1987) and continues to take place. In broad terms, the debate is between, on the one hand, linguists in the Hallidayan school who see genre as text-type and who have been instrumental in devising curriculum programmes that currently run in several Australian states; and on the other hand, educationalists who see the composing of writing more in terms of individual and collaborative growth and development.

18 In May 1994, at the time the writing of this book was completed, the School Curriculum and Assessment Authority (SCAA) issued a further set of proposals for English (1994) that were intended to act as a basis for the curriculum for five years from September 1995. They were a result of the 'slimming down' of the curriculum in the wake of the Dearing Report (1994). Changes from the 1993 proposals were minimal, though the fact that argument retained some space within a slimmed-down curriculum was heartening. As in the previous orders and proposals, the main location for argumentative work was seen to be in Speaking and Listening, with significant elements of argument embedded in the curriculum for Key Stages 1, 3 and 4 (in Key Stage 2, the emphasis seemed to shift to passivity in the face of 'information'). In the Programmes of Study for 'Reading', there is more emphasis on reading 'arguments of non-fiction texts' at Levels 1–3, though again the world of discourse appeared to divide into 'literature' and 'information', or fiction and 'non-fiction'. As argued in the body of the chapter, this binary distinction tends to sideline argument. The same is true of the Programme of Study for 'Writing'. The National Curriculum for English assumes that argument is a sub-category of non-fictional, informative communication.

Essentially, then, successive changes to the National Curriculum have not radically affected the perception of the place of argument within it. There has been more highlighting of argument, as in 'Pupils' reading should include texts with challenging subject matter that broadens perspectives and extends thinking' (SCAA, forthcoming, p.13), but no realignment of the curriculum to accommodate argument in writing and reading at primary/elementary levels, nor sufficient diversification of argumentative forms at secondary/high school levels.

In the 1994 (SCAA, forthcoming) version of the National Curriculum, the ten levels of attainment set out in the 1990 version were capped at eight levels, with the General Certificate of Secondary Education (GCSE) system for examination at 16 accounting for assessment at Key Stage 4.

19 When the results are broken down by school, there is close correspondence between the three schools. Fifty per cent of students in two of the schools found narrative easier, and 52 per cent in the other school. The only surprising result from this analysis showed that the only *class* to prefer argument to narrative (of the six classes overall) was the 'bottom set' at the only one of the three schools to 'set' its classes. I assumed that if narrative is generally thought to be easier than argument, then this class might reflect the general opinion. Students in the class, however, said that they preferred argument because you 'didn't have to make it up' (see Clarke and Sinker, 1989) and because they had 'lots to argue about'. Perhaps their status as 'bottom set' gave them the impetus to argue about the injustice of their lot. There is room for further research here on how the different modes are perceived by students of different 'ability'.

20 I have not addressed the narrative side of the research undertaken for the doctoral project in the present book. Readers interested in attitudes towards narrative and in the structures and composing processes used by young writers in this respect are referred to the thesis itself Andrews (1992a) and to Applebee (1978), Wilkinson *et al.* (1980), Cook-Gumperz and Green (1984), Cowie (1984, 1985), McKeough (1986) and Anthony (1986) among others.

Chapter 2

Some Solutions

> If you don't mind my saying so, my mind is bursting with ideas. (Paul)

Perception of the problems associated with the composition of written argument have often been followed by suggestions as to how these problems might be solved. Many of the problems outlined in the previous chapter, for example, have been the basis for a rethinking of approaches to argument, and I will be looking at some of these suggestions here. The suggested solutions are all very different, and no single one of them can provide a panacea for the problems surrounding argumentative writing. This chapter will look in turn at these various approaches, weigh their differences, present them again in book form so that the quality of thinking about the problem can be acknowledged (many of them appeared in publications with small print runs, in journals and sometimes not in print at all), and build on them in subsequent chapters.

LINGUISTIC TECHNIQUES

One of the researchers on the APU team mentioned in the first chapter was Janet White. In an independent paper (1987) she presents a challenge to the assumption that 'argumentative/persuasive writing is an especially difficult, intractable genre for children' (p. 1). She traces the sources of the assumption to associations with cognitive complexity (largely within the Piagetian tradition), particularly that which assumes argumentative discourses are only possible with older children, once 'formal operations' have been established. School practice typically isolates one method of writing – the four-(or five)-paragraph essay with the structure:

State a proposition.
State the reasons which might oppose it.
State the reasons which might support it.
Draw a conclusion.

In turn, this is reflected in panel discussions on television and radio, clearly also within the adversial tradition. White is adamant that the conventional situation regarding the teaching of argument is, to say the least, limiting, and in her subsequent discussion of the issue, refers more positively than Gubb (1987) to possibilities of transition from spoken to written forms. Eleven-year-olds seem to exhibit more of the characteristics of speech in their written arguments than 15-year-olds, who have acquired more of the written conventions of the mode. Often, students in the survey to which she refers were able to offer rudimentary proto-arguments, 'indicating that they either displayed in skeletal form a basic structure of a written argument, or contained some of these features — that is, an opening proposition, followed by a reason/explanation, followed by a summation' (White, 1987, p. 10).

This structure differs from the standard four- or five-paragraph model in that it contains no counter-argument, whether seriously introduced in order to exhibit balance, or raised merely to shoot down. From White's researches, it appears that 'causal connectives are left implicit, to be inferred from juxtapositions of sentences rather than being given lexical realisation' (1987, p. 14). In what is a critical passage as far as the current book is concerned, White goes on to question the relationship between narrative and persuasive discourse offered by Dixon and Stratta (1986a), discussed later in this chapter. She suggests that they imply that moving from one to the other entails moving 'from the particular to the general, thus raising the level of abstraction...[secondly] the connections between the general statements have to be logical or rational, to make sense and stand up to criticism' (1987, p. 10). Rather than being an issue of 'levels of generality', White sees the problem as being one to do with 'knowledge of the functions of language' (p. 11), and with young writers 'not knowing how to use (written) language for anything other than an informal anecdotal/informative function' (pp. 11–12). If narrative can carry persuasive import, she argues, need there be such a distinction between narrative and argumentative levels of discourse in the first place?

There can be no doubt that narrative can fulfil a persuasive function. Every novel does so, to differing degrees, and the persuasive function is even more obvious in forms like the fable, parable or Japanese koan (a very short story with the essay-like function of revealing a truth about Zen). As persuasion is one kind of argument, it might be said that all narratives are argumentative, to one degree or another. Here, however, we are talking about argumentative *function* rather than *mode*. One could argue, as does Winterowd (1975, p. vii), that all spoken and written communication is suasive and therefore that all communication is rhetorical. This seems to me to be taking the case for the argumentative function too far. That is why it is worth preserving a distinction between narrative and argumentative modes, and why the work of Dixon and Stratta is important to consider here. What appears as a difference of position between White on the one hand, and Dixon and Stratta on the other is, indeed, merely a difference in emphasis. The latter would probably accept White's assertion that narratives carry persuasive weight; and White, in her turn, would probably concur with their interest in widening the range of discourses available to emergent writers.

There is one further point to make with regard to White's work. She concludes:

> Overall, it would appear that there are few pupils who are not alert to the use of writing to persuade, but that most would benefit from systematic study of the great variety of linguistic techniques which speakers and writers draw on when taking an authoritative stand on issues of controversial interest. Such a study would entail the analysis of formal structures used in constructing arguments to show how these were functional in making meaning, and would far exceed the fossilised preoccupation with a for/against schema.
>
> (1987, p. 16)

Along with the following paragraph, which urges a reappraisal of the 'difficulties' of argumentative writing, this forms a convincing argument for critical consideration of the field; but the suggestion that 'systematic study of the great variety of linguistic techniques' might be one of the answers to the problem of writing argument is one of 'case not proven'. While in principle this suggestion is sound, such techniques have not always taken root in practice. What are the linguistic techniques implied here? Mostly they are aspects of text structure, from the phrase and sentence level up to the macro-level of the structuration of the text itself.

At one level, they are manifested in phrases like 'to begin with', 'a second point', 'on the one hand', 'nevertheless', 'in conclusion' and so on. These phrases are useful in that they mark turning points in an argument. If arguments do proceed by 'turns' − not only in the exchanges of spoken argument but also in the angles taken in the development of a written argument (see the definition of 'argument' on p. 2 as 'the angle, arc or other mathematical quantity from which another required quantity may be deduced, or on which its calculation depends') − then these phrases are useful. The problem with such an approach, is that it is almost purely formal; that is to say, there is little consideration of what is being said or of why it is being said − this is formal teaching without rhetorical consideration, and as such is bound to be seen by students as arid. What it needs is a closer linking to the function and intention of the discourse in question. Nevertheless, the emphasis on formal structures at phrase and text level *and the way they link the two levels,* is a useful contribution to the search for solutions to the composition of argument.

TEXTBOOKS

Textbooks that purport to teach argumentative skills are a likely source of further emphasis on linguistic techniques, and a sampling of three such textbooks from the 1980s confirms this view. As Northrop Frye pointed out, evidence of a systematic understanding of a subject can be seen in the ability to write an elementary textbook explaining its basic principles, but that may or may not be the case in the field of the essay. The three examples of such textbooks discussed here are Johnson (1980), Jenkins and Summers (1982) and Pirie (1990), all of which are designed for the secondary age range.

Johnson argues that any form of persuasion is a kind of argument, so that advertisements, anecdotes, headlines *et alia* all come within the field of argument. When it comes to overt, formal argument she defines two routes, and these might be read in relation to Dixon and Stratta's 'levels' of abstraction: they are that of deductively reasoned arguments, working through general principles; and of inductively reasoned arguments, working through 'example'. Chapters in the book cover such areas as 'Appraising accurately', 'Persuasive tactics', 'Persuading, informing, bias and fact' and 'Arguing to solve problems'.

Jenkins and Summers's book is also divided into stages: 'Gathering material', 'Paragraphs', 'Planning the essay' and 'Beginning and ending'. It then moves on to 'Words', 'Sentences' and 'Figurative language' before looking at different topoi. The book insists that writing an essay 'is like building a house: you cannot begin until you have all the materials ready to hand' (1982, p. 1). The building metaphor is interesting, and one we have already met. It happens, however, that this is not the way houses are built. Houses may be commissioned by developers, and are designed by architects, who take a continuing interest in the construction of the buildings as they evolve and move toward completion. Materials are ordered and arrive on the site at appropriate stages in the construction of the building, and almost never all before the construction takes place.

The building blocks of the essay are seen as paragraphs, to which the second chapter of the book is devoted. This makes the assumption that paragraphs are always indicated by topic sentences and that an argument will proceed paragraph by paragraph. As indicated in Chapter 5 of the present book, this is not necessarily the case in the work of 12- and 13-year-old writers.

Planning is seen as essential, and 'tone' may determine sequence or suggest that the structure can vary from the chronological. This is an interesting notion that is not pursued by Jenkins and Summers in *Approaches to Essay Writing*. However, much attention is paid to beginnings and endings, with various kinds of beginning suggested according to purpose: beginnings which contrast with the main body of the essay, direct opening, statements of position, dramatic openings and anecdotes. Similarly, endings might be straightforward, take the form of questions or simply sum up what has gone before.

Both textbooks mentioned so far classify the constituent parts of different kinds of essay and then translate these into pedagogy. Of the two, Johnson (1980) provides a wider foundation of argumentative discourse for students to build on, but both books derive from classical notions about the composition of arguments. Neither book takes into account developments in the understanding of writing processes or matters of arrangement on the macro-level.

Pirie (1990) is more forthcoming about the process of composing an argument for a critical essay, and suggests that apprentice writers 'revise the ordering of [their] main points until [they] are satisfied that [they] have found the most illuminating and persuasive sequence in which to lead [a] reader through them' (p. 54). There is an admirable emphasis on fitness for purpose. Yet the advice on paragraphing reflects that of Jenkins and Summers: that 'each paragraph must be recognizable as a logical next step in a coherently developing argument' (p. 58) and 'must advance at least one major idea' (p. 60). Further advice on the sequencing of the essay suggests that the form might proceed according to a 'thesis/antithesis/synthesis' pattern, via 'proposition and proof' chronologically or according to 'the text's own order' (p. 68). Ponsot and Deen (1982) similarly offer six 'essay shapes' with which to work, but even these consist of fairly rigid two-part structures.

Pirie's book is one of the few I have come across which deals with arrangement and rearrangement at the macro-level. Advice on the writing of essays in departmental notes for guidance of students at university level also tends to miss out the whole question of rearrangement, assuming that the planning of a piece of writing is sufficient, and that there is a direct relationship between the structure of the plan and the finished essay. As evidenced in the work produced by the students in the section on the structures of argument writing in Chapter 5 (see pp. 100–105), this is not necessarily so. Changes in the order of constituent parts may take place at any time during the process of composition.

Two of the best textbooks to appear in recent years have emerged from Australia:

Issues and Persuasion and *Issues, Persuasion and the Press* (Béchervaise, 1990; Béchervaise and Trethowan, 1993). The first moves beyond the three textbooks discussed above in that a substantial part of the book is devoted to locating the issues (the topoi or 'places' of argument). It thus embraces more of classical rhetoric than the previously mentioned books, which focus largely on the formal stylistic requirements of argument. *Issues and Persuasion* goes further, addressing invention, arrangement and audience as well as style. Among its sections are those on personal opinion, common techniques used in argument, ambiguity, irrelevance, point of view, the order of presentation, evidence and argument in media other than print. The second book is equally comprehensive in range, and pays particular attention to the presentation of issues in the press and via electronic media.

LEARNING FROM THE RHETORICAL TRADITION

There are several strands to the rhetorical tradition but perhaps it is best to say at the outset that the 'rhetoric' I am referring to here is not the 'rhetoric' that is used disparagingly in phrases like 'mere rhetoric' and 'political rhetoric', meaning cant, pure verbiage, words rather than action, an insincere and often devious manipulation of language for persuasive ends. Rather, it is rhetoric in the contemporary sense of 'the arts of discourse' with all the associations of discourse embedded in social contexts. I want to build a case for the close relationship between argument and rhetoric later, but here I will concentrate on versions of rhetoric that are ultimately Aristotelian in origin and that have informed many recent approaches to the teaching of argument. In later chapters I will suggest that the versions of rhetoric I am presenting you with here are inadequate to the task of accounting for argument in all its forms and contexts; this does not mean to say that there is not a good deal of mileage in pursuing classical rhetorical teaching for some of the journey.

Earlier we saw that there was no clear guide to the arrangement of arguments in either Aristotelian or Ciceronian rhetoric, and that the *Ad Herennium* accepted that it was often necessary to employ 'changes and transpositions' in the sequence of an argument when the cause itself obliged us to do so. That enlightened view − of writing or speech driven by the contingencies of the situation − does not accord with Renaissance practice, best represented in the *Progymnasmata* of Aphthonius (Nadeau, 1952). Aphthonius covers a range of forms in what is, in effect, a writing primer. These include fable, tale, proverb, comparisons, descriptions as well as forms which are not now current, like the encomium (a speech bringing out the good points in someone) or the chreia (a brief bit of advice bearing appropriately on some person). All these might be considered aspects of argument, and yet the pedagogy is primitive. Each text-type is defined briefly, then subdivisions and examples of the type are described. An example follows, with the form presented in various styles. In other words, the pedagogy is simply that of providing a model which students imitate. Learning to argue, or learning to discourse in this community is clearly such a conservative activity that the forms themselves seem to count for all. In many ways, the similarities with some of the practice of genre theorists is startling.

The problem with models, however, is that although they may help students to recognize and write a limited repertoire of 'fixed' forms, there is no guarantee of transferability from situation to situation – indeed, no consideration of situation at all. Nor is there much room for invention or subversion, or the creation of new text-types. Models often leave the emergent writer with little sense of voice or scope, and the writing that emerges is thin and derivative. There is also the problem of the sequence in which models of different types are introduced.

In classical, Renaissance and Enlightenment practice, argument – supported by the rational paradigm – had a high profile. The repertoire of forms looked like a panoply of argumentative forms; or, at least, what they had in common was an argumentative function. In addition to the list cited above, colloquies, essays, epistles, declarations and orations were composed. But as Womack (1993) points out, with the disintegration of the universe of classical discursive competence during the course of the eighteenth and early nineteenth centuries, that repertoire 'came to look elaborately and oppressively formalistic' (p. 43) and the essay – gaining momentum from its introduction to England by Montaigne and Bacon at the end of the sixteenth century – came to be the sole survivor, carrying much of the burden of explicatory and argumentative expression right through to the present.[1]

Perhaps the fiercest attack on 'classical rhetoric for the modern student' comes from Knoblauch and Brannon (1984, pp. 4–5), who suggest that modern rhetoric (in the full contemporary sense of the word):

> emphasizes the process of composing more than the features of completed texts, thereby distinguishing itself from both ancient rhetoric and literary criticism. It is preoccupied with the writer's choice-making in the development of texts, the exploratory movement of mind, the discovery of connection among ideas, the progressive testing and reformulating of statements.

This much is true enough, but Knoblauch and Brannon see the ancient and modern perspectives on rhetoric as 'incompatible' (p. 5), partly because there is 'a closer connection between language and thought, discourse and knowledge than ancient speculation has supposed'. As teachers, they are surely right to attack the pedagogy that makes writing a 'perfunctory, ceremonial exercise' (p. 27) through the use of mechanical formulae, and they provide a useful caveat against the dangers of taxonomies:

> Whether a given text is regarded as argumentative or persuasive is surely less a matter of its objective features than a matter of the situation in which it was composed and the disposition of its readers to react in certain ways.
>
> (p. 27)

A dissatisfaction with classical structures is also expressed in the British context by Hackman (1987) who is critical of 'traditional practice' in which writing 'exists as a pre-fabricated structure into which [the writer] pours her meanings' (p. 6). Her arguments are telling, particularly with regard to the constraining effect of such structures on learning itself:

> The rhetorical conventions of the literary essay are ancient, inflexible and limiting. They are derived from classical models, based on an epistemology quite out of place in modern education. Cicero's oration formula (exordium, narrative, partition, confirmation, refutation, rebuttal and peroration)[2] is recognisable in the structure of most A level essays, particularly those which seek to 'discuss' this or that aspect of a text... The problem with the old model is that it ignores the processes by which a reader makes sense of the text,

bypassing the learning processes in an anxious rush to see the evidence of learning as end-product. Teachers understandably end up teaching essay-structure rather than literature.

(p. 7)

She elaborates on the effects of such an approach later in the book. As I have suggested with regard to models and given structures, Hackman points out that the provision of such ready-made supports has the opposite effect from that intended: it tends to sap the students of the pattern-making energy that is necessary to the formulation of ideas on a subject.

Hackman accepts, however, that language forms are artificial and that there is no 'natural personal language' which takes shape without some attention to structure. It should also be remembered that although the general point of students having to use outmoded models of essay-writing is a fair one, classical practice as recorded in the *Ad Herennium* was open to flexibility with regard to the arrangement of texts.

In arguing against the revival of the classical rhetorical tradition, and against its connection with modern rhetorics of 'process', Knoblauch and Brannon (1984) go too far towards the Scylla of expressiveness without form, caricaturing their antagonists in the process. Such polemic obscures the possibilities of integration between the classical rhetoricians and genre theorists on the one side, and the process theorists and individualists on the other. Hackman is more moderate, suggesting that attention to shape and structure is an important element in the process of composition, but that such considerations are more useful in the 'earlier stages of writing' (1987, p. 71).

THE PROVISION OF READING MATTER

As pointed out earlier, classrooms and libraries at both primary/elementary level and secondary/high school levels are often short on argumentative texts. When we look under non-fiction, often the closest we get to argument is exposition (see Mallett, 1992, for example). It is worth listing what kinds of texts might come under the heading of argument − a list that will provide the basis for a further consideration of the range of argument later in the book, for both reading and writing purposes. Argumentative texts include:

> advertisements
> letters of complaint/persuasion
> leading articles (in newspapers and magazines)
> campaign literature (local, national and international), including manifestos
> speeches
> credos
> philosphical and other dialogues
> parables, fables
> fiction (to varying degrees)[3]
> polemical drama and poetry
> essays, including critical/literary essays

Of this list most of the argumentative texts do not take book form. Arguments on the whole are shorter than novels or plays, biographies or information books, which tend to be the staple of libraries and indeed of the programme for most English lessons in secondary schools. Arguments are ephemeral to the bulk of the library stock and hard to preserve. If they are collected in book form, they lose the context that is so important to them (whereas fiction, in general, provides its own bookish, relatively sealed context). Exceptions are books like Terry Jones's *Attacks of Opinion* (1988), a collection of his columns for the *Young Guardian; Say What You Think* (Moger and Richmond, 1985); Orwell's essays, or, say, collections of articles by Miles Kington. Argumentative texts are more ephemeral than literary texts because their function is usually to change things in the world, to bring about action. Once that action has, or has not been brought about, the *means* to the end of action is jettisoned and forgotten. Perhaps that is why film and radio are good media for argument: their closeness to speech and their immediacy of impact are able to carry argument more effectively. When libraries free themselves of the tendency to stock fiction and information (in both printed books and via information technology), they might take on more argument. The usual experience in reading, however, is to suspend or ignore the argumentative function.

One school in which argument was given much higher priority was that of Hazel Brown (reported in full in Cambourne and Brown, 1989). In a three-year longitudinal study, Cambourne and Brown recorded and analysed practice in Brown's classrooms (during which time she taught one Year 3 and two Year 5 classes). When wanting to develop in her pupils an ability to recognise and produce writing in different registers,[4] she followed a sequence of activities over a two- to three-week span, each involving two hours per day. The overall strategy was one of *immersion* in the register in question, including tactics such as demonstration, response, individual reading, sharing/discussion, retelling, writing independently and generating criteria. Of these, the latter two were usually practised and explored after the other four had been in operation — sometimes concurrently — for some time. In the case of the teaching and learning of argument, the teacher 'read as many examples . . . as possible (e.g. letters to the editor, anti-smoking literature, conservation literature)' (pp. 48–9), a stage in the process of learning which was always followed by a period of up to 20 minutes of sustained silent reading in the same register. Sometimes, prior to asking the pupils to write in the particular register, the teacher would think out loud as she composed to demonstrate the problems in composing in that register and how to overcome them. Discussion, exploring the features and contexts of the writing in question, would take place during the two- to three-week period, and small groups of children would be formed for an activity called 'retelling procedure' in which individuals would make predictions about the content or direction of an unseen text written in that particular register. After writing and sharing, children would generate criteria, in groups and as a whole class, as to what they thought distinguished the register in question.

Although the pedagogy described above is not exclusive to argument, it does show how one teacher has tried to overcome the problem of lack of exposure to argumentative texts via a varied programme. Pedagogically, despite its emphasis on the acquisition of the written 'register' rather than on the functions of argument or on the situations in which argument might be necessary (an emphasis which might lead to rigidity and over-formality), the pattern of classroom activity is very much in accord with that suggested in the excellent *Small Group Learning in the Classroom* (Cook *et al.,* 1989) which suggests a movement from engagement through exploration, transformation and publication to evaluation: a structure which shows interesting parallels with Labovian narrative structure (see Labov and Waletsky, 1967) and some models of arrangement in argument.

SUGGESTIONS FROM THE CANADIAN RESEARCH

I suggested earlier that some of the most extensive work on the differences between products and processes in narrative and argumentative writing has taken place in Ontario. In this section I want to look at the suggestions made by that research for helping students to write argument more effectively.

Pringle and Freedman (1985) suggest, as strategies for dealing with the poor performance of students in argumentative writing, the following:

> There should be more exposure to good argumentative models at all levels, from 'good adult prose ... to student writing' (p. 125). Students should be encouraged to respond to the ideas presented in such prose in much the same way as they respond initially to stories – that is, without particular attention to structure. 'In the upper elementary high school years, some analysis of the structure of the models, especially in the context of their own writing, will be profitable, as long as this supplements rather than replaces the reading' (ibid.).

> The competing model of persuasive discourse (commercials, billboards, political speeches) 'will have to be combatted' (ibid.).

> Children should be given the opportunity to write arguments in primary school. The range of topics should be determined by the students, rather than imposed by teachers (ibid.).

> Children should not be asked to compose 'for-and-against' essays until they have mastered writing which 'upholds and substantiates only one side of the potential debate' (ibid.).

> Children need to acquire 'a wider sense of the composing process, so that they may develop and explore their ideas in a first draft (or drafts) and then learn how to reorganize such ideas in an appropriate argumentative structure in later drafts' (ibid.).

What is even clearer in their most recent essay on the topic (Freedman and Pringle, 1989) is that there is a need to distinguish between conative/persuasive discourse on the one hand (see the second recommendation above), and more purely argumentative discourse on the other. One further point emerging from this recent re-examination of the earlier work is that exploratory argumentative writing might well result in 'a failure in the realization of the conventional structure for arguments' (1989, p. 78), but that such a failure 'is a small price to pay for the growth implied' (ibid.).

In an earlier report (Pringle and Freedman, 1980, p. 33), they had also suggested by implication that because both grade 8 and grade 12 students in their Ontario study did not build elaborate logical structures in making their arguments, but tended to make separate points that were only related to the topic rather than to each other, more work on the development of abstract conceptualizing might help the students write better arguments. In discussing this problem, they refer to Vygotsky's distinction between 'complexes' and 'concepts'; it is to this distinction, its place in a broader hierarchy of cognitive development, and its relationship to models of narrative and argumentative development that we now turn.

LINKS BETWEEN COGNITVE DEVELOPMENT, STORY AND ARGUMENT STRUCTURE

There is a passage in Piaget (1977, p.219) which might well have been written by Vygotsky:

> Reflection is an internal discussion... In social conflict is born discussion, first simple dispute, then discussion terminating in a conclusion. It is this last action which, internalised and applied to oneself, becomes reflection.

This is close to Vygotsky's central contention that human consciousness is achieved by the internalization of shared social behaviour. The dialogic principle (see p. 57, below) in the formation of thought will have a bearing on our understanding of the genesis and structure of oral and written argument, which attempts to link 'thoughts' to each other. Indeed, Vygotsky quotes Piaget in 'Genesis of the higher mental functions' (in, Light *et al.*, pp.32−41) when he suggests that 'Reflection may be regarded as inner argumentation.' He goes on to say, in his own words, that 'all that is internal in the higher mental functions was at one time external... In general we may say that the relations between the higher mental functions were at one time real relations between people' (ibid.). The nature of the links between social engagement, story, argument and cognitive development is a more pressing concern, because there seems to be a connection between the development from 'heaps' and 'chains' to 'complexes' and 'concepts' in Vygotsky's theory of cognitive development on the one hand with both narrative and argumentative structures on the other − and thus an implied link between narrative and argumentative structures.

Vygotsky proposed 'a sequence of different behaviours from random activity to logical reasoning' (Britton, 1970, p. 208) in the development of concepts in children. The first identifiable stage is that of 'heaps', that is to say apparently random collections of items which seem to have no relation to other 'heaps'; the second, 'thinking in complexes', a kind of grouping by family resemblances. Complexes are characterized by having a unity (unlike 'heaps') but this unity is best depicted as a kind of constellation; there is no clear thematic unity. Third comes the 'collection' in which a central unifying idea is linked to the individual components in a star shape; fourth, the 'chain complex' in which the items are linked to each other but not to any central unifying idea. The penultimate stage is that of the 'pseudo-concept', in which there is a central unifying idea and a linked chain of satellites, but no overall network of links between the two; this stage corresponds to an 'empty structure' or a concept offered by a teacher, but not fully experienced as such by a pupil. The final stage is that of the fully-fledged 'concept' in which not only is every satellite linked to the central idea, but they are logically linked to each other.

Applebee (1978), in his study of stories told by children between the ages of two and five, has based his modes of organization on Vygotsky's stages of concept development. Figure 2.1, based on Applebee's formulation, depicts the six stages, indicating possible parallels with development in argumentative competence as the third element in each list.

The identified stages in the formation of narratives are heaps (of unconnected perceptions), sequences (concrete and factual rather than abstract and logical), primitive narratives, unfocused chains, focused chains and fully-fledged narratives. It is

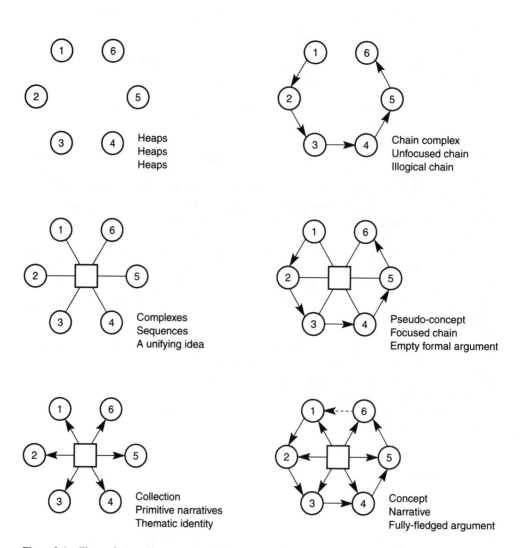

Figure 2.1   *The evolution of concepts in relation to narrative and argumentative structures.*

this last stage at which 'stories begin to have a theme or moral' (Applebee, 1978, p. 66) and in which 'the ending is entailed within the initial situation. At this stage the incidents are linked both by centering and by chaining and are thus more fully controlled' (ibid.). Although this formulation is Vygotskian, Applebee also refers to the Piagetian model of cognitive development, tracing responses to literature in terms similar to those of Moffett (from 'retelling' to 'evaluation') and following the course from pre-operational to formal operational thought processes.

If we think of the construction of essays (one particular form of written argument) in these terms, we can see that there is also a correspondence between the cognitive development model proposed by Vygotsky and the stages in the movement towards the writing of a fully-fledged essay. Essays may begin with the 'heaping together' of unconnected perceptions. Once a central informing idea is found (which will become the theme of the essay) these heaps begin to take on significance in relation to that central idea (the stage of 'thinking in complexes' – the stage which Pringle and Freedman found students stuck at in their writing – or 'sequences' of illogically connected points). This significance is reinforced in the next stage, that of 'collections' (corresponding to 'primitive narratives') in which the sequential logic is poor but thematic identity is clearly established. The fourth stage seems a different and perhaps parallel approach: it is that of the 'chain complex' (corresponding to 'unfocused chains' in narrative structure) in which sequentiality is strong but without a unifying central theme. In the fifth stage there is a combination of the second and fourth stages: a bringing together of a clearly defined sequence and a central theme. This stage of the 'pseudo-concept' referred to by Applebee as the 'focused chain', corresponds to the empty, formal essay which is achieved in form but which displays no real connection between intention, theme and sequence. Lastly, the pattern which represents the 'concept' and corresponds to the fully-fledged narrative can also be seen to correspond to the fully-fledged essay. It would be characterized by relevance throughout, with each section relating to the central theme; there would also be a clear and significant sequence to the points made.

What is striking about such an overlaying of three models is that not only does it shed light on the emergent structure of arguments, but it seems to accord with perceptions of the quality of arguments composed by students. Furthermore, the stages as depicted in Figure 2.1 seem uncannily close, visually and structurally, to the plans devised by secondary/high school students for their arguments, as we shall see in Chapter 5.

THE CONTRIBUTION OF DIXON AND STRATTA

Dixon and Stratta take a grounded approach to the problems posed by attempts to compose argument; their work in the 1980s in this field is substantial (Dixon and Stratta 1981, 1982a, 1982b, 1982c, 1986a, 1986b; Dixon 1989). They see the difficulties with argument as manifold. These include the inappropriateness of the 'for-and-against' model – a form that is almost exclusively school based, as they see it – for developing writers; the legacy of the classical rhetorical tradition with its exercises without real engagement or context; the tendency of English teachers in the late 1970s and early 1980s to focus on imaginative literature and writing at the expense of argumentative practice; and the resultant paucity of argumentative material in GCSE coursework folders.[5] These and other factors have combined to make the area of argument problematic for young writers in schools. So far, Dixon and Stratta's position is similar to White's, and they share a view that the standards of public argument 'are appallingly low' (1986a, p. 9). Their position differs, however, in certain key respects. They see 'narrative' and 'argument' as belonging to a continuum which moves from the particular to the abstract; in this respect their position is informed not so much by Britton as by Piaget and Moffett. Their focus is more on the emergent 'voice' of the individual writer and less on the forms and structures of discourse that are available to young writers.

As far as the present book is concerned, the most important insights of Dixon and Stratta are as follows: their distinction between advocacy and dispassionate argument; the distinction between 'action-oriented and belief-oriented argument' (1986a, p. 9) which, however, do shade into each other; differences in structure that result from these different functions; the suggestion that there might be an analogy between the structures of discussion and those of written argument; and the suggestion of a continuum from narrative to argument.

The first four of these insights shed light on the question of the structures of argument. Although structure *per se* is not the principal focus of Dixon and Stratta's work (their focus is more on the functions of argument and forms resulting from those socially situated choices), there is some discussion of structure, and the implications of their work are considerable. Argument might be seen to progress structurally from assertion through refutation, qualification, evidence, logical extension and rhetoric, and arguments that are ruminative (in a sense, these are pre-argumentative) rather than advocative or confrontational will have different structures. The more personally based and less public arguments may well develop differently, beginning with a question or meditation and developing through reflection, philosophizing or speculation to an inconclusive ending. Furthermore, they make the following assertion about the effect of spoken genres on written ones:

> It is in . . . serious discussion, or civilized conversation, as we might call it, that we suggest the foundations of connected argument or discussion are laid.
>
> (1986a, p. 13)

The essential points here are that there are several kinds of function of argument in the real world; each of these types has its own kinds of structure; it is limiting to reduce this variety to an artificial school-based model of argument which draws on only one aspect of rhetorical structure. Argument then, can be explorative rather than confrontational.

In the fifth insight, Dixon and Stratta acknowledge the complexity of the relationship between narrative and argument and suggest (1986a, p. 9) that 'narrative as a form of discourse has its limitations' in that it does not make its line of argument explicit. They see narrative as grounded in particularity and as standing on a continuum, at the other end of which are argumentative discourses. Narrative and personal expression infuse these upper reaches with liveliness, commitment and feeling, so that argument in this sense (committed, not detached, 'rational' and 'cold') does not 'lose sight of structures of feeling' (1986b, p. 72). If we 'move on from narrative . . . into typifying, summing up people's characters, generalizing and arguing. . . we are constantly moving back into [narrative] and out again' (ibid., p. 49)

The sensitivity to a range of functions exhibited in the work of Dixon and Stratta enables them to see not only that present conceptions of argumentation are limited, but that structures vary according to function and that within any single piece of argumentative writing there may well be a range of different kinds of language. The abliltiy of students 'to move backwards and forwards with ease from concrete particulars to abstract ideas' (ibid., p. 84)[6] is a manifestation of the flexibility already evident in young writers. But as the authors point out,

> it is the multiplicity of purpose that often makes the writing of prose so complex in its demands on young writers, for each 'purpose' arises from a tacit question, and the difficulty is how to put these questions together in an integrated string.
>
> (ibid., p. 83)

There is much that Dixon and Stratta have to offer in their publications on argument. While the developmental dimension of their work, grounded as it is in notions of movements away from egocentricity and in related notions of 'spectator' and 'participant' involvement in situations, is not strictly within the remit of this book, it is possible to synthesize aspects of their and White's work as we try to form a picture of how writing takes shape in the argumentative mode.

FROM NARRATIVE TO ARGUMENT?

In the late 1980s, encouraged by a movement in narrative studies in education which was probably then at its peak, I developed a hypothesis that difficulties in the composing of argument could be overcome by using narrative as a bridge to argument. Specifically, I embarked on doctoral research which hypothesized that children's competence in narrative structures as they reached secondary/high school could somehow be transformed into facility with argumentative structures. As I report in Chapter 5, that hypothesis was not confirmed, but other possibilites were thrown up by the writing of the students whose work I examined.

The general assumption is that narrative is deeply embedded in children's experience and is prior to the experience of and competence in argument. I have no argument with the first of these assumptions. Writers like Fisher (1987), Rosen (1984) and Fox (1993) have written eloquently and convincingly about how narrative manifests itself in storytelling, in the fiction we provide for children to read, and even how narrative paradigms operate to order and make sense of experience for us. General comments like Barbara Hardy's 'narrative is a primary act of mind' (1977, pp. 12–13) and James Moffett's notion that for a time, for children, narrative must do for all (1968) (i.e. be the processor through which all communication must be filtered) have set the tone for a generation of studies and programmes based on the primacy of narrative.

What is questionable, I think, is the assumption that narrative comes first. Barthes (1966) notes – almost in an offhand way – at the end of *Introduction to the Structural Analysis of Narratives* that it is perhaps not coincidental that a child learns to speak a fully formed sentence at about the same time as learning to tell and read stories. The implication is that the mind is ready to structure material in narrative fashion and that sentences are also structured narratively; and thus that narrative is operating in a multi-levelled way on the discourses of young children. This may be true (though my observation of very young children suggests that this fusion starts much earlier) but it is also observable that dialogic, sometimes argumentative exchanges can take place between children as young as 18 months, and that in proto-linguistic ways, exchanges of this sort take place even earlier. The difference between the two positions is that the argument hypothesis is supported by social theories about the learning of language, whereas – until recently – narrative was of interest because of the extended monologic discourses that were observable in speech and writing, and so was more readily recorded in print.

Despite Wilkinson's (1990) challenge to the notion that narrative is 'primary', national curricula continue to see narrative as the place from which children start their journey in acquiring a working knowledge of their own language. The English National Curriculum, for instance, in all its versions has narrative preceding argument, and the general progression is from storytelling to story-writing, from discussion in speech to essay-writing. Just as this curriculum seems to assume that storytelling stops at secondary school level, so too it assumes that the writing of argument does not take place until the end of junior school. The problem is caused by seeing argument in terms of the literary essay rather than in more open dialogic terms. Moffett's influential model of a movement from drama (what is happening) though narration (what happened) and reporting (what happens) to hypothesis/argument (what might happen) – a model very much predicated on a movement from the particular to the general as well as from the self outwards – similarly sees narrative coming before argument.[7]

Rather than debate which of these powerful modes of organizing language and exchange between people – narrative and argument – comes *first,* it is more productive to look at the close relationship between them, and to accept for the moment that argumentative discourse in its proto-forms has as much claim to primacy as narrative in its proto-forms. Let us think first about the common ground between narrative and argument as modes of discourse. Putting aside the functions of a particular discourse for the moment (the functions of argument will be discussed in Chapter 7), it is clear that within the broad categories of narrative and argument as modes there are many forms which share characteristics of both. The most obvious of these are narratives which carry an explicit message. In Labovian terms (see Labov and Waletsky, 1967) these are narratives in which the *evaluation* – an essential part of narrative in any case – is spelt out. Examples are parables, fables and other *exempla.* As we move along the spectrum towards more 'purely' narrative forms – that is, forms in which the evaluation is embedded and perhaps hidden (as in chronicles), or indeed, in which the point of the story or tale is given by its context among other stories and tales (as in conversation around a meal, for example) – we find forms like the anecdote and told story. More formally and in written form these become stort stories, novels, diaries and so on. At the other end of the spectrum, towards more purely argumentative forms, we find the political speech, persuasive pleas, objections and essays.

There are several important distinctions to make here, as the field we are discussing can easily become clouded. Narratives can have argumentative function as well as incorporating elements of argumentative mode in their make-up. Arguments can also incorporate narrative in their make-up, but the narrative function of argument is less obviously evident (unless an argument is included in a narrative – like dialogue in a narrated novel – for a particular purpose, in which case the function is ultimately argumentative). This sounds complicated, so a diagram may help clarify the relationship (see Figure 2.2).

Although the different text-types like chronicle, anecdote, essay and so on can be arrayed on this spectrum with a certain degree of confidence (and are conventionally seen as belonging to that mode of communication), there is room for lateral blends and mixes as well as the inter-level flexibility we have just been discussing. For example, a novel – clearly a narrative form on the whole – can include lists, recipes, letters, essays and dialogue, just as an essay can include lists, recipes, reports, anecdotes and stories. Furthermore, even relatively modest and generic forms like the recipe can include stories, advice, anecdotes and other independently recognizable text-types. In other words, text-types (or 'genres' in 1980s linguistic parlance) are rarely 'pure' but are often found to embrace other text-types; their hybridity is often manifested in mixes or by one text-type subsuming another, but there can also be blends of text-types that do not, as yet, have names. Some of Orwell's essays are very close to stories, for example; the prose poem is a classic example and the Japanese koan is another.

I hope the above discussion has at least put a question-mark over the polarized distinction between narrative and argument. Another way to look at the distinction is in

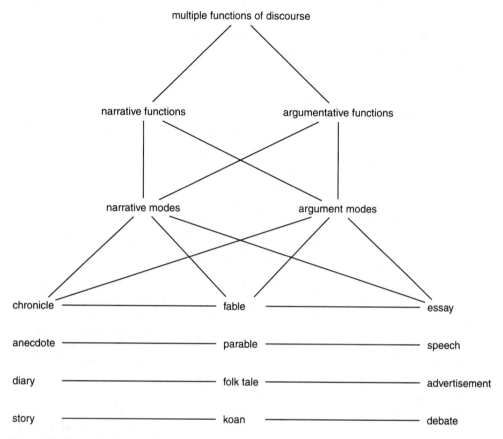

Figure 2.2 *Some functions and modes of argument.*

terms of levels of generality. It is true to say, in general, that narratives tend to be expressed in specifics – *this* place and *this* time – and that arguments tend to be expressed in generalitites, working from premisses and positions and assumptions and then proving or disproving these either by logical deduction or by reference to different kinds of evidence.[8] The evidence is usually located 'on the ground', as it were. Deductive arguments work from the general to the particular whereas inductive arguments work the other way. The very existence of inductive arguments, however, points to the fact that the relationship between specifics and generalities is never very clear cut, and that arguments tend to move backwards and forwards between the general and specific levels, just as readers' responses to a story move backwards and forwards between immersion in the details of the story and interpretation and criticism of it (see Protherough, 1985). Both modes, then, are able to play the whole range of levels, and in many ways the art of the good arguer or storyteller is to be able to operate and signify at those different levels, *integrating* the levels in an apparently seamless way.

Two writers have explored the interrelationship of narrative and argument in some detail. Hesse (1986, 1989a, 1989b, 1992) argues five main propositions with regard to the relationships between stories and essays. The first is that stories within essays do not prove points in the way that conventional wisdom argues. Secondly, story in an essay is not the same as narrative. Thirdly, the borders between story and 'not-story' in essays are hazy and cannot be determined merely by the presence or absence of narrative. Fourthly, narrative essays make points by giving propositions a place in story; propositions are seen as events in the essay-as-story. Fifthly, the persuasive form of narrative essays is less mimetic or ethical than formal. In short, this means that narrative can serve five functions in relation to the essay: to illustrate points, present information, occasion the essay, structure the essay and *be* the essay.

Fox (especially 1989 and 1990) finds in the spontaneous storytelling of 4- and 5-year-old children the genesis of argumentative structures. In 'Divine dialogues' (1989, p. 35), she notices:

> two major forms of dialogic, discursive argumentation. There is one in which the child as narrator conducts a dialogue, either directly or as a more obscure unidentified narrator, with an imagined listener. Here the text that the child narrates propels itself forward with questions, hypotheses, explanations and propositions, which are essentially addressed to itself, and which make explicit the particular problems which the story must address. The second type of argumentation is in a more dramatic...mode, where characters in stories stop and discuss problems and their possible solutions.

This is not just a question of narrative with an argumentative function – indeed, the function of these stories could only be said to be argumentative in the very loosest sense – but of argumentative rhetorical strategies embedded within narrative discourse. In her discussion of the stories of Sundari in 'The genesis of argument in narrative discourse' (1990, p. 30), Fox eschews a discussion of the syntactic or narratological in favour of a look at the 'range of rhetorical devices at [the storyteller's] disposal' (ibid.). These include knowing the difference between narrating time and story time, knowing the difference between the narrator's and the characters' points of view, and 'moving back and forth from one to the other in a very complex way'. Fox does not elaborate, but believes that it is in the practice of this kind of rhetoric at an early age that 'all the linguistic and intellectual tools required for later "rational" or "disembedded" discourse lie ready to be used' (ibid.).

If children of pre-school and infant age are indeed either able to argue explicitly, and/or are able to embody within narrative and other discourses devices and strategies that we can identify as argumentative, the implications for theories of cognitive development and for the staging of school curricula are considerable.

THE CRITICAL THINKING MOVEMENT

Any book on learning to argue must take into account the work of the 'critical thinking' movement which, over the past generation, has been suggesting new approaches to the teaching and learning of thinking. The imperative is there because behind argument as expressed in verbal and/or visual language is thought; and informing thought are reason and systems for producing thought.

There are reasons to explain the fact that the focus of the present book is argumentation rather than critical thinking. First, argumentation is social, dialogic (or multi-voiced) and tangible. You can see evidence of it, and therefore subject it to critical analysis. Because it constitutes an observable field of discourse, it can be delimited and compared to other kinds of discourse. Implied by this contrast between argument and thought is that the latter is less tangible: how can we tell when a thought begins and ends, and how can it be distinguished from feeling? How can we be sure that in discussing a thought put forward by an individual we are talking about exactly the same thing? The objection of imprecision could be levelled at thoughts and feelings manifested in language too, of course (verbal language being relatively more imprecise than mathematical language or musical notation), but relative to thinking and rationality, argument (the verbal manifestation of exchanges of points of view) looks more tangible. In addition, one of the aims of this book is to bring expressiveness and feeling back into the argument fold, rather than see feeling and intuition as diametrically opposed to rationality. Critical thinking, on the other hand, emphasizes the development of 'higher-order thinking skills' and these (from some points of view) tend to be seen as refinements away from feeling, however central they are to the operation of democracies and organizations. My third reason for distinguishing the development of argument from critical thinking is a pedagogic one: critical thinking is in a re-emergent state of excitement about its substantive and procedural approaches. While proponents of critical thinking would argue that their methodologies are sensitive to context, my impression to date is that the advances in substantive content and missionary zeal of the movement have temporarily occluded developments in methodology. The field of argument, on the other hand, emerging from a fossilized practice of debate and essay, is a field of pure methodology and strategy, grounded in dialogue.

To make such caveats at the beginning of a section on the relationship between argument and critical thinking may seem ungenerous, but they are necessary if we are to break through to the common ground between the two fields (just as was the case with narrative). Indeed, the common ground is more extensive, and the revival of interest in recent years in argument, critical thinking and rhetoric indicate many shared assumptions and practices. But it is also necessary to make one further distinction as we enter the field of critical thinking: between critical thinking itself and its parent discipline, philosophy. Philosophy is a *discipline,* 'the pursuit of wisdom, or of knowledge of things and their causes' and 'the study of the general principles of some particular branch of knowledge, experience or activity' (both *OED* definitions). Critical thinking is more of a process, an activity, 'thinking that facilitates judgement because it relies on criteria, is self-correcting and is sensitive to context' (Lipman, 1991, p. 116). In other words, critical thinking is more grounded than philosophy, more contingent on its context, more practical, less likely to speculate than to redirect its participants towards action. In a sense, critical thinking is philosophy recast for the purposes of application in educational contexts, particularly, as it happens, primary/elementary school contexts which are perceived to be a rich field for the development of such practice, given the dearth of philosophy in the school curriculum as a whole – a dearth seen by the proponents of critical thinking as a 'colossal gaffe' (ibid., p. 263).

To sum up the distinctions between philosophy, critical thinking and argumentation: philosophy is a discipline which embraces critical thinking and other forms of reflection; critical thinking is more of a process, akin to philosophical method but more of a skill than a discipline; argumentation is important to both, but is yet a further means to the ends of critical thinking and philosophy. Despite its position in relation to the other language arts, it tends to be seen as a 'lower order skill' in comparison to critical thinking's 'higher order skill'. As with many kinds of hierarchical definition, the relationship between philosophy, critical thinking and argumentation is relative.

In many ways, then, the introduction of critical thinking and argument into the primary/elementary school curriculum go hand in hand, and both stand in opposition to the prevailing assumption, derived from Piaget and elsewhere, that such activity is not possible at this level. Resistance to philosophy at this level is not new. In *The Republic,* Plato argues that dialectic (note the dialogic origin of philosophy) can only be introduced to those who have completed many years of training:

> And there's one precaution you can take, which is to stop their getting a taste of [philosophical discussions] too young. You must have noticed how young men, after their first taste of argument, are always contradicting people just for the fun of it; they imitate those whom they hear cross-examining each other, and themselves cross-examine other people, like puppies who love to pull and tear at anyone within their reach.
>
> (Book 7, 539b)

The same position was enshrined in the medieval universities where the seven liberal arts were seen as introductory to the study of philosophy; and in a contemporary view by Mary Warnock (1988, p. 57) who suggests that philosophy is not 'an appropriate subject for study in schools'.

Critical thinking, in opposition to these points of view, tries to encourage a critical, reflective disposition in children that is able to value and to see through indoctrination or attempted inculcation of narrow sets of values. It tries to help children think for themselves rather than accept pre-packaged education and ideas; the very 'traditional subjects' that Warnock and others are promoting are often seen by the critical thinking movement as areas of the curriculum which do not produce thinking by their emphasis on content and skills. The compartmentalization of the curriculum in this way – a vestige of late nineteenth-century categorizations of learning – is seen as fossilized and inhibiting in the late twentieth century.

One of the central figures in the critical thinking movement is Lipman (see 1982, 1983, 1985, 1987, 1988, 1991; Lipman and Sharp, 1978, 1979; Lipman *et al.,* 1980), whose work since the late 1960s in devising 'Philosophy for Children' programmes is a useful marker from which to take bearings. Two of his principal methodological approaches are to use story as a vehicle for philosophical method and to build up communities of enquiry which are committed to high-level reasoning. The stories used are very like the parables we referred to in the section on narrative: they are stories written with a purpose – to elicit reflection on reasoning and thinking, epistemology, logic and the philosophy of nature, language, value or art – rather than stories with any literary verve, and as such they come over as deliberate, with an ulterior motive, and somewhat dry. Methods of working with the stories are also rather limiting, because of the ulterior motive of the activity: children read episodes or sections of the stories in turn as an 'exercise in moral reciprocity' and are then asked for comments on the story, which are written on the blackboard. Teachers ask questions which elicit responses from the children. These approaches seem to try to develop a community of inquiry while appearing to reinforce power relations in the classroom. Questions seem to come from the teacher, in the time-honoured way, rather than from the pupils; despite the attempts of the stories and the eliciting questions, possession of the discourse seems to remain that of the teacher.

So teachers using these novels have two choices. They can ask children to read portions of them aloud, or they can read the stories themselves. Neither approach is without its difficulties, but the former may be more problematic, since poor readers are likely to be discouraged at the outset, and may come to look on philosophy as one more subject in which they are unable to 'shine'. To suggest that this problem is circumvented by a procedure which allows a child to 'pass' when it is his or her turn to read aloud is surely mistaken, as this is likely only to reaffirm the poor reader's inability to perform as well as his or her peers. On the other hand, should teachers decide to read the material themselves, this may become a laborious task and so may lead to boredom for pupils. If a programme is to be pedagogically liberating, one way to obviate this difficulty might be to offer children a number of media through which to study philosophy (see Costello, 1988, 1989).

In the development of a community of inquiry and in movement beyond the concrete to the abstract in primary/elementary school learning, however, Lipman's continuing commitment to the development of critical thinking is a potent one, and is shared by many other contributors to the field.[9] According to Burwood (1993, p. 10) critical thinking skills can be summarized as:

- the ability to summarize information accurately
- the ability to interpret and evaluate this information and assess additional evidence
- the ability to adjudicate between various positions
- the ability to ask pertinent and impertinent questions
- the ability to identify assumptions and reasoning errors
- the ability to draw out implications and make conclusions
- the ability to reason and argue a topic through and to develop and present new arguments

One heartening aspect of the critical thinking movement is its commitment to exploration of ideas through language, a commitment which seems lacking in de Bono's recent work on argument. In *I Am Right, You Are Wrong* (1991), de Bono eschews not only the adversarial model of argument that seems to pervade Western thought and institutions (an eschewal I would partly share in seeking new ways of framing argument) but also dismisses the role of language in bringing about change through argument. In this blanket dismissal, he seems to assume that language is inherently adversarial in the way it frames issues and experience, rather than seeing that words (*pace* Vygotsky, Kress) enable us to denote difference. In a summary of his objections to argument (1991, p. 272), de Bono claims:

> The argument process is central both to our traditional thinking system and also to such practical institutions in society as law, politics and scientific progress. We need seriously to reconsider the effectiveness of the method. If argument is intended as 'exploration' of the subject, there are much better methods.... The validity of argument depends on certain assumptions about absolutes and also on a lack of imagination. The polarizing, distorting and conflict-generating aspects of argument have long been self-evident.

I am in agreement that the adversarial model needs to be overhauled − indeed, that is part of the function of this book − but the contention that argument 'depends on certain assumptions about absolutes and also on a lack of imagination' is a deliberate reduction of the range of argument for − ironically − argument's sake and is challenged in the evidence of what children produce, as reported in the rest of the book. Looking for a Zen-like solution to a seemingly intractable problem that has been petrified by adversarial argument is one way to avoid argument; but it doesn't take into account that the imagination and different points of view generated in argument may well come up with a better solution. Furthermore, de Bono's attack on critical thinking (e.g. p. 273), suggesting it is not as important as creative thinking, misses the point of the critical thinking movement, which sees creativity as generated by and through its approaches, rather than diametrically opposed to them. Thus de Bono falls into exactly the kind of argument he is trying to criticize: an adversarial win/lose game.

OTHER APPROACHES TO IMPROVING THE QUALITY OF ARGUMENT

Planning is an important element when considering the advances already made in helping students of all ages to write better argument. One of the most distinctive contributions to understanding the nature of planning in different modes of discourse has been made by Bereiter and Scardamalia (1987), who make the distinction between 'adult' and 'novice' writers in their study of the psychology of written composition. Moving from notes to final text 'is primarily a matter of editing in the case of younger students' (p. 15) (by which they mean working on what is fully evident in the plan rather than transforming it in the final text). For adults, on the other hand, 'going from notes to text involves going from a multi-level data structure, often set out in non-linear form, to the creation of a linear text – a major transformation' (ibid.).

It was certainly borne out in the plans for narrative writing in one of the empirical studies underpinning the present book that moving from notes to text is primarily a matter of 'editing' for 12- and 13-year-old writers, but not so in the execution of the plans for argumentative writing. These are discussed fully in Chapter 5.

In a postscript to the chapter on the development of planning in writing, Bereiter and Scardamalia admit that their study is based on planning in expository writing. They refer to the widely held belief that young writers are more advanced in their ability to produce narrative than exposition, but note that it does not follow that 'their planning abilities are more sophisticated in narrative. It could simply be that a good narrative can be produced with less planning than is required to produce a good exposition (however "goodness" is to be equated across the genres)' (p. 213). Burtis *et al.* (1983) carried out a replication of the study undertaken by Bereiter and Scardamalia, altering the task to that of planning and then writing a story; Bereiter and Scardamalia report that the 'results were identical to those for expository writing' (1987, p. 214). Furthermore, 'the notes of some of the adults, but not the children (at grades 4, 6 and 8, ages 9, 11 and 13), in narrative planning had the same structural quality found in the adult notes of argument planning' (Burtis *et al.,* 1983, p. 2).

Burtis and his colleagues conclude that, rather than being more advanced, 'if anything, planning in narratives lagged behind planning in arguments' (ibid.). This is an interesting conclusion, but there is nothing paradoxical about this situation, as Bereiter and Scardamalia seem to suggest (1987, p. 214). We might only view this as paradoxical if we see one form of planning as 'lagging behind' another, as if it might be supposed to 'keep up' in some way. As will be demonstrated in Chapter 5, the composing processes in narrative and argument are different.

Benoit's concern is with the structure of spoken arguments between pairs of pre-school children, though she refers to the conventional approach to the subject as being focused on the making of arguments by individuals within a cognitive developmental perspective:

The child progresses from an egocentric stage capable of making simple assertions, to an adaptive stage in which reasons accompany claims, to a diversification stage in which a repertoire of reasons are available and strategic considerations dictate selection.

(1983, p. 72)

This stage analysis is similar to Piaget's distinction between primitive and genuine arguments, in that primitive arguments employed by the pre-operational child contain only implicit reasoning for claims while genuine arguments explicitly tie claims to reasons and are produced by children in the stage of concrete operational thought (Piaget, 1926, pp. 83–6). Benoit's approach differs from the conventional in that she sees argumentative interactions as 'rule-governed and socially organized events' (1983, p. 74) and arguments as 'emergent productions which are sequentially constructed by interactants through structural forms' (ibid.). The major difference in approach is that there is an attempt to chart the principles of the emerging structural patterns in the composition of argument, whereas 'the previous research tends to view argument as a fixed form' (ibid.). This perception is a useful addition to our emerging notion of how argumentation proceeds.

However, the underlying argument structure perceived is adversarial. This may seem inevitable, given that the field of research is spoken argument, but as Phillips (1985) has discovered in his research into the talk of 10- to 12-year-olds, argumentation (one of five categories of talk examined) seemed to be oriented in favour of cooperativeness rather than confrontation, creating a discourse style 'which asserts rather than argues'. His conclusion is that 'it might be beneficial to frame discussion topics in ways which invite speculation and leave conclusions open instead of requiring children to reach a decision' (p. 79).

For Benoit, on the other hand, 'argument structure' at its simplest level simply requires the child to follow a partner's assertion with a denial. This seems a limiting view of argument. Other work in the field of discourse analysis and cognitive development has included that by Delia *et al.* (1979), who conclude that the increased command of persuasive strategies that appears in children from kindergarten through to grade 12 (17 years) calls upon 'progressively advanced levels of social perspective-taking' (p. 254) and also exhibits a sensitivity to register. They suggest that:

> if the child is to develop control over communication at the abstract level of tactics and strategies, it is essential that constructs be developed for representing personality dynamics and motivations. By adolescence it is those persuaders who have developed a greater number of such constructs who adapt their messages to their target's perspectives at the highest levels.

(ibid.)

Bearison and Gass (1979) and Clark (1985) contribute further to this line of inquiry, concluding that teaching strategies can be devised to improve performance in argumentation.

Work in England has concentrated less on the identification of strategies that will enhance arguing in young children than on discovering existing argumentative strategies in their speech and writing, and on developing contexts in which argument might flourish. In relation to positions taken by Wilkinson and Fox, already discussed in this chapter, in the past few years there has been a steady increase of interest in the learning and teaching of argument in junior school children (aged 7–11). Reid (1991), in an action-research study, attempted a range of different argumentative structures with her Year 4 (8- to 9-year-old) class, from lists and short statements on what made the children 'angry' through comic-strip dialogues and face-to-face speech bubble confrontations to 'balanced' arguments. Most of the assignments set were dialogic in nature, with the dialogue taking place either within the text created or between the writer and a respondent – notably the headteacher of the school, with whom the children argued about the right to play marbles in the playground at breaktimes. In Piagetian terms, Reid noticed a capacity in the children to 'decentre' in advance of the conventional assumption; in Vygotskian terms, there was clear indication of the children's ability to embody social dialogic principles within univocal written work. The results of the study show that the children's perception of the difficulty of the assignments closely matched that of the teacher/researcher, but that the children actually enjoyed the difficulty of some of the assignments. We will return to later work by this teacher in Chapter 4.

Reid's explorative approach to children's argumentative writing contrasts with Frowe's (1989) work in developing oral competence in argument in Year 6 (10–11) children. Here, as with many of the North American studies, the emphasis is on teaching argumentative skills. Frowe discusses the giving of reasons to support arguments, contradictions, *ad hominem* and *reductio ad absurdum* arguments in his exposition of the capabilities of these children, and concludes that 'Primary teachers are in a unique position to promote the habits of mind necessary for good argumentative reasoning' (p. 63).

Working in the same field of developing argumentative talk, but with a different emphasis and approach, is Dyke (1991) who examines the relationship between social and cognitive skills, and asks the question: 'What happens to argument as you increase the size of the group who are arguing?' This is an interesting question as far as the present book is concerned, because it may have implications for notions of structuring on spoken and written discourse. What has been implicit in several of the works discussed so far is that arguments are often divided into two-part basic structures (either 'for-and-against' or 'statement and proof') and that these structures are seen to be conventional. We have also seen that it is possible – indeed, has been the case – that structures may consist of anything from two to seven parts in theory. It seems, then, that argument has been conceived as either taking place between two people (or two groups of people) or as being produced by a single person in argument with another party; or by a single person who tries to embody both points of view. Throughout these various types of argument runs a common strand: a conception of argument as essentially adversarial. Might it be possible, however, that as we conceive of argument as taking place in groups of three and upwards, not only will the dynamic of the argument change, but as a result (in concert with other factors) the structuring of the argument might also change? Although Dyke does not pursue this question, it is one that is addressed in the following chapter.

Bean and Wagstaff (1991) touch on this question in their chapter on the persuasive aims of writing. They suggest that, in bridging the gap between spoken and written argument, 'it is the teacher that must take on the role of the dialogue partner and support the child's line of thought and argument through the giving of cues, reassurance and general conferencing' (p. 99). Caution would have to be exercised with this procedure, however, in order to ensure that the child retained ownership of the argument and did not become over-dependent on the teacher in generating argument.

Bean and Wagstaff suggest further that support of this kind can put the emphasis on argument as exploration rather than as confrontation between two adversaries, and that such exploration 'should become the natural development of classroom discussion' (pp. 99–100). What seems to be overlooked here is that classroom discussion can take many forms, from whole-class discussion directed by the teacher to pair, small-group and debate-style discussion, each of which will have different implications in the notion of transference from speech genre to written structure.

In examining writing in the 'poetic' and 'transactional' functional categories in the work of two children, one at either end of the middle-school age range (9–14), Mallett and Newsome (1977) notice a general pattern emerging from a comparison of the two bodies of work that has some bearing on the present inquiry. Kerry (aged 9) 'writes in the expressive and poetic functions with proficiency and control. In the transactional function she has great difficulty, especially when she is required to organize material on a non-chronological principle' (p. 208). Cathy (aged 14) has consolidated what is already achieved by Kerry, and has made 'dramatic gains' in all kinds of transactional writing: 'Her remaining problem is with those assignments which demand the presentation of a balanced and supported argument on controversial political and social matters' (ibid.).

One further study that is close in subject matter to the present inquiry is developmental, and focuses on narrative and argumentative writing. Crowhurst (1987), in 'Cohesion in argument and narration at three grade levels' focuses on the written work of students at grades 6, 10 and 11 (ages 11, 15 and 17). She uses Halliday and Hasan's (1976) taxonomy of cohesive devices, and found that there was a decrease in the use of causal conjunctives from grades 6 to 12, and that this was largely the result of a decreasing use of 'so' (which at all three grade levels was the most common causal conjunctive). At grades 10 and 12, causal relationships were more likely to be expressed by subordination. For temporal conjunctives, there was also a decrease, 'but the differences were confined to narration' (p. 196). This result was largely explained by the decrease in the use of 'then'. We will find in the empirical study of the present research that conjunctives of this kind are most prevalent in the work of the seemingly weaker writers, and that subordination or ellipsis takes place as writers develop competence in giving their work cohesion. I also found that conjunctives of each kind (as defined above) are evident in both narratives and arguments. Temporal conjunctives are not confined to narrative, and casual ones are not confined to argument, as might be assumed. Throughout, there are more conjunctives used in narration than in argument (and the majority of these in each case in the narrations are additive), but one has to question whether every instance of the use of 'and' in a narration is a structural one, and furthermore, what degrees of structural importance are evidenced by this conjunctive, and by others in the analysis. While the analysis of such conjunctives is a useful element in the overall analysis of the cohesion of texts, it must be remembered that structure involves more than the appearance of surface conjunctives. Crowhurst admits as much in her summary (1987, p. 199):

> The most interesting and important finding of the study was that, for some types of cohesive devices, similar mean scores obscured very different uses of cohesion resulting from different writing behaviors.

She concludes that 'questions must be raised about the usefulness of frequency counts of types of cohesive ties as measures of writing maturity and writing quality' (p. 200).

Questions must then also be raised about teaching methods which focus on the level of cohesive ties, assuming that children will learn to argue if they are taught to use the nuts and bolts of an architectural structure, rather than everything from the design to the large-scale structuring of a building.

SUMMARY

Various approaches to helping students to argue have been discussed in this chapter as a preface to the development of new approaches. I have drawn on the best of what has been produced over the last ten years or so as well as taking a critical stance towards the developments in order to highlight differences. Some of the contributions to solving the problems of speaking and writing argument are as follows:

- to teach students a range of linguistic techniques, mostly to do with the cohesiveness of the text;
- to locate issues and strategies of argument, particularly in the press but also in other print and electronic media;
- to learn from the rhetorical tradition, particularly with regard to the arrangement of arguments;
- to discover good models of argument which can act as a guide to students as they try to compose in this mode;
- to understand more about cognitive development and how it relates to developments in narrative and argumentative competence;
- to build on competences in expressive and narrative writing;
- to explore further the relationship between narrative and argumentative composition in both speaking and writing, looking for both common ground and differences between the two modes with a view to changing assumptions about their relative positions on a map of discourse types;
- to accept that advances in argument may go hand in hand with developments in critical thinking;
- to look closely at the kinds of planning and other pre-writing, pre-compositional strategies that are best suited to argument;
- to begin to see argument as a dynamic discourse that is firmly located in social contexts, and to see that these contexts may well affect the kinds of argument that take place.

It is this last direction in particular, along with implications for argument seen from a dialogic and multi-voiced perspective, that we will now pursue.

NOTES

1 For a more extensive discussion of the influence of classical rhetoric on modern pedagogical practice, see Corbett (1965) and Cockcroft and Cockcroft (1992). For an extensive history of rhetoric, see Vickers (1988), and for contemporary reformulations of rhetoric, see Leith and Myerson (1989) and Andrews (1992b).
2 Note that this seven-part structure adds yet another version to the array of structures we discussed in Chapter 1. The additional section in this account of Cicero is the sixth, 'rebuttal'.

3 The relationship between fiction and argument is a complex one, and is discussed more fully in the sections on narrative in Chapters 5 and 7.

4 'Register' is the term used by Cambourne and Brown to distance themselves somewhat from, but at the same time to correspond to, 'genre' in the Australian 'genre theory' context. As a term, it lies somewhere between the use of 'genre' in an Australian context − as text-type − and its use in a North American context as 'social action'. As Cambourne and Brown make clear, 'By "registers" we mean types of oral and written discourse which serve specific functions. A sermon, a joke, a debate, a plenary session at a conference, are all examples of oral registers which have a specific linguistic function. They also have a characteristic linguistic organization which in part serves to define this function' (1989, p. 43). I have not used the term 'register' in this way in the rest of the book as I take it to refer to a distinctive lexical and stylistic selection of the language in different social and professional contexts.

5 GCSE is the General Certificate in Secondary Education, the standard examination at the end of compulsory schooling in England and Wales.

6 I deal further with the concrete and abstract in relation to argument in the following chapter, under 'Levels of abstraction', p. 67ff.

7 In later textbook versions of the model (e.g. 1981, 1986) Moffett disclaims that programmes of study from 'narrative to essay' are necessarily sequential, preferring to call the arrangement an 'array'.

8 A different view of argument − one not based on statement and proof − is put forward by Kaufer and Geisler (1991). They see argument proceeding along a main path along which 'faulty paths' are pointed out. This view is discussed in Chapter 7. The path/journey metaphor suggests parallels with narrative development.

9 The journal *Classroom Philosophy,* in embracing education, philosophy, moral education, thinking skills and narrative approaches to these, indicates the range of current interests (available from The Centre for Philosophy for Children, Old Acres, Charvil, Berkshire, UK RG10 9QL).

Chapter 3

Spoken and Written Argument

'I think that the voice has a lot to do with how good your argument is. You can use your voice like plasticine: you can mould it into the argument, bringing your voice high and then letting it drop down.' (Simon)

The relationship between speech and writing is a complex one. In general terms we can say that speech is characterized by shorter utterances, by a grammar that is different from writing, by the fact that sentences are often left unfinished or are finished by someone else in the conversation, by its relatively ephemeral nature, its sensitivity to context, its closer reciprocity with listening than writing has with reading, its more obvious dialogic or multi-voiced nature, and so on. Conversely, writing can be characterized as generally consisting of longer utterances or statements, as a 'second order symbolic system' that is dependent on speech, as a more permanent medium than speech and (perhaps therefore) afforded more status, as a means of communication in which the audience is usually more distant and less personal than in speech, as a medium which allows more time for reflection before a response is made, and so on.

There are plenty of exceptions to these generalizations; so many, in fact, as to put a question-mark over the general rule rather than to prove it. Take the following examples. A note is left on the front door for friends who are expected to call round: 'In garden. Please come through side gate.' The language of that note fulfils its function perfectly but it is a language without a main verb in its first 'sentence' and without articles ('the', 'a'). Imagine the family sees the note, goes round the side of the house and greets the other family in the garden. There might well ensue extensive ritual exchanges to begin with, but these might soon be followed by one of the members of either family holding court with a long story about a recent close shave or humorous incident. Within the normal patterns of talk over tea or a picnic, a story like this is unlikely to go on for more than two minutes before it is responded to in kind or with general approbation; but as a chunk of spoken discourse, it is likely to be longer than anything that is written during the afternoon.

Rather than think about argument solely in terms of spoken and written forms, should we also consider what argument is like on an informal/formal axis? There is room for both approaches, and in this chapter I hope to begin to map the possibilities for comparison between spoken and written argument in relation to formal and informal argument.

IS ARGUMENT SEEN AS PRIMARILY ORAL?

In Chapter 1, while setting out the problems surrounding the teaching and learning of argument, we saw that the English National Curriculum sees argument as taking place primarily in speech. I would argue that, from one point of view, this assumption is a valid one. The speech-based understanding of discourse is essentially a Bakhtinian one, suggesting that not only argument, but all kinds of written discourse have their informing origins in speech; it is also a view supported by Vygotsky, who sees the acquisition of speech as the first step in the development of thought – a 'first order symbolic system' which is further represented by writing, and which, generally speaking, is acquired *before* writing.

If speech precedes writing as children learn to communicate, and if speech precedes or informs writing in cultural production, both contemporaneously and historically, what is the particular relationship as far as argument is concerned? Is it true to say that argument is primarily oral in nature?

Argument, as a mode of discourse (whether in speech or writing) assumes that there is a specific audience. That audience is more immediate than the audience of many narratives, which are usually written (though not spoken) for an imagined audience. The proximity of audience in argument is a result of the fact that when arguing a case or putting forward a point of view, it is with the intention of *changing* the mind or position of the other(s) with whom one is arguing. There is little point in arguing your position if the audience is undefined. For a start, you wouldn't get any feedback or response to the argument, and would feel as though you were whistling in the wind. One of the distinctive features of an argument is that it defines itself in relation to other positions and points of view, and depends on these other positions in order to orient itself and try to make changes within that set of positions – just as in the view of argument put forward by Kaufer and Geisler (1991), of which more in Chapter 7.

In this respect, argument is a natural dimension of speech. Both share a more immediate sense of audience than narrative (or description or lyric expression). As defined at the beginning of this book, argument involves exchange and interchange of views, and such communication takes place more rapidly and more efficiently, perhaps, in speech.

If argument is primarily oral as a mode of discourse, it will show some of the characteristics of speech which were outlined at the beginning of this chapter. That is to say, it will be highly context-dependent, contingent upon circumstances and power relations, ephemeral, subject to shorter utterances on the whole than narrative; it will be dialogic or multi-voiced and social. Furthermore, it will follow the modulations of the speaking voice more closely than narrative, as suggested in the epigraph to this chapter. To put it another way, the speaking or writing of argument will gain more from tuning itself to the rise and fall of the voice in its everyday range than narrative (which may incorporate voices but which is more likely to follow the rhythmic relations apparent in speech than relations of tone and pitch – because narrative is more to do with organizing *time*). It is not only tone and pitch that are important to argument; volume is another aspect of sound and music that has a bearing on argument.

It is perhaps not coincidental, given the close relationship between speech and argument, that argument and argumentation have resurfaced as areas of interest over the last ten years or so. There are a number of related reasons, which will now be set out.

FACTORS BEHIND THE RISE OF INTEREST IN ARGUMENT

One of the factors behind the rise of interest in argument and its revival to stand alongside other major modes of discourse in education is the rise in oracy. Since 1965, when Andrew Wilkinson coined the term 'oracy' to refer to a range of speaking and listening practices (in contrast to 'literacy'), speech has taken an increasingly important role in learning, the curriculum and in assessment. Landmarks over the last thirty years have included the publication of *Language, the Learner and the School* (Barnes *et al.*, 1990) which established the close connection between learning and talk, in particular the role of different kinds of question from both teacher and students in a range of classrooms; the Bullock Report (DES, 1975) which emphasized the importance of talking and listening across the curriculum; the inclusion of oral examinations in the CSE examination,[1] which consisted, for the most part, of 'talks' given by candidates to a pair of examiners who then questioned the candidates on the topic of their presentations; and the advent of GCSE in the mid-1980s in which for the first time 'Oral Communication' was a compulsory part of English for all students at 16. It is worth stopping the chronicle of events at this point to record that the advent of GCSE, in requiring teachers to think more about oracy for all their students and as an integral part of education – along with the scope offered by assessment by coursework rather than by final examination – greatly widened the range of oral activity in classrooms. Students were now interviewing each other, preparing simulated news broadcasts, engaging in role play, linking drama and English ever more closely together, discussing and arguing over topics and texts in small groups, storytelling and asking more questions (partly as a result of directed activities relating to texts) *as well as* engaging in debate and speeches/presentations to the class. In other words, what had been represented in the curriculum as a formal tip of the iceberg in the range of speech genres used, now broadened to the rest of the iceberg. Competence in debate and the giving of talks was seen to be dependent on exposure to a much wider range of forms (many of them more informal in nature).

It is important to record these developments in English and also to say that other subjects were following suit, or were in advance of English in the recognition of the importance of speech to learning. A notable example was mathematics, in which the publication of the Cockcroft Report *Mathematics Counts* (DES, 1981) not only signalled the value of students talking about their maths as they worked on problems, but also of teachers assessing mathematical competence through talk. Some years earlier, in the teaching of modern languages, the shift to communicative competence in a second language was transforming teaching into a more interactive, oral activity.

By the time the National Curriculum was being formulated, subject by subject, in the early 1990s, 'speaking and listening' had considerable presence, both in English and in other subjects. As far as English was concerned, teachers and industrialists fought hard to ensure that oracy was given equal status with reading and writing, and managed in the first stage of the implementation of the orders to gain a third of curriculum time, with writing and reading having the other two-thirds between them. I say 'fought' and 'managed' because the government at the time was not keen to see speaking and listening given so much space. A third of curriculum time, however, still did not represent equality with literacy; but a third did seem reasonable compared with the 20 per cent that this part of the English curriculum was reduced to in later government guidelines.

We have already looked at the place of argument in the National Curriculum for English. But argumentation is not restricted to English, as is further evident in Chapter 6 where we look at argument in a number of disciplines at sixth-form and higher education levels. Because of a strong emphasis on skills and processes in the curriculum, counterbalancing that on 'knowledge' and 'information', a good deal of argument — or, at least, the elements of argument — is required in most subjects. In music, for example, 11- to 14-year-olds are expected to 'analyse music critically, using appropriate vocabulary', 'evaluate compositions and performances heard in class' and 'express opinions and preferences' about music. These requirements all come under the heading of 'appraising' music. In geography, often assumed to be a school subject which is high on the accumulation of information, there are elements of argumentation, even at primary/elementary school level. Particularly within two Attainment Targets, 'Geographical Skills' and 'Environmental Geography' (which is more obviously to do with issues than human or physical geography), students are asked to 'give reasons why people make journeys of different lengths', 'interpret relief maps' and, at the very start of schooling, 'express personal likes and dislikes about features of the local area'. Later, at secondary/high school level, these develop into 'consider the conditions that produce river and coastal flooding', 'analyse the factors ...', 'give an account of the relationship between variables' and 'give evidence' to account for hypotheses about the environment.

In mathematics, again at very early stages, students are expected to talk about their work and make predictions, speculate on 'what would happen if ... ?', make generalizations and hypotheses and test them and 'use appropriate language to justify decisions when placing events in order of likelihood'. Later, they are asked to 'construct an extended chain or argument using "if ... then" appropriately', justify solutions, interpret diagrams, and handle abstract concepts of proof and definition. To give one more example, in history at the primary/elementary level, students are required to explain, give reasons for events and historical phenomena, suggest multiple causes for events, make deductions from sources, and comment on the usefulness of a historical source. At secondary level these activities are refined, and in addition students are expected to make judgements about reliability and value, show how different causes are connected and 'discuss in a group what importance to attach to political and religious causes of the Civil War'.

Similar empasis on argumentative skills is to be found in technology, art, physical education and modern languages (to a lesser extent). What is surprising is that science and English, the two subjects in which one would expect the greatest stress on argument, put least emphasis on it.

In all subjects, the expectation is that justification, interpretation, commentary, the giving of reasons, the making of deductions and other aspects of argument will take place largely in speech.

SPOKEN ARGUMENTATIVE RHETORIC TO CONTEMPORARY WRITTEN PRACTICE?

For Aristotle, rhetoric is a counterpart of dialectic — a dialetic of conversational argument and discussion. This important first principle distinguishes Aristotle from rhetoricians who might see the art of rhetoric as divorced from the quality of arguments. The connection between rhetoric and dialectic mirrors the connection between argument and thinking. Because rhetoric and dialectic are closely associated, the nature and techniques of proof (for example, the enthymeme)[2] are central to Aristotle's thesis. His reasoning goes as follows: what rhetoric is principally concerned with is proof; proof is a sort of demonstration; the strongest of rhetorical proofs is the enthymeme; the enthymeme is a kind of syllogism. Competence in syllogistic reasoning is thus central to Aristotle's conception of rhetoric.

In relation to persuasion (which is only one of the functions of argument), Aristotle is clear that the function of rhetoric is not 'so much to persuade, as to find out in each case the existing means of persuasion' (1926, 1354al). In other words, Aristotle sees argument as highly contextualized, and sees the function of rhetoric as to 'find out' the best means of persuasion. The fact that the particular contexts in the *Rhetoric* are deliberative, forensic and epideictic[3] does not mean to say that there are not many more contexts in both private and public life in which rhetoric may be useful. Rhetoric provides arguments that are sound, in that they are derived from dialectics, and moral, in that the art of rhetoric sees itself as dependent upon moral standpoints. Indeed, the moral character of the speaker is seen as one of the kinds of proof available, along with 'putting the hearer into a certain frame of mind' and the speech itself. It is the third of these on which I will continue to focus here and more specifically still, the neglected aspect of composition: 'arrangement'.

In focusing on arrangement (structure), we must be aware that this forms but one stage in the composing and performing stages that were identified by classical rhetoric. These were *inventio,* or what we would call now the 'creative' aspect of composition (but which for classical rhetoricians was concerned with *topoi,* or the places and locations of arguments); *dispositio,* or arrangement of the parts of the discourse at macro-level; *elocutio,* or what might be termed 'style' (choice of lexis and syntax); *memoria,* the faculty of remembering and preparing for delivery; and *pronuntatio,* the actual elements of performance.

Following the principles of his conception of rhetoric, Aristotle sees the necessary parts of a speech as the statement of the case and its proof, though to these can be added the exordium (beginning of the speech) and epilogue, with the possibility of dividing the statement into a narrative of the facts of the case and a division of the topic addressed (i.e. a 'defining of terms'). There follows, in this part of the *Rhetoric,* extensive advice on the deployment of the various parts of a speech.[4]

Following Aristotle, Cicero, in *De Oratore* (1893), outlines the structure of a speech as consisting of an introduction, statement, proof and conclusion, but in the *Ad Herennium* (assumed to be by Cicero), this pattern is further refined as introduction *(exordium),* statement of the facts of the case *(narratio),* outline of points or steps in the argument *(divisio),* proof *(confirmatio),* refutation *(confutatio)* and conclusion *(peroratio).* Not only are Cicero's views on arrangement of significance as far as the present book is concerned; the way in which some of the books are written is also of interest. *De Oratore* is written in dialogue form, but in order to elucidate a dogma rather than to explore a topic in dialectical (Platonic) fashion. The style is almost novelistic, and takes the shape of narrative in its exposition; the oratorical principles are revealed in a story involving characters that is set some thirty-six years before the date of composition (55 BC). A key point, too, is that more than two characters are involved in the conversations, so different angles can be explored (with the concomitant disadvantage that the conversation may stray from the strictly logical progression that is more likely in a dialogue).

To return to the question of arrangement, Corbett (1965) notes that the rhetoricians acknowledged that on some occasions 'it was expedient to omit certain parts altogether...or to rearrange some of the parts', for example introducing the refutation before the *divisio* or *confirmatio*. This flexibility is evidenced by beginning a speech with 'the statement of facts', or using the proof immediately after the introduction and before the statement of facts. At other times it is advantageous to omit the introduction (either because no one can listen to it 'with patience' or because the subject matter or situation demands that we dive straight in.[5]

An example of a contemporary 'rhetoric' for the teaching of oral argumentative discourse is a programme devised by Hountalas and Craigen (1991). Like all contemporary rhetoricians, they move away from the three contexts of Aristotelian rhetoric and array types of argument on a spectrum from the informal ('whether to order pizza with anchovies or not') to the formal ('a disagreement as to who will be the better political party'). Although four reasons for arguing are laid out − to win, to work off aggression, to clarify and to learn − the 'basic principles' of the art seem to be concerned with winning, with the other three functions acting in a subsidiary role. In the major section on the technique of argument, we move from general strategies − who speaks first? who has the last word? strengths and weaknesses − to support strategies and rhetorical devices like rhetorical questions, emotional appeals, eye contact and body language, understatement and overstatement, voice and what to do if you make a mistake. In pedagogical terms, programmes for oral argument often take the form prescribed by Hountalas and Craigen. I shall comment on these stage by stage, as they form a useful basis for reflecting on the state of argument teaching in secondary/high school classrooms. In the following exchange, the roman type indicates material by Hountalas and Craigen; the italic type represents my response:

> Choose a topic that has content which can be managed by the level of students you teach or have the students generate topics in which they are interested. The topic must be such that two positions can be established (pro and con) and on a subject that the students care about... Also the topic should be chosen for which there is some short documentation available so that there is a basis for the development of an argument.

> *The emphases on the students generating topics and on the availability of documentary evidence are useful, though notice that the model of argument assumed is the 'pro and con' one we encountered in Chapter 1. Also, should the documentation be provided for the students or should they be taught how to find documentation, and how to use it? Perhaps that question is answered in the next suggested stage...*

> Gather materials and resources so that students know where they can find information relating to their position [then] have students work in groups of four so that students can work in pairs on the pro or con of an argument.

But students sometimes object to having to argue against their own conviction. Is it really as useful to make argument an academic exercise in this way as it would be to have students argue their own point of view while anticipating the objections to it and thereby devising ways to counter those objections? What happens when there are more than two points of view expressed around the table?

The group then discusses the issue, defends [its] positions, and critically examines the positions of the opponents. The opponents should listen carefully and/or take brief notes that could be used in further discussion. [They] can then evaluate the strengths and weaknesses of their arguments and those of their opponents.

And stay within the formal constraints of this kind of argument?

The programme devised by Hountalas and Craigen is one of the most thoroughly developed to date for a school board and is an excellent example of its kind. It still assumes, however, that argument takes place in a sealed classroom — hence the emphasis on the formal aspects of learning to argue. Further considerations of audience and context are necessary if argument is to take on a more effective role in the curriculum. With all this attention on the internal mechanisms of arguments, we must not forget that rhetoric has its roots in political and judicial practice, and that its application to literary or oral style is but one aspect of its extensive and integrating power. Our present focus on argument is closely intertwined with such a conception of rhetoric.

What I hope has revealed itself is that reflection on the patterns of oral argument may have implications for the way in which we write arguments; that dialogue and multi-voiced discourses are not only possible in writing — they are necessary if we are to extend the range of the written repertoire, give more energy and access to written forms, and ultimately revive monologic forms such as the essay.

ARGUMENT AND DIALOGUE

An idea — or nexus of ideas — that can be neatly divided into two opposing halves, or mutually supporting halves, has a great deal of attraction for the human mind, because it appears to simplify what may well be a much more complex picture. Questions like 'Are you saying A or B?', constructions of argument in schools as a case of 'for and against', the reduction of possibilities for action to two (only one of which can be pursued), the large-scale divisions in politics, Hegelian patterns of thesis and antithesis applied to thought and social change, stereotypes to distinguish national characteristics — all these are simplifications for and of the mind so that issues can be remembered and action taken. Often, polarizations such as these are justified with the argument that 'truth' is generated through the clash of opposites.

It is not always the case, however, that two voices, two views on a particular issue need to be diametrically opposed, or that the two voices of dialogue need operate from the same power base (the very word 'dialogue' has associations of mutual understanding and a common goal). Take Socratic dialogue, for example. Here is an extended stretch of such dialogue in which Socrates questions Lysis in order to bring the boy to an understanding of the relationship between free will and happiness:

SOCRATES: I dare say, Lysis, that your father and mother love you very much?
LYSIS: Certainly, Socrates.
SOCRATES: Then they would wish you to be as happy as possible?
LYSIS: Yes.
SOCRATES: Is a person happy when he is a slave and cannot do what he likes?
LYSIS: I should think not.
SOCRATES: So if your father and mother want you to be happy, they always try to please you?
LYSIS: Certainly.
SOCRATES: So they let you do what you wish, and they do not punish you or prevent you from doing what you like?
LYSIS: Oh, but there are many things which they stop me from doing, Socrates.
SOCRATES: What? They want you to be happy, yet they prevent you from doing what you like? Let's say you want to ride one of your father's chariots in a race. They will not allow you to do it?
LYSIS: They will not allow me to do so.
SOCRATES: Whom will they allow to do it?
LYSIS: There's a charioteer, and my father pays him to do it.
SOCRATES: They let a hired man do whatever he likes with the horses, but they won't let you?
LYSIS: Yes.
SOCRATES: Well, answer me now. Are you your own master, or do they not even allow that?
LYSIS: They do not allow it.
SOCRATES: Who is your master?
LYSIS: This servant and teacher here.
SOCRATES: Is he a slave?
LYSIS: Of course. He is our slave.
SOCRATES: It's a terrible thing for a free man to be governed by a slave. Just what does he do with you?
LYSIS: He takes me to my teachers.
SOCRATES: These teachers also give you orders?
LYSIS: Of course they do.
SOCRATES: But then why are they so anxious to prevent you from being happy and doing what you like? All day you keep under the control of another person. You can do nothing you desire to do. You, Lysis, are the master of nobody and can do nothing.
LYSIS: Why, Socrates, the reason is that I am not old enough.
SOCRATES: I doubt that is the reason. Your father and mother do permit you to do many other things and do not wait until you're of age. For example, if they want anything read or written, I guess that you are the first person in the house who is asked.
LYSIS: Very true.
SOCRATES: And are you allowed to write and read the letters in any order you please? You can take up the lyre and neither your father nor mother would interfere?
LYSIS: That is true.
SOCRATES: Then what can be the reason you are allowed to do some things and not others?
LYSIS: I suppose because I understand one and not the other.
SOCRATES: So the reason is not that you are not old enough, but that you do not have enough knowledge.
LYSIS: I think so.

(New York City Board of Education, 1981, pp. 14−15)

I am not presenting this dialogue as an example of good teaching. Socrates is too much in control of the direction of the dialogue to give Lysis the room to make the advances on his own. His 'I think so' at the end seems like resignation as much as enlightenment, and throughout he is 'set up' by Socrates to give the answer that Socrates needs for the next stage of his exposition. Take the question that Socrates puts to Lysis about the charioteer. Lysis is not allowed to ride one of his father's chariots; rather, his father pays a charioteer to do it. Socrates 'moves the goalposts' in asking 'They let a hired man do *whatever he likes* with the horses, but they won't let you?' Clearly, a hired man cannot do whatever he likes with the horses any more than Lysis can do 'whatever he likes'. Socrates is bending the argument to his own ends. Surely, too, it is an over-generalization to say 'Lysis, you are the master of nobody and can do nothing.' Lysis fulfils the role of a stool pigeon, a convenient aid to the exposition of Socrates's argument.

Nevertheless, this *is* argument. Various ideas are aired in considered, dialogic script. Issues such as the relationship between free will and happiness, the relative position of slaves and masters, the function of parental control, and reasons for such control are presented in a form that is grounded, concrete and has implied narratives behind it. It is thus probably more accessible and memorable that a straightforward monologic exposition of the issues. Its operation – despite Plato's attacks on rhetoric[6] – is decidedly rhetorical in that it manipulates the power relation between its two characters through language.

This discursive, expositional argument takes the form of a dialogue. Bakhtin (1981) sees the Socratic dialogue as a 'remarkable document that reflects the birth of scientific thinking and of a new artistic-prose model for the novel' (p. 24). It arises as *apomnemoneumata,* that is 'recollections' of personal memories of real conversations. These conversations take the form of dialogue framed by a dialogized story in popular spoken language.

Such qualities of dialogue, connections with memory and narrative, real conversations and the closeness to the speaking voice are a long way from the conventional forms of argument, like debate and essay, that I have characterized as part of the problem with gaining access to argumentative discourse. Debate is highly ritualized; the school essay – unlike the journalistic essay – is monologic, formal, and hidebound by the 'for-and-against' model. It militates against thought rather than providing an arena or vehicle for it.

The dialogic principle, on the other hand, is beginning to revive argument, making it more accessible, more sensitive to modulations of the speaking voice and more open to collaboration between writers. Just as, for Bakhtin, the novel 'can be defined as a diversity of social speech types...and a diversity of individual voices, artistically organized (1981, p. 262) so too the essay, if we erect it into a classic meta-genre characteristic of the argumentative mode in writing, can be defined in the same way. The links and relationships between the multiplicity of voices that find their way into the composition of essays and other forms of argument are also more or less dialogized. Furthermore, just as Bakhtin argued that stylistics as a critical approach to the novel had focused merely on the level of variations in syntax and vocabulary, so too it seems that approaches to the writing of argument have concentrated on elaborating stylistic variations on the essay, seen as a fixed canonical form derived from classical rhetoric and the Renaissance tradition of Montaigne and Bacon. But we have already proved that neither the classical tradition, nor the essays of Montaigne and Bacon, exhibits the formulaic patterning that the modern apologists for the school essay claim. They are guilty of reifying the tradition for their own purposes, which I would suggest are to limit the essay to a 'high' form accessible only to a small minority of the population and which has been used to differentiate performance through assessment. Hence its position at the 'pinnacle' of the discourses available in the National Curriculum, and hence its prevailing hold on expression at undergraduate level.

I am suggesting, then, that what Bakhtin claims for the novel is not only true of the essay too, but perhaps also of other meta-genres (as distinguished from modes) like the 'report' or the quasi-form, 'description'.[7] Each is informed by a dialogic principle.

If we follow Bakhtin's argument further, we will see that the hegemony of rational argument as expressed in essays and debate, from the point of view of the Romantic celebration of the individual as opposed to the celebration of interaction and collective action in society, is a convenient way of preserving the individualistic ideology. Rationality is seen as hierarchical and the essay as monologized. Similarly, in an assessment designed to differentiate and pitch individual against individual, monologic forms are prevalent, not only in writing but in speech too (the 'talk', the speech within a debate, the 'presentation'). The 'other voice', the respondent to whom you are addressing your language is, in fact, the examiner, and as such is distant, impersonal and will not respond in kind. And so, just as Socrates puts Lysis through an intellectual ordeal of shooting at his feet in order to make him dance, so too teachers who rely heavily on the examiners' technique of firing questions at their students are exploiting their power over the discourse of the classroom.[8]

There are further implications in privileging a dialogic view of the writing that can take place in a classroom. Writing such as parody, writing in polemical style and ironic writing seem underused in writing curricula even though they are common in vernacular speech among children as well as adults. It is as though the monologic conception of writing as self-sufficient, 'imprisoned, as it were, in the dungeon of a single context' (that of the classroom and its simulated, closed-off environment — itself a microcosm of larger forces in educational institutions inhibiting the expression of students) is not able to admit the principles of speech, in which 'messages [can be exchanged] with other messages' (Bakhtin 1981, p. 274). That is why 'the specific feel for language and discourse one gets in stylizations, in *skaz,* in parodies and in various forms of verbal masquerade, "not talking straight" and in the more complex artistic forms for the organization of contradiction' (ibid., pp. 274–5) do not figure in the repertoire of national curricula. They are subversive, and argument covers a great many of these forms because it demands an audience, it responds to injustices, contradictions and platitudes — above all, it questions authority, assuming that there is always more than one voice, more than one viewpoint. As such, it gives the necessary space for real expression of individuals and groups on society, rather than the muted expression allowed by 'approved' monologic forms that do not question or threaten the bases of expression.[9]

If communication — in writing as well as in speech — is essentially dialogic; if, as Bakhtin suggests,

> the living utterance, having taken meaning or shape at a particular historical moment in a socially specific environment, cannot fail to brush up against thousands of living dialogic threads, woven by socio-ideological consciousness around the object of an utterance; it cannot fail to become an active participant in social dialogue.
>
> (1981, p. 276)

then what are the further implications for argument, which is the mode that not only most fully embodies exchange, but also in its various forms can take dialogic or multi-voiced shape?

ARGUMENT AND THINKING

It has been evident so far in this book that it is hard to seperate the development of argument from the business of thinking. We can also put this equation in its reverse form: it is hard to separate thinking from the business of argument. In Chapters 1 and 2 I suggested that 'thinking' *per se* was a problematic area for students and teachers wanting to develop argumentative skills; and that the critical thinking movement had contributed a great deal to the revaluation of how we teach thinking. At the same time, I felt unease about some of the pedagogical techniques of the critical thinking movement. That unease is related to my sense that what is missing from the critical thinking formulations is, if not a sense of dialogue, then a sense of the rhetorical situations that shape thinking.

The writer who makes this connection, and whose work in rhetoric and social psychology acts as an important stepping stone in the argument of the present book, is Michael Billig in *Arguing and Thinking* (1987). He sees the best of classical rhetoric as providing more than handy guides – indeed, as the social and political situations have changed, the specific rhetorics cease to be useful guides. Rather, the value of rhetoric is that it reveals the importance of argumentation in human thought. He suggests that psychologists – and, we might add, the philosophers and critical thinkers – interested in thought processes have shown a tendency 'to venerate logical thinking to the neglect of the sort of rhetorical or argumentative thought to which Protagoras's maxim ["There are two sides to every question"] applies' (1987, p. 5). Thus rhetoric needs argument, or it is reduced to style manuals; in turn, thought needs argument in rhetorical context because thought processes are modelled on public debate (and other forms of argument).

Billig lays particular stress on Protagoras because he was 'the first person who asserted that in every question there were two sides to the argument exactly opposite to one another' (p. 41). In an important paragraph, Billig writes:

> A rhetorical approach stresses the two-sidedness of human thinking and of our conceptual capacities. A rhetorician is brought face to face with the contrary aspects of thought, and the teachers of rhetoric specifically aimed to develop a mental two-sidedness in their pupils... Protagoras trained his students to argue both sides of an issue, and in his treatises he compiled pro and con arguments which might be of use to both prosecutors and defenders.
>
> (1987, p. 49)

This two-sidedness is seen to be related to the human power of contradiction and the role of anti-logos in thought, so that Protagoras's maxim can be applied to psychological theory itself. In adolescence it may be particularly apposite to develop the contradictory spirit, supported by the powers of argument, as the development of a separate, argued stance seems central to the shaping of identity at this stage. Similarly, Ricoeur characterized argument and criticism as driven by suspicion, with narrative as a code which is 'obeyed'; Dr Johnson, fired by a spirit of contradiction, found talk dull unless spiced with the exploration of difference.

I have already suggested, however, that the human propensity for seeing ideas in terms of opposites – either/or, black/white, man/woman, us/them – can be limiting to thought. We need to add to Billig's insight into the connection between rhetoric, argument and thought something extra: a sense that argument − and thus thought itself − can be shaped by more than two voices. When I refer to models of communication as 'dialogic', it is this two- or multi-voiced possibility that I mean.

TOWARDS A DIALOGIC MODEL OF COMMUNICATION

I am going to pursue a train of thought which suggests that argument is the most ostensibly dialogic of all the modes, and that its re-emergence in models of discourse for education is overdue, by using John Dixon's paper 'Writing in response to each other' (1994b), itself a response to an article by Paul Richardson (1991). It's an ideal 'paper' to use, because it assumes much of the background I have just been exploring and it takes us one step closer to matters of argumentation and communication in the classroom. It is also written with the characteristic energy of the spoken voice, and seems like a conversation. For that reason, I am going to switch from the voice of a writer acting as intermediary between you, the reader, and the terrain which I am trying to cross − the voice I have been using so far for most of the book − to a voice that engages directly with what Dixon 'says'. You will have to reorient yourself to assume the position of someone overhearing or witnessing a conversation. Extracts from Dixon's paper here are presented as JD, and my own responses as RA:

JD: [The] idea of 'written dialogue', and its wide range of academic uses, struck me forcibly while reading Charles Bazerman's analysis of the arguments between Isaac Newton, Christian Huygens and others in the 'Correspondence' of the Royal Society (Bazerman, 1988). On that occasion, it turned out, the relationship of contributors was increasingly antagonistic; on this one, it's more a matter of friendly difference. As it happens, Leslie Stratta and I have recently suggested that teachers might distinguish between these two poles by calling them, respectively, 'argument' and 'discussion' (Dixon and Stratta, 1986).

RA: I too was struck by the Bazerman analysis, though I'd want to argue that an exchange between scientists could include both discussion and argument in the way you define them. As I've tried to say earlier in this book, however, I'd prefer to see 'argument' and 'discussion' as operating at distinctively different levels of analysis, with 'discussion' being a friendly exploration in words, and 'argument' being the mode that embraces discussion as well as dispute. I don't see them as opposite ends of a spectrum, because that suggests argument is acrimonious or antagonistic. If you like, argument is a mode and discussion a speech genre.

JD: I want to focus...not on 'language' [and its hierarchical categories] but on people 'interacting' through the medium of linguistic − and other − signs. As far as 'genres' are concerned, this will make a fundamental difference.

RA: Agreed. Perhaps we are moving in the same direction if I suggest that we are interested in genres a social action[10] rather than as text-type, and that this reorientation is entirely in line with seeing language from a rhetorical perspective, with particular speakers communicating to particular audiences in distinctive situations, rather than in a vacuum. Going back to the 1960s and 1970s, for a moment, you feel you have to remind Richardson that...

JD: ...by the time of *Language, the Learner and the School* (Barnes *et al.,* 1990) some teachers in England and Wales had already begun to analyse classroom dialogue across the academic curriculum, and there were teachers in maths, science, and so on who were just as interested as those in English and the Language Arts. From this point on, changes in social ways of 'making meaning' – a phrase picked up from Halliday's team in the early 1970s – were a precondition for any major changes in writing. We were trying to implement a 'negotiation' model of learning, instead of a 'transmission' model (Barnes, 1976).

RA: You remind me that, in the later chapters of the present book, the work of Barnes and others in that period has to be my starting point, because the implications of a dialogic view of communication are as much to do with classroom interaction as they are to do with the kinds of writing students undertake. But I don't think that movements beyond the 'narrative' and 'expressive' in that period in terms of writing fully took on board the implications of such a view of communication. The 'transactional' seemed more to do with 'information writing' – projects and so forth — than argument. In other words, in rhetorical terms (a tradition that movement was explicitly trying to move away from) the language examined was largely monologic. Classification of types of discourse, though, is always problematic.

JD: Before making any attempt to classify the range of utterances and texts we would hope to encourage in classroom dialogue, it is worth raising some preliminary questions. For example: a) should we expect the average utterance or text to have a single function, or several? b) how do listeners and you, the reader know what function(s) are in play at any given moment?

RA: I'll try to answer the first of your questions. In your own answer, you suggest that utterances and texts are probably going to be multi-functional. I agree, and explore the multiple functions of argument in particular in Chapter 7. That does mean that we need a multi-levelled, perhaps multi-dimensional 'model' of language use if we are to have one at all. Like you, I find myself objecting to the classification of extract from a piece of polemic as in the 'factual' category, sub-category 'argument'. That seems altogether too hierarchical, and I would want to make a clear distinction between argument and 'factual writing': a distinction that isn't made in many of the National Curriculum statements or in examinations, and which seems to blur thinking about the non-fictional area. The second of your questions is an important one, but leads me away from the topic of this book towards the reading and interpretation of argumentative texts – an area that *does* need research.

JD: When we ask ourselves what kind of categories to put down for the benefit of students and colleagues, the simplest answer seem[s] to be: give an illustrative range of 'speech/dialogic act verbs'. [These might number thousands].

RA: Again, that fits with a rhetorical conception of language use because each situation will demand a different kind or combination or blend of language. The problem is that such a plethora of different speech acts can generate no theory; there can therefore be no critique of what goes on in each speech act. At the far end of the spectrum that runs from structuralism and 'universal grammars' at one end to individualized, context-dependent speech acts at the other, the categories become impossible to define and less than useful. They are either too general or too specific. Argument, which is a broad term covering a wide range of potential dialogic acts, stands in a useful middle ground between the two ends of that spectrum, and also between function and form. This conception of argument has already accepted the dialogic principles you outline – indeed, they are integral to it.[11]

PROBLEMS WITH EXISTING MODELS OF DISCOURSE: MOFFETT, BRITTON

A dialogic approach to the understanding of discourse raises many problems that we are still in the early stages of trying to solve: problems of how to categorize different kinds of speech and writing, problems with the notion of 'genre' (as text-type), problems with assessment of school talk and writing. These problems are there to be solved over the coming years, and will be addressed in the later chapters of this book, once we have looked in more detail at the kinds of speaking and writing possible in classrooms. For the moment, however, there are other problems to be solved before we move on. These are more to do with existing models of communication, each of which has limitations as far as a new theory of the role of argument in a dialogic model of communication goes. In this section I will look at models put forward by Moffett (1968), Britton *et al.* (1975), Kinneavy (1971) and D'Angelo (1975), looking in particular at how they characterize the relationship between narrative and argumentative modes of discourse.

Moffett (1968) incorporates narrative and argument within his scheme, which is based on levels of abstraction. Before proceeding to expound and criticize this model, it is worth revealing that Moffett is more interested in structure than is usually assumed. Bringing this aspect of his work to light will reinforce the present argument that some consideration of the *arrangement* of narrative and argumentative texts will contribute towards a fuller understanding of writing processes. Although seeming to be inflenced by Chomsky on the structure of sentences (though transforming that work into a pedagogical context through an emphasis on conjoinings and embeddings at the syntactic level) and more generally by structuralism, Moffett maintains a distance from such influences, which helps to illuminate the question of structure more brightly. For example, he suggests that 'in the act of talking about structure we reify it into substance. The form of one man's short story is the content of another man's critical essay' (p. 2). This sensitivity to the nature of structure helps to break down the antagonism between those who favour the teaching of structure and those who see structures as 'empty' and, worse, as 'tyrannical' or 'constricting'.

> Anything is a structure. If we presuppose that some things are structures and other things are substantive elements which go into structures, we have trapped ourselves at the outset. Everything is both, which is to say that things and relations are matters of conceptual option.... By calling something a structure we mean that we are preferring to strip it of context, in fact to make it itself a context for some smaller structures.
>
> (ibid.)

Moffett's own 'structures' are based on the communication triangle of speaker, audience and 'object', with a 'notion of hierarchy of abstraction' informing the model. There exists a 'symbolic hierarchy going from the codification of our world that most nearly reflects the structure of that world to codification that more and more resembles the structure of the mind' (p. 10). That is to say, the model is essentially rhetorical and the 'structures' are not 'rigid' and autonomous, but a reflection of the situation of communication. That is exactly how structure is viewed in the present book: as a response to the demands of a rhetorical situation, often in response to a particular utterance by another.

But there are limits to how far we can accept the formulations of Moffett. He sees different kinds of discourse as resulting from shifts in relations between persons, so that the 'rhetorical distance' between speaker and listener 'and the increasing abstractive altitude between the raw matter of some subject and the speaker's symbolization of it' (p. 10) define the form. This notion of abstraction – central to Moffett's thesis – underpins the relationship between narrative and argument, and is one with which we have already had cause to argue.

In Moffett's model, the dramatic mode comes at the bottom of the hierarchy in that it records 'what is happening'. Next comes 'what happened' represented by narrative and linked to 'reporting'; above that, 'what happens' and the kind of generalizing evidenced in exposition; and finally, 'what may happen': logical argumentation and theorizing. According to this model:

> the logic of lowest verbal abstraction is chronologic (narrative) because it conforms most closely to the temporal and spatial order in which phenomena occur.... After playing historian, we play scientist: we assimilate a lot of narratives into a generalization by the analogic of class inclusion and exclusion. First I collect lots of anecdotes about Henry's behavior and then I conclude he is a bum.
>
> (p. 34)

From the analogic level the next move is to the tautologic by which general assertions are transformed into other general assertions. Furthermore, 'most high order discourses contain, like parentheses within parentheses, successive embeddings of the lower orders which they have subsumed' (p. 46). This last point seems indeed to be the case: descriptions and dialogues are often subsumed by narratives, which in turn might form parts of arguments. And yet at the same time, it is possible for arguments to be framed by narratives and for narratives, in their turn, to form part of descriptions or dramatic dialogues. The notion of one level subsuming another seems too hierarchical, too neat.[12]

The notion of progression from narrative towards argument is understandable if we take into account that Piaget is more of an informing presence than Vygotsky in Moffett's work; this very dependence exposes a weakness in the model. The narrative sequence – from interior monologue to third-person narration – posited within the level of 'what happened':

> corresponds closely to Piaget's description of the evolution of learning in the child. What hinders the growth of understanding, he says, is an unconscious preference for a limited local point of view. Learning is a matter of 'decentering'.... We achieve decentering by adapting ourselves to things and people outside ourselves and by adopting points of view initially foreign to us, as the anonymous narrator does with his single, dual and multiple points of view.
>
> (p. 148)

In the 1981 anthology, Moffett's position regarding sequencing is clearer than in the 1968 volume. By 1981 he had come to the conclusion that 'sequencing *en masse* can occur only grossly over a very long haul and that specific sequencing should occur on an individual basis' (p. 5). The sequence or 'array' was spiralled rather than laid out in a temporal line, bringing it more into accord with Bruner's notion of curriculum development and contemporary critiques of the National Curriculum for English, which has tried to impose a linear model on a subject that is largely recursive in its approach to language development.

The 1986 anthology lends a slightly different emphasis to the model. The move is away from a notion of four levels of modes of discourse and from dependence on the work of Piaget towards a more broad-based taxonomy which progresses from notation, recollection and investigation to imagination and cogitation. This is still a model based on levels of abstraction, though not necessarily a teaching sequence. In the 'Cogitation' section of this anthology there is a movement from a 'dialogue of ideas' through 'dialogue converted to essay', 'statement through story', 'generalization about oneself', 'generalization about anything', 'personal essay', 'review', 'comparison' and 'evaluation' to 'causal analysis'. Thus the 'sequence' begins in dialogue and ends in monologic (written) analysis; it begins personally and ends impersonally; it begins in drama and ends in the formal written essay. Incorporated within this sequence are stepping stones from narrative forms to argumentative forms. It is not clear where narrative becomes argument, and each of the modes is highly differentiated within itself as well as being broadly distinguishable from other modes. Fiction — but not poetry — is more happily integrated within the proposed range than previously.

Moffett's work has been discussed at length because it provides the most extensive account of relationships between narrative and argument as modes of discourse, at both the theoretical and the practical level.

Britton and colleagues, in their report based on project work carried out between 1966 and 1971, *The Development of Writing Abilities (11–18)* (1975), preferred to devise function categories than rely on the 'time-honoured textbook categories of narrative, descriptive, expository and argumentative' (p. 1). They suggest that these traditional categories or 'types of intention' 'will not serve as a conceptual framework for the study of writing' (p. 4), derived as they are from eighteenth-century categories (as defined, for example, in Campbell, 1776) and nineteenth-century versions of these (as in Bain, 1866). The interesting shift in this rhetorical tradition is from functions, as defined by Campbell, to the modes defined by Bain ('five leading kinds of composition, namely, Description, Narration, Exposition, Oratory and Poetry': p. vi). It is as if types of writing have been created by custom, and habitual use has given them an identity as recognizable products in themselves. Function has been reduced in significance, and the feeling that modes or genres of language constrain and limit expression is given credence. It is from this position that Britton and his colleagues — reacting to practice fossilized in the 1950s and early 1960s — list the 'shortcomings' of this particular rhetorical formulation. These are that such categories as narration and exposition are derived from an examination of the finished products of professional writers; that this tradition is profoundly prescriptive and shows little inclination to observe the writing process; that what the tradition actually provided was a collection of 'rules' about the best sorts of things to say in various argumentative situations. One of the most telling criticisms from this group accords with my own perception of the misunderstandings arising from not distinguishing between narrative and argument as modes and functions: that 'narrative can scarcely be seen as an intention in the same sense as persuasion or exposition might be' (p. 5); and that the four categories (narration, exposition, description and argument) are not equal in status. Rather, 'many pieces of writing employ one mode to fulfil the functions of another' (ibid.). As will become clear in Chapter 5, the more rhetorical approach adopted in the studies on which this book is based did not seem to reveal any lack of flexibility in process or attitude to writing in either narrative or argumentative form; nor was there any sense of 'prescription' in the way the writing was conducted.[13]

The particular relationship between narrative and argumentative modes of discourse is painted in stark contrasts by Martin (1985), who discusses argument under the umbrella term of 'factual' writing — an unhappy term for someone who sees all writing of this kind, in which he includes procedures (how something is done), descriptions, reports, explanations and expositions, as infused with ideology. Argument comes under the category of exposition, but a distinction is made between analytical exposition, which tends to appear in written form, to show little personal expression and to support the status quo; and hortatory exposition, which tends to be spoken and to challenge the status quo.[14] I find these categories unsatisfactory, and the broad and detailed distinctions made between spoken and written versions of analytical and hortatory too generalized on the whole. These problems, compounded by the polarized distinction between narrative and expressive forms on the one hand, and 'factual' ones on the other — leading to a conspiracy theory that society suppresses children's need to argue — suggest the dangers of the simplified debate about discourse and its uses in education. But Martin puts forward a thought-provoking argument on the relationship between power, ideology and argument which I will take up in the final chapter.

LEVELS OF ABSTRACTION

Moffett (1968) and Donaldson (1978), from their different perspectives, insist that abstraction can — and perhaps should — incorporate sensory material from the 'real world', narration, images and other forms of reification. This point is also made by Bakhtin (1981, p. 258), who suggests that 'in order to enter our experience (which is social experience) [meaning] must take on the form of a sign... Without such temporal-spatial expression, even abstract thought is impossible.'

This does not mean that there must necessarily be a fusion of the abstract and the particular, but it does mean that they are more intimately related in discourse than some of the developmental theories we have been considering allow. Dixon (in Dixon and Freedman, 1988) notes that Moffett incorporates the need for theorizing to be 'on a two-way street' (Moffett, 1968, p. 29) shuttling between abstract formulation and concrete reappraisals of the emergent theories. Dixon and Freedman use this perception to analyse further the nature of abstraction in language. This question has particular bearing on our inquiry into the relationship between narrative and argument.

Freedman's individual contribution, 'Levels of abstracting', examines the models developed by Moffett (1968) and Britton *et al.* (1975) and finds that 'the dominant voice is at times undercut by a sense of the problems inherent in the models presented' (Dixon and Freedman, 1988, p. 55), even though in the application of these models such problems have largely been ignored. We must pursue some of Freedman's questions in some detail as this paper would seem to take thinking about the relationship between narrative and argument to the limit of its development to date.

The first question posed by Freedman is one that might be asked of the present study: is the model (that is created to explain relationships between kinds of writing) psychological or merely formal? She defines the Moffett and Britton models as formal but notices that statements made in Moffett (1968) and Britton *et al* (1975) 'can be interpreted as making either claim' (Dixon and Freedman, 1988, p. 56). A second question concerns the focus of my attention in examining texts in the following three chapters. As already noted, Dixon has pointed out that Moffett himself was aware that most mature texts 'reveal a movement up and down among propositions with respect to levels of abstracting' (ibid., p. 57). In which case, should the attempt be to try to determine a dominant level of abstracting for each text?

Thirdly, is 'a conflation of genre with level of abstracting empirically valid or theoretically useful?' (ibid., p. 63). Two points must be made here before this question is discussed: I have already attempted to clarify the relation between mode and genre, but accept that the term 'genre' may cover the broad categories identified by Moffett (narrative, argumentation, etc.); and the conflation to which Freedman refers is that posited by Moffett in his hierarchy of kinds of discourse. Freedman suggests that specific levels do not correlate with specific genres, and gives as example one of the very 'genres' with which we are concerned in the present study:

> An examination of actual samples of texts will reveal that some genres, at least, can be presented at differing levels of abstraction. Consider for example, the argument,[15] a genre that is valued highly in school writing. At least in North America, the term is used to describe texts that are animated by a single thesis, often made explicit at the beginning and recapitulated at the end. This thesis is developed through a logical set of steps and/or illustrations. Digressions are avoided, and the linearity is expressed through explicit connectives. Most commonly, the register ranges from the upper levels of informal to highly formal.
>
> (ibid., p. 63)

She continues:

> It is true that argument cannot be written at the level of record or report [Moffett's categories] (although specific passages within arguments may be presented at these levels). On the other hand, although most arguments written by schoolchildren are more likely to be classified as high-level analogy, some are clearly tautologic or theoretic. And certainly, many examples of adult arguments fall into the latter category. In other words, while some genres may tend to higher or lower ranges in the scale, there is no clear identification of genre and level of abstracting.
>
> (ibid.)

Freedman also seems right to point out that the assumption that narrative is an imitation or real-world sequences is a false one as 'temporal sequencing. . .is not identical with narrative structure' (ibid.). Narrative is as much a selection from available material as argument, so narrative cannot be equated with report as it is in the Moffet model. Freedman makes this point in a way in which, in turn, we may find reason to argue in the concluding chapter:

> To tell a story (that is to present a sequence of events according to a narrative schema) involves an imposition of mind-made structure in precisely the same way that writing an argument does, with one important difference. The schema is not invented by the writer (in the way that the organizing thesis for an argument is so invented or created); it is provided by the culture and consequently often exerts its influence on a text through non-conscious processes.
>
> (ibid., p. 64)

In the same publication (Dixon and Freedman, 1988) Dixon makes an observation that will prove to be an important one as far as the present study is concerned. He suggests that forms like annals, chronicles, personal stories, arguments, sets of instructions and descriptions (or expositions) are all familiar social forms, some more restricted than others. Stories, discussions and even arguments, on the other hand, are very varied in structure. It is an insight which not only reinforces the notion that narrative and argument are best seen as modes of discourse, but it also throws us back to rhetoric and context, because it places a question-mark over the very ability of 'structure' to account for the nature of different kinds of writing.

FURTHER RHETORICAL MODELS: D'ANGELO, KINNEAVY

A discourse theorist concerned with both syntagmatic and paradigmatic structure in composition is D'Angelo (1975). This is not the occasion on which to discuss his 'conceptual theory of rhetoric', but within it more attention is paid to arrangement than in other contemporary rhetorics. D'Angelo observes that for many writers of classroom textbooks, the conventional wisdom of 'beginning, middle and end' is all that is offered the emergent writer, regardless of the type of writing attempted. This advice is considered to be 'so general as to be almost worthless' (p. 55). Other writers of such texts are observed to make a more formal distinction between 'spatial patterns', 'temporal patterns' and 'logical patterns' and these, in turn, are sometimes aligned with the traditional modes of discourse: respectively, descriptive, narrative and expository/argumentative writing. Perhaps D'Angelo's most telling contribution to the subject of the present book is that rather than aim to revive classical structures or seek any other kind of prescribed pattern to aid composition, he is at pains to point out the connection between invention and arrangement: he is able to bring together those who profess that 'form ever follows function' on the one hand, and those with a preference for formal approaches to composition on the other:

> Following Aristotle's system, I take form to be closely related to the formal principle (i.e. one of the causes of a mode of being) which produces discourse. In other words, in the inventive process, the writer begins with a mental image or plan of the discourse which is to be produced. This image (which is extrinsic to the discourse and represents the efficient cause) corresponds roughly to the order of discourse itself (which is intrinsic and represents the formal or material cause).
>
> (1975, p. 56)

D'Angelo thus provides a level of analysis between that of content and form, namely that of the classical 'topics'. The topical categories of definition, partition, classification, enumeration, exemplification, cause and effect, comparison and contrast are seen as 'formal patterns of arrangement' (p. 57) for organizing discourse. They differ from the conventional patterns mentioned above, however, in that they are both organizational and topical; they are not static but are 'symbolic manifestations of underlying mental processes' (ibid.); they are idealizations 'which the rhetorician is free to abstract from actual discourse' (ibid.); and they are to be considered 'universal patterns of discourse' (ibid.). As Adams (1984) suggests, D'Angelo, in linking forms to composing processes, is working very much according to the principles established by nineteenth-century rhetoricians on both sides of the Atlantic.

There is a paradox here. Although rhetoric offers the possibility of high-level theories of discourse, it also works at the pragmatic level of offering choices and strategies for working one's way through a composition (see Reid, 1987; Andrews, 1992b). D'Angelo's approach seems to suggest that rhetoric idealizes and abstracts patterns from discourse rather than providing patterns which may inform structures that actually appear in discourse. On the other hand, one could read D'Angelo as arguing a similar line to that of Dixon, mentioned above: that the choice of structure within any given composition is so varied, but that these variations are informed by certain underlying or overarching principles at the topic level.

D'Angelo makes an assertion later in the same volume that must also be mentioned here, only to be disproved in the research reported in Chapter 5: that 'formal patterns of arrangement on the paragraph level and on the discourse level obviously share structural characteristics with formal patterns of style on the sentence level' (p. 105). Not only is it a partial fallacy that syntactic structures provide the template for discourse structures, but it is a false assumption that 'patterns of arrangement on the paragraph level' are necessarily related to discourse structures. It is clear in the scripts analysed in the empirical study (Andrews, 1992a) that the paragraph does not always accord with the underlying structure of the composition, whether in narrative or argumentative form. Nash (1980) is closer to the mark when he suggests that 'in the rhetoric of prose the paragraph functions as a viewfinder, freely used to define the groupings and transitions of a compositional design. With its help the writer may frame a dominant motif spanning a number of subordinate details, or may perhaps outline a sequence of related propositions.' (pp. 8–9)[16]

The last major contemporary theorist in the field of rhetoric that we must consider, and whose work pertains to the relationship between narrative and argument, is Kinneavy (1971, 1983, Kinneavy *et al.* 1985). He prefaces his work with a caveat that the fields of discourse and composition are in the 'pre-paradigm period' (1971, p. 2) and that as a result 'little experimental evidence can be cited as conclusive' (ibid.) – though that might be said of all research in discourse.

Kinneavy is probably best known for his theory of the aims of discourse, based upon the 'communication triangle' whose three points are the speaker/writer or 'I' of the communication (associated with the expressive); the audience or 'you' of the communication (associated with the persuasive); and the real world or 'it' of the discourse (associated with the referential). While it is not directly relevant to the concerns of the present book to provide an exposition and critique of this model, it is one to which we will have course to refer in discussing the modes of discourse.

In an early statement in the exposition of his theory, Kinneavy notes that the dominance of the modes of discourse over the aims in the nineteenth century was a stress on 'what' rather than 'why'. At the outset, this formulation is one to argue with. Modes, by definition, do not deal with the 'what' of communication but with the 'how', the ways in which discourses relay or embody what needs to be communicated. Nevertheless, Kinneavy's next point is not only acceptable but important to our present concerns, that 'narrative or definition or description are determined by a kind of reference, not by an aim of language use. Narrative, as such, is not necessarily oriented to any aim: there can be scientific or exploratory or persuasive or literary narratives, and the same holds true of descriptions and the other modes' (ibid., p. 28).

Kinneavy is critical of periods in which the study of modes has precedence over the study of the aims of discourse because of 'a substitution of means for end' (ibid., p. 29). We can, however, defend the focus of the present book by arguing that the modes of discourse are the 'highest' level of analysis within language itself (as defined semiotically) and that limited though this level of analysis is, it nevertheless attempts to account for observable features of language in use. Elsewhere in this chapter, it has been accepted that a study of the modes of discourse must be informed by the level of content and intention, and perhaps also (if we are to take D'Angelo on board too) by the level of topics. Kinneavy himself (ibid., as on pp. 35–6 for example) is not always clear enough about the distinction between the aims and modes of discourse.

Kinneavy refers back to the modes (then called 'forms') of discourse established by Bain (1866) — narration, description, exposition and argumentation — and to make them more strictly modal, renames them narration, description, classification and evaluation. These modes might be arrayed in a different order to accord with Moffett's scheme,[17] but more importantly for our present concerns, they are seen as not being exclusive of each other. A qualification is attached to this general principle, however: that 'in a given discourse there will often be what Morris (1946) calls a "dominant" mode' (p. 37). In the present book, I have taken narrative and argumentative writing to be two major dynamic (perhaps *the* two major dynamic) modes of discourse as exhibited in school work in English, and as such we are drawing more on the conventional history of the modes than on Kinneavy's formulation. What his re-naming of the modes does confirm is that arguing is an aim of discourse as well as a mode, unlike narrating, which is merely a mode. If there are 'different logics for each of the aims of discourse [as well as] different logics for each of the various modes of discourse' (Kinneavy, 1971, p. 107) and further, if 'it is the logic of discourse, almost as much as any other single factor, which establishes a discourse as being of a given aim or mode' (ibid.) then it follows that a study of the 'logic' or syntagmatic arrangement of these discourses — both in the process of composition and as 'products' — is the right area on which to focus for purposes of comparison between narrative and argument.

Orienting yourself in relation to models of discourse is important, because it enables you to see possibilities that perhaps were not open to you previously. This is the function of good theory: to make sense of what happens and to offer new possibilities as well as the prospect of change. Having spent much of this chapter on the more general alignment of argument in relation to speech and other modes of discourse, let us now return to the practical before exploring possibilities in primary, secondary and tertiary education.

WHAT MIGHT A DIALOGIC APPROACH MEAN IN PRACTICE?

We have already seen that it is possible to extend the argumentative repertoire in speech. One major way in which dialogism can be effected in writing classrooms is through collaboration, and I can do no better than refer you to Morag Styles's book *Collaboration and Writing* (1989) for a full exploration of how that can work in primary/elementary and secondary/high schools. Here I wish to consider how the dialogic principle affects the act of writing, and whether there are any spoken forms or approaches that can be translated into the written medium.

How does the dialogic approach affect the act of writing?

If we free ourselves from the convention of seeing writing as a solitary act, as it is often practised in schools and universities, and almost always prepared for assessment in this way, then we begin to see writing in the way it operates in the public domain. At work, in the composition of novels and other literary forms, among teachers and lecturers, writing is more often than not a *collaborative* act. This collaboration can take various forms. In the preparation of a research bid from lecturers in a university, for example, the idea of bidding will first be mooted and discussed. A formal meeting might ensue, probably unminuted but perhaps leading to the making of notes on the elements of the proposal. One of the group will offer to write an initial draft of the bid, perhaps running to three or four sides of paper, and then will circulate it for comments. These will come in the form of marginal written comments, spoken response or fuller written feedback and then either the originator of the first draft or another member of the group will take on the revision of the draft. A number of drafts may be made before the group as a whole is satisfied with the proposal. When it is finally sent off, the 'principal investigator' or head of the research team may or may not be the person who did most of the actual writing. This model of writing is probably not uncommon in industry and, indeed, anywhere that people work in a team.

In this model of writing, editors of text are almost as important as writers. In traditional publishing practice, manuscripts (a misnomer now that most scripts are submitted in type and on disk) are submitted to publishers. They are read by commissioning editors who make suggestions as to the revision of the text. They then go to desk editors ('copy-editors') who make further suggestions or alterations concerned with content, sense, consistency, accuracy, layout and a number of other aspects of the text. The manuscript is then returned to the author, who makes the appropriate changes or negotiates the changes with the editorial team. Editors are hardly ever mentioned in the credits of book production in Britian, and yet they play a crucial part in the making of the text. Consider the part Ezra Pound played in the coming into being of *The Waste Land* (see Eliot, 1971).

In schools, this kind of collaboration does happen, but it tends to do so in situations removed from the assessment of writing. The making of a newspaper, the co-composition of a text on a word processor, a jointly worked out design brief or the writing of a playscript are often undertaken collaboratively.[18] Unlike collaborations in the public domain, these writing acts tend to be carried out *in situ,* with one student acting as scribe and the others as the providers of ideas. In the writing of playscripts, a group of students may each write the script, offering the ideas for the parts to which they have assigned themselves. This is a slow, laborious process, and probably much unlike the writing of a playscript for the theatre (collaboration takes place after the script has been written to transform it into a stage production). We have also seen in the last fifteen years a move away from a classroom of individuals writing for a teacher-audience towards a community of writers working towards publication by reading each other's drafts, conferencing, editing and proof-reading each other's work (see, for example, Graves, 1982).

Are there any spoken forms that can be translated into the written medium?

Before we discuss particular forms, here is a table showing a range of spoken and written, informal and formal types of communication:

Table 3.1. Spoken and written, informal and formal forms of argument.

	Informal	Formal
Spoken	Conversation Rows, quarrels Discussion Question and answer	Pair work Small group work Interviews Role play Debate Simulated meetings, court cases, etc. Real meetings TV and radio panel discussions Symposia TV and radio advertisements Games involving argument Speeches Problem-solving
Written	Personal logs Reading and project logs Notes 'Thinking aloud' Plans Drafts (and discussion of them)	Written dialogues Poems that argue Tracts Essays Written symposia Design briefs with justifications Parodies and satire Persuasive reports Advertisements of all kinds Literary essays References and testimonials Parables and fables Question and answer, notes and queries Proposals Collaborative writing Stories Plays

Like all tables and schematic accounts of what is possible in discourse, this has its limitations. It is two-dimensional and does not reveal the subversive energy that parodic, ironic and other forms of positioning can bring to an argument. It also divides rather too neatly the written from the oral, the formal from the informal. But what it does reveal is that there is a large number of spoken and written forms, that not only relate closely to each other but that are rarely used in the curriculum. Some of the most underused are parable,[19] dialogue and symposium, notes and queries, playscripts that explore issues, think-aloud protocols, real meetings, problem-solving and real rows and quarrels.

SUMMARY

This chapter has set out the case for seeing argument in terms of dialogue and ultimately in terms of the dynamics of speech. The rise in the influence of speech in language studies over the last thirty years, and the resultant or concurrent rise in the importance of speech in school curricula, have more recently given rise to an increased interest in argument. The main points made in this chapter are that:

- the relationship between speech and writing is complex and there is no direct transference of spoken argumentative forms to written forms. Nevertheless, there is much to be gained from seeing writing in terms of dialogic principles, both as regards the relationship between utterance and response and in the new dialogic written forms that can enter the repertoire;
- it is useful to think, not only in terms of differences and similarities between speech and writing, but also to see argument on an informal/formal axis;
- the relationship between narrative and argument is much closer than has been assumed;
- models of discourse that do not take into account the speech dynamic, that conflate exposition and argument or that separate argument from its expressive roots are likely to be unsatisfactory models;
- the concrete/abstract axis is yet another way of looking at argument, and yet I have rejected the notion that argument exists only at the abstract end of that axis, preferring to see it as playing the whole range of the axis and integrating the particular with the general;
- such realignments of argument as summarized above allow us to generate new forms of writing for the classroom. Some of these have been set out in Table 3.1 as a preface to a description of them in use in classrooms and at university level.

It is to accounts of what has taken place and what is possible in educational settings that we now turn.

NOTES

1 The Certificate of Secondary Education operated for examination at the end of compulsory schooling from the early 1970s to the mid-1980s, and was aimed at the 80 per cent or so of the school population who were not entered for the General Certificate of Education (GCE). Both examinations were replaced in the mid-1980s by the General Certificate of Secondary Education (GCSE), a unitary examination.
2 In Aristotle's use, an 'enthymeme' is a rhetorical argument as opposed to a demonstrable one; an argument based on probable grounds; for Cicero it is a striking antithesis closing a rhetorical period; and in logic, a syllogism in which one premiss is suppressed. A syllogism is a three-part argument: the first two parts are premisses from which the third proposition, or conclusion, is drawn. 'Syllogistic argument' is sometimes used to mean argument that proceeds from the general to the particular.
3 Deliberative rhetoric is either hortatory or dissuasive, and concerned with the giving of advice in private or in a public assembly; forensic is accusatory or defensive and concerned with investigation; epideictic rhetoric is concerned with praise or blame. Aristotle sees the first as future oriented, the second as past oriented and the third as located in the present.
4 For the detail of Aristotle's advice on arrangement, see Aristotle (1926) III, xiii ff; and for a full discussion of the question of *dispositio* or arrangement, see Barthes (1988) p. 76ff.

5 Research evidence on the importance of order in the presentation of persuasion is inconclusive. Hovland (1957) cites two studies – Lund, 1925 and Cromwell, 1950 – which are inconclusive as to whether the first speaker or second has more effect. There is a similar lack of conclusiveness about the order or presentation within a single discourse, despite Aristotle's advice that weak points in one's argument should go 'in the middle'.

6 See especially Vickers (1988) for a defence of rhetoric against Plato's accusations.

7 Bakhtin sees a dilemma facing stylistics and the philosophy of discourse, and suggests as a solution to it 'oft-neglected rhetoric, which for centuries has included artistic prose in its purview. Once we have restored rhetoric to all its ancient rights, we may adhere to the old concept of poetic discourse, relegating to "rhetorical forms" everything in novelistic prose that does not fit the Procrustean bed of traditional stylistic categories' (1981, p. 267). Later, he suggests that 'All rhetorical forms, monologic in their compositional structure, are oriented toward the listener and his answer. This orientation towards the listener is usually considered the basic constructive feature of rhetorical discourse. It is highly significant for rhetoric that this relationship towards the concrete listener, taking him into account, is a relationship that enters into the very internal construction of rhetorical discourse' (p. 280). The relation of argument to rhetoric is discussed in Chapter 7 of the present book.

8 Bakhtin (1981, p. 272) suggests that 'Every concrete utterance of a speaking subject serves as a point where centrifugal as well as centripetal forces are brought to bear [and so] the authentic environment of an utterance, the environment in which it lives and takes shape, is dialogized heteroglossia, anonymous and social as language but simultaneously concrete, filled with specific content and accented as individual utterance'. The move towards dialogue and the iconoclastic attitude towards the fixed canonical forms in the present book can be seen in terms of a broadly centrifugal movement away from notions of individualized, Romantic 'voice' and towards 'voices', even within apparently single utterances by individuals.

9 From the perspective outlined in this section, we can begin to see that attempts to impose a monologic culture on students in schools in the form of *National* curricula are part of a centripetal drive to erase difference – perhaps to close down thought itself.

10 See Carolyn Miller (1984) and Freedman and Medway (1994) for a view of genre, not as 'text-type' but as situated in the world of action, of language operating in the world (rather than the world of discourse).

11 So now, has narrative, in the form of Ian Reid's ground-breaking *Narrative Exchanges* (1992). As far as this range of speech acts is concerned, John Dixon has suggested in a recent letter (May 1994) that some speech-act verbs were 'central' or 'nuclear'. Such verbs – like saying, asking and telling – enter into a range of syntactic settings which further confirm their semantic range. 'In this sense,' writes Dixon, 'the theorist need not be faced with thousands of differentia; they can be grouped under less delicate, more ambiguous central verbs. Discuss and argue, you might say, were an obvious couple of central verbs in a new terrain – explicitly dialogic, not monologic.

12 Moffett (1981) admits that his original formulation was unable to account fully for poetry, where specifics and generalities can be fused in the image. I would argue that such actions of language are not limited to poetry, and discuss the question further in Andrews (1991b).

13 See Britton *et al.* (1975) pp. 146–61 for a discussion of conative (language used to instruct or persuade), informative and theoretical writing under the broad heading of the 'transactional function'. Although transactional writing formed 63.4 per cent of the total sample in this study, only 1.6 per cent was allocated to the persuasive category and 4.1 per cent to the theoretical category, bearing out the small proportion of argumentative writing in schools noted in the first chapter.

14 Martin uses a terminology that is largely Hallidayan in origin and is not employed in the present book. He calls 'genre' the purpose of a text and 'mode' the way in which it is transmitted.

15 Here Freedman means a specific North American school genre, the argumentative essay.

16 D'Angelo (1975, p. 125) does mention a feature of arrangement that is under-researched and yet which might shed light on the nature and processes of composition, viz. repetition: 'Repetition is certainly a major principle of arrangement, yet I know of no rhetoric or composition books in which repetition is handled as a major structural principle.' To repetition, we might add its development, rhythm — a feature that forms a part of the analyses of poetic texts but which has not been applied to the analysis of transactional texts.

17 Kinneavy (1983) has outlined the similarities between the models suggested by Moffett (1968), Kinneavy himself (1971), Britton *et al.* (1975) and D'Angelo (1975) in an attempted synthesis of the four.

18 See also Flower *et al.* (1994) for studies of collaboration in writing.

19 Erikson (1984) quotes a former janitor turned youth worker on the rhetorical importance of anecdote in explaining: 'He said that in counseling young men it was not a good idea to confront them directly with their situation or tell them in so many words what they should do. Rather, he preferred to tell what he called parables. These would be introduced with the phrase "I knew a fellow once who...". The story was actually about the young man addressed. The parable was an argument using devices analogous to the classic figures of speech, synecdoche (using a part to stand for the whole and vice versa) and metonymy (use of concrete attribute to refer to abstract entity meant)... The youth worker emphasized that it was not necessary to state the underlying point of the story explicitly — indeed, that would be inappropriate. The young man could be counted on to get the point for himself, and this allowed him to save face.'

Chapter 4

Argument, 0–11

'Emma, I thought you said a minute ago that you like playtimes.' (Carly)

This chapter marks the beginning of the second half of the book, in which practical applications of some of the suggestions made in the first three chapters will be explored. It is particularly exciting to consider the possibilities of argument in the first eleven years of life as this is the period – in schooling, at least – where argument has been assumed not to be possible.

The problems associated with the speaking and writing of argument have been largely diagnosed from research in secondary schools and within the subject 'English'. Work on argument and other modes of expression in the primary school, however, has usually been termed 'Language', though there is a move at present – partly prompted by the framing of the National Curriculum as *English 5–16* – to call the area of language practice and study 'English' too.

The difference between primary school language work and secondary school English is reflected to an extent in the kinds of project undertaken by schools involved in an extensive action-research project between 1991 and 1993 (the Esmée Fairbairn project; see Appendix 1). The projects in the ten primary schools selected for this research are less bound by the discipline 'English', and are more cross-curricular in nature; whereas the projects in the ten selected secondary schools all took place within English lessons. Although in some cases the work in secondary schools could be considered to be cross-curricular in theme, there was no interdisciplinary element to the work.

It may be that the recent nature of English as a secondary subject – its literary, expressive credentials – influenced secondary English teachers in the Esmée Fairbairn project into thinking that written outcomes had to be conventionally essay-like, in opposition to the prevailing narrative and expressive tradition. Oral work seemed less hidebound, and the prevalence of small-group discussion, simulations and debates suggests that secondary teachers saw more scope in extending the range of argument in speech than they did in writing.

There is no such grip by the essay on the argumentative imagination in primary schools. Speech also seemed to be the principal medium through which to argue (including role play), though there was a good deal of written work too, in various (less generically defined) forms. Two advantages that the primary school teachers enjoyed over their secondary colleagues were (1) that argument work was not bound by subject constraints; and (2) despite the time constraints imposed by the National Curriculum, there was still more flexibility in the primary timetable to allow for project work to find its own rhythms, rather than to be determined by the structure of the timetable.

Before we look at the results of the project, it is necessary to go back to pre-school experience in order to see what pupils bring to school in terms of argumentative competence.

ARGUMENT AS A PRIMARY ACT OF MIND?

In an article published in 1990, and in various papers and publications before that in the mid-1980s (1986a, 1986b, 1989), Andrew Wilkinson challenged the notion that 'narrative is a primary act of mind transferred to art from life' (Hardy, 1977, p.12). He suggested that differentiating (as posed to synthesizing) analytical activities such as the recording of evidence, evaluating, persuading, classifying, deducing, arguing – activities which all come under the heading of 'argument' – developed alongside narrative competences and that neither was primary when compared to associative thinking. Each mode is distinguished by its forms of validation. In argument, validation takes the form of the provision of reasons or 'proof', sometimes in the form of evidence. Wilkinson quotes several exchanges between 2-year-old children which show them providing not just one, but often multiple reasons why a situation should be seen one way rather than another.

As I write, my own third child is coming up to 2 years old. She shows many proto-characteristics of argument. One of her favourite words is 'No'. She says this in various tones and volumes, usually – of course – in resisting being made to do something against her will (like go to bed, get a coat on to go out, eat her breakfast). With two parents and an older brother and sister, there are plenty of people to resist. Although she can say many other words at this point, she never says 'Yes'. Assent is shown simply by going along with the request or by a quiet little hum. Language is thus used to resist and to define her identity in these cases, and it is a language of opposition rather than a language of assent. It is perhaps not too far-fetched to see her enacting what Ricoeur calls the 'vow of suspicion' rather than the 'vow of obedience'. The first turns into argument, the second into narrative in which we 'suspend our disbelief'. By the age of 4 or 5, children have devised a wide repertoire of argumentative strategies for getting their own way.

These argumentative turns are usually brief, like the single word 'No' and developments from that. But as well as being provided with opportunities for exchanges of this kind, Wilkinson argues that children should also be given opportunities to argue at length, in speech and in writing. This requires the provision of conditions and situations in which such extended argument might take place, and it may be that 'we have made a virtue of not doing so' (Wilkinson, 1990, p. 17). I wish to discuss at this point the example Wilkinson provides of an extended argument, because I think there is more to say about the piece than has been said so far. He quotes Catherine aged 5 years 2 months who orally presents 'a piece of straight exposition and explanation which owes nothing to narrative structure' (ibid., p. 16):

Well I said to these kids – you know the loops they have to do, she did those but not the first part you have to pull up. She just did that and I said that's wrong, you've got to learn – I can't spend all my life doing that and this knot and this knot and all the others as well. So I never can do that all by myself. And if there was another child could help with the shoelaces to do them in my classroom they could come to both of us but there isn't so I'm the only person and I get busy doing shoelaces and now I'm worn out . . .

This is the first part of her argument, and Wilkinson is right that the argument is clear. In his summary he gives the rest of her case:

'the children can start tying their laces but do not know the final processes. If there were someone else in the class to help I would be less worn out, but there isn't. Children of five should know how to tie their shoelaces. Kelly, particularly since she is taller than me, should know how to do them. One solution would be for children to wear slip-on shoes for PE. But if they don't I really need a team to help me. As it is, I despair, thinking of my classmates arriving at adulthood without being able to tie their shoelaces.'

(ibid., p. 17)

I'm not sure though, that Catherine doesn't also use narrative in her expression of her position. 'Well I said to these kids . . .' is a classic opening for a story told by a child. The 'well' is like a tuning fork struck to indicate the beginning of a tale and we are immediately into reportage. The utterance begins in the past tense, moves into the present ('I never can do that all by myself') and ends in the future ('when they're an adult they'll have to do it by themselves'). As a whole, then, the utterance is framed at the start within narrative. It's more of a whinge than an argument, though you could say that the dominant overarching function is argument.

My point in analysing the passage further is to suggest that utterances are rarely 'pure'. In this case we have a mixture of narrative, exposition and argument; but there is no doubt that we *do* have argument and that the 5-year-old is adept at presenting the various aspects of her case.

DIALOGUE WRITING AND REVIEWS

In a book of accounts by teachers of the emergence of authorship in young children entitled *Writing with Reason* (Hall, 1989), two essays stand out – among the many excellent ones in the book – as contributing to the overall development of argumentative writing. The first is typical of many of the contributions in that it lays considerable store on dialogic exchange. Jeanne Price describes how 3- and 4-year-old children in a nursery exchanged letters with a large model of a ladybird, having first conversed with the model. In the exchanges, they were set problems by the ladybird which they had to answer in writing, and were also asked to 'do a bubble talk letter', i.e. represent speech in print. As Price concludes, 'It is difficult for young children to understand that different voices can operate within a text. By using bubble talk, one can introduce a fundamental aspect of speech punctuation, that of separating out the 'saying' from the reference to who is 'saying'' (p. 13). More than that, I would suggest, the children were representing more than one voice in a written text, and moving not only towards the representation and punctuation of speech, but also towards the acceptance and inclusion of multiple voices within a text – an important step in the development of argument skills in writing.

In another account, Susan Williams describes how a class of 5-year-olds wrote reviews of books they liked. In many ways, the approach follows that of Cambourne and Brown (see Chapter 2, p. 32) in that the pupils were immersed in the form of review writing; but there is a much surer sense of the pupils developing their own writing. After reviewing books they liked, the pupils went on to become more critical in reviewing their own work and then on to writing guidelines for reviewing. They thus developed powers of reflection, wrote for real audiences within their own classroom (the reviews were displayed) and also engaged in activities that demonstrated the close reciprocity between reading and writing.

In these and other accounts, we see evidence of the benefits of dialogue writing, of collaboration, and of the connection with the development of argumentative competence in writing. There is acknowledgement of the presence of the speaking voice in the work, the development and supporting of points of view, the expression of opinions, the toing and froing of the teacher's and children's voices (or versions of them in role), and the telling of stories through dialogue. In the taking of different perspectives, there are the beginnings of reflection in writing. Not only is the emergence of authorship and writing ability demonstrated and seen to be important, as Vygotsky has shown us, because of the extra dimension of symbolic representation it affords us; there is also specific representation of multiple voices in writing (sometimes in collaboration, sometimes alone) and perhaps the consequent emergence of a sense of self among others through this very social approach to composition.

ARGUMENT AT INFANT (5–7) LEVEL

This section begins with accounts of work on argument in three primary schools that took part in the Esmée Fairbairn research. At the start of this research project, the intention was to focus on children from ages 7 to 16. Teachers from the ten primary schools involved were keen, however, to try argumentative work with infant (5–7) children, either by themselves or in collaboration with colleagues on the staff. Each of the projects reported here is different from the others, though there are common elements too which I will try to draw out.

What makes me angry

At Minster School, the aims of the teacher were to give children experience of developing their powers of argument in different contexts and to devise some means of assessing and recording any development that took place (Andrews *et al.,* 1993, pp. 74–87). With a Year 1 (ages 5–6) class, activities included the choosing of a toy from a catalogue and the articulation of reasons for the choice; discussion of the question 'What do adults do that make you feel really angry?'; discussion of the book *Fourteen Rats and a Rat-Catcher* (Cole and Cressey, 1988); encouraging children to 'be the other person' (as in imagining the point of view of a mother wanting to get a child to bed); and writing on topics such as 'Should toys be allowed on the playground?', letters to the head of the infants about the issue, the pros and cons of playtime and writing about the killing of 'minibeasts'.

The written statements of what made the children angry are, on the whole, brief and include such positions as 'My mum won't let me watch telly because I won't sit down on a chair' and 'I don't like tidying up because it's a messy job. My mum makes me do it.' As well as the assertion of a position (the proposition), there is the proof. But it is in the discussions between pupils of this age that the development of argument is at its most interesting. Four children — Carly, James, Emma and Richard — have been asked to discuss the pros and cons of playtime, and have been given guidance about the proprieties of discussion on tape; they have also been asked to consider the good points before the bad points. Here is an extract from their discussion.

RICHARD: What do you think about playtimes, Carly?

CARLY: I think they are quite good because you can play and my best friend is Anna. I keep on saying 'Can I play with Anna, can I play with Anna?', because everyone wants to play with me but I really like playing with Anna the most.

RICHARD: James? Emma?

EMMA: Well I think playtimes are good because sometimes people want to play with you and they are kind to you when you fall over.

● Yes.

RICHARD: James?

JAMES: Sometimes you can meet people, play with people.

RICHARD: What I think is playtimes are pretty bad but I like them. They are pretty nice things.

CARLY: Have we all heard ourselves loud and clear?

● Yes.

● Good.

RICHARD: I think that's a good question because you get fresh air in the outside.

● Yes.

● It's really, really hot.

● Yes but . . .

CARLY: Look outside now. It's quite sunny. That's part of the good things.

RICHARD: And sometimes when it's sunny we are allowed to have out coats off.

CARLY: Yes. That's the best thing really.

JAMES: We can go on the grass.

RICHARD: Yes that's a good part.

EMMA: I think the bad thing is when a bully pushes you over. I don't think it's fair when nobody helps you.

RICHARD: Yes.

● Everybody is laughing.

● Yes.

RICHARD: It is awful when you fall over and people laugh.

● It's really awful.

● You've got to go and tell Miss, don't you?

CARLY: Emma, I thought you said a minute ago that you like playtimes.

EMMA: Well it doesn't mean actually playtimes are nice. It's bad and good.

CARLY: Yes. I think it's a mix, isn't it?

EMMA: Yes, it's a mix, a mix, a mix.

RICHARD: But sometimes playtimes are good but sometimes . . .

JAMES: Boring.

JAMES: It is not fair when we can't go out in the rain.

● Yes.

CARLY: I think it is quite good when it rains because I love indoor play because then we can draw and do things like that.

EMMA: Yes.

EMMA: Well I think the thing is when it is raining the heavier it gets the heavier it gets. We get all soaked wet and we fall over and it's not funny and because it's not funny I think we keep falling over and it's not very good when you get wet and it's not very funny when you get wet because you get all soggy and you've got to get some new things from school and then bring them back and what if you forget them?

Richard acts a chair for the first part of the discussion, asking for an initial expression of opinion from everyone in the group, and generally supporting the contributions of others. The others all offer reasons as to why playtimes are good, ranging from the purely personal (Carly's '... because you can play and my best friend is Anna. I keep on saying 'Can I play with Anna, can I play with Anna?' because everyone wants to play with me but I really like playing with Anna the most'). Carly's 'because you can play' is extended in Emma's 'because sometimes people want to play and they are kind to you when you fall over'. Richard then moves the discussion on to a more general level – 'because you get fresh air in the outside' which is taken up by the others to include being able to 'go on the grass'. What is particularly interesting at this point in the discussion is that Emma introduces a 'bad' thing about playtimes: 'when a bully pushes you over'. What's worse is when no one helps you and 'everybody is laughing' at you. Next follows the most interesting part of the discussion, I think:

CARLY: Emma, I thought you said a minute ago that you like playtimes.
EMMA: Well it doesn't mean actually playtimes are nice. It's bad and good.
CARLY: Yes. I think it's a mix, isn't it?
EMMA: Yes, it's a mix, a mix, a mix.

Carly takes up Emma's switching to the 'bad things' about playtime, as though Emma was contradicting herself. As Emma makes clear, playtimes are 'bad and good', so she is hardly contradicting herself – only appearing to do so. I believe what these 5- to 6-year-old children are revealing here are two important principles in learning to argue: that it is possible to 'take up' what others say and not only add to or amplify their comments, but also *challenge* and oppose them; and that the development of a position may be more complex than at first appears. It may involve qualifications, multiple stances and disclaimers, as in Emma's 'it doesn't actually mean playtimes are nice. It's bad and good.' In the children's terms – as Carly and Emma perceive with excited repetition of the word – it's a 'mix'.

A question we should ask at this point is, 'Why has the teacher asked them to discuss the topic in this way?' I think the benefits are clear. First, this is a topic that is close to their hearts, although they probably have not conceived of it before as the location of an exploratory argument. Secondly, by addressing it in the formal situation of the classroom (and the further formal requirement of a taped discussion), they are able to 'stand back' from their experiences and feelings and reflect on them. Thirdly, the 'pro and con' (or 'for-and-against') model they have been offered enables them to approach the topic in a systematic way, even if it is limiting. It helps them structure the discussion, but at the same time it probably limits the nature of the discussion. Once the 'mix' of feelings and viewpoints has been identified, the pupils revert to the original pattern and then move on to a slightly different and more motivating issue: what happens on wet playtimes. With the hindsight of reflecting on a transcription, this might be a moment at which the group could be asked to develop arguments for what to do about wet playtimes, thus moving the argument from the academic (the pros and cons of playtimes) to the active (what do we do about wet playtimes?).

A further interesting section of the discussion takes place during the listing of the 'bad points' about playtimes. The children have suggested that you can fall over on the playground and bump your head:

CARLY: When I went out at playtime I saw Beth with a lump on her head.
JAMES: My sister did it one Sunday and she had to go to the hospital.
EMMA: Yes, but . . .
RICHARD: When I went to swimming lesson on the two weekends I couldn't help falling over in the water.
CARLY: I think we are talking about playtime. It doesn't matter, it doesn't matter. Anyway that's still helpful.
RICHARD: It is helpful.

As often happens in arguments or discussion, points are substantiated by anecdotes. Perhaps Emma's 'Yes, but . . .' (again, indicative of an awareness of the complexity of argument) was to be an attempt to bring the discussion back from what she perceived to be a diversion. She is foiled by Richard, however, who comes in with another seemingly diversionary anecdote to do with bumping one's head rather than with the problems of playtime. Carly brings the discussion firmly back in its central topic, but then follows her reminder with 'it doesn't matter, it doesn't matter. Anyway that's still helpful', to which Richard adds 'It is helpful.' The group then moves on to another point, more obviously connected to the central topic.

This last exchange interests me, partly because it is typical of discussions to wander off the point, partly because of the assertion with which the girls bring the discussion back to its central topic, and also because of the polite acknowledgement that the errant contributions are 'helpful'. The children may have revealed that they are aware that there are moments when, with subtle deployment of strategies and by using their teacher's language they must get the discussion back to its main focus, even if a secondary or subsidiary line has been followed for a while. The harmonic nature of this kind of discussion – the importance of balance and resolution – are in evidence.[1]

Debra Burnett, class teacher, recorded in her evaluation of the work with this class the following:

In the early stages of the project I felt sure that all of my class of 5/6 year olds were able to verbalise an opinion of some sort. They had all, at some time, asserted themselves, but could they express verbal and written opinions coherently and could they justify their opinions? As a junior trained teacher, I was very interested in discovering just what 5/6 year olds could do.

All of the children were prepared and able to give a single spoken reason to support an opinion – if the subject matter was important and personal to them. Throughout the project, this seemed to be an important factor with regard to motivation, enjoyment and sustaining a discussion.

Although all the children could make a personal statement, in the initial stages of the project, the majority of them were not able to discuss issues with each other. They simply said what they felt – full stop! I had not realised how much experience the children would need in actually learning to listen and respond to each other. I had made the assumption that successful day to day discussion was a transferable skill. Also, I had not considered how limiting equipment, such as the 'Coomber' [a multi-outlet cassette recorder] could be.

The children initially concentrated more upon this than upon the discussion. Both of these areas have shown a marked improvement throughout the project and developing these basic aspects should not be neglected or undervalued.

A proportion of the children (approximately 25%) were able to assert a verbal opinion and support it with a number of reasons, which they had not been able to do at the beginning of the project. It is difficult to decide whether this is due to the experiences and opportunities presented to the chidren, or whether it is a question of maturity.

Several children showed an increasing ability to present an oral argument which was coherent and followed a logical structure. Interestingly, these children were not all high ability children. Richard, for example, was a poor reader, not able to write any words at all and yet he was a forceful speaker who was able to think through an argument. For example, when discussing the merits of indoor/outdoor playtimes, Richard states:

> We're allowed to play out when it's snowing, but we're not allowed to play out when it's raining. That's the point!

Richard, along with several other children, also began to use acceptable/conventional forms of language in argument – 'the main question is...' 'However...' etc.

I believe this improvement in the type of language used was directly related to the experiences and examples provided, as the vocabulary was not used by the children in other situations.

Although all children experienced success in oral argument, written work tended to limit the amount of reasons provided. In most cases, the children did not have the secretarial skills necessary to put all their ideas on to paper. Therefore, for writing tasks the volume of writing required was limited – I was far more interested in specific quality than in quantity.

(Andrews *et al.*, 1993, p. 75)

Argument through role play

In Appleton Primary School, the emphasis was on improving the speaking and listening skills of 6- and 7-year-olds using a series of role-play situations. Imagining that it was shipwrecked, the class focused on the need to prioritize activities. The children were encouraged to exchange ideas and voice opinions and certain ground rules were established:

- There was no need to raise a hand to speak. A break in the conversation could act as the necessary starting point.
- There were to be no personal and unkind remarks.
- One could make a comment simply agreeing or disagreeing with any party if one wished.

The teacher, Pamela Rose, offered her own account of what happened:

> At first, comments made were suggestions for possible actions, and others agreed or disagreed as they chose. Most disagreements were based on 'what if' arguments: '... I understand what you mean, but what if X happens?'
>
> There were numerous tangents and complete blind alleys! However, over the weeks that followed, many children who had been initially hesitant became more prepared to voice an opinion. Some enthusiasts became even more enthusiastic – one to the point of verbal 'bullying'. More factors were added to the scenario. The plot thickened! Decisions were debated and made.

I noted two particular 'jumps forward'. Both were concerned with what seemed to be developing ability to look beyond the argument/opinion and to examine the motives/actions of the 'arguer'.

The first was an occasion on which a number of children were able to distinguish between a reason and an excuse. We were discussing possible courses of action should a schoolfriend fall into the sea. Some children realised that 'I can't swim' is a valid reason for not jumping in to rescue the friend. 'I don't like X' may be thought of as an excuse for a lack of action.

The second example came from a very bright child who realised that there was a contradiction between the words and the actions of a friend. Stephen believed that X was a suitable course of action. Nicholas disagreed and noted that Stephen was saying 'X' but doing 'Y' — and the two were contradictory.

(ibid,. pp. 56–7)

The pupils debated and discussed the various courses of action they might take on the island. One distinctive feature of the dialogue which took place was that much of it was conducted without reference to the teacher. Typical statements made or questions asked by children were:

'Can I just ask you something?'

'I agree with you ...'

'Someone could say ...'

'I didn't agree with you.'

'I don't think it's fair.'

'If one way it's right and in another way it's wrong.'

'What if...?'

'She's just making an excuse ...'

Here is an extract from the transcript of the discussion. This is a lengthy extract, but the length is necessary to show how the argument is sustained. It reads like something from *Lord of the Flies* — with girls as well as boys:

PR:	Do you think that we need to have somebody who is in charge, or do you think that we could manage without that?
PAUL:	I don't think we should have somebody in charge 'cos they could be bossy. So I think we could manage without one.
FIONA:	I agree with Paul. If you have a boss, they always boss you around.
ROGER:	I don't think we should have a boss because if you're saying something and I thought 'Oh, it's not a good thing. I don't know why they're bossing us around.'
FIONA:	I think we all should be a boss. We all could be in charge.
MARY:	If you had one boss, you could have good ideas and other people could have good ideas.
PAUL:	If the boss didn't have a very good idea, the other people might have a better idea. So we don't need a boss anyway.
PR:	Could I ask William to come in here because I don't think he agrees with this?
WILLIAM:	I think we should have not a boss but bosses. I think we should just have the boss of every group. The people who thought of it (the activity) should be the boss.
PR:	Who would those people be?
WILLIAM:	Simon, Tony, Samantha and me.

PR:	Do you think you'd be a good boss?
WILLIAM:	At home I am quite bossy.
PR:	Do you remember when you were talking about organising your group? You said you would listen to what people had to say and then you would let them have a vote.
WILLIAM:	If somebody else had a good idea, I'd let us have another vote and then we'd get good ideas.
PR	What would you do if someone didn't agree with your good idea?
WILLIAM:	I'd just tell them that it was a good idea and then we'd have another idea.
TIM:	I don't think that's really fair, because if they have ideas I don't see why they can't do their ideas.
WILLIAM:	I just want to say something, if somebody has an idea to make one big thing, then they would need help to make that big thing.
DAVID:	But it might not be a big thing, William, it might be a small thing. And I think having a boss would be a good idea, because they wouldn't know what to do, would they, without a boss?
PAUL:	I quite agree with the voting, because if you had good ideas and the boss didn't agree with them, you could have another vote, or else he'd just ignore them.
RACHEL:	I wouldn't like having to have a boss because they would be a bit bossy.
DAVID:	Bosses are meant to be bossy.
RACHEL:	I know they are meant to be bossy, but they might not be bossy, might they?
FIONA:	I don't think it's a good idea because they might ask us to do something we can't do. We might hurt ourselves.
WILLIAM:	I've remembered what I was going to say. I didn't agree with David because if somebody's idea got the most votes, I'd try it out to see if it worked. And then if it didn't work. I'd tell them that it was a silly idea and I'd get another idea.
PR:	I'd like to bring Richard in now because you didn't want to be in any of the groups did you, Richard? Do you think there should be somebody in charge?
RICHARD:	I think there shouldn't be anybody in charge.
SAMANTHA:	If there was somebody in charge, the other people might get fed up.
PR:	Would you like to be in charge?
SAMANTHA:	I don't think it would be fair on other people.
WILLIAM:	Samantha, I want to say something here. Even though your idea was quite good, I don't agree with what you've just said. Because when your group goes off, they won't be able to know what to do. They need to have someone to show them where to go and lead them.
PAUL:	Well I quite agree with Samantha, because if I was the boss of a team I wouldn't like to be organising because they would all get fed up.
PR:	Would you get fed up if someone was telling you what they thought you ought to do?
PAUL:	Yes.
WILLIAM:	So, Paul, how come you're not getting fed up because you're in David's group and you've got a boss?
	[Long silence]
WILLIAM:	Don't explain what you're saying, Paul because I don't think you knew what you were saying and if you don't have a reason . . .
PR	Paul, why did you choose to go into David's group?
PAUL:	Because I thought it was an important thing to look for food and shelter for the night.
PR:	Would you have gone into that group if you had thought that David was not a very good leader?

PAUL: I know he can do things very well and he's never bossy. He never gets cross.
PR: Is that right, David? Are you that sort of person? Don't you ever get bossy?
DAVID: Not all that often.
TOM: I think I'd like to have one person in charge and if people in the group had good ideas, we'd listen to those ideas and if they were sensible, we'd try them out.
WILLIAM: Tom, your idea is just quite like mine, except he isn't voting. You're just choosing ideas there. So it's exactly the same as mine that idea. I'd pick the idea that got the most votes. And then the one with a few less. And then I'd keep going down until I'd find a good one that would work.
JOHN: I'd go into Tom's group, because if I was going to say something, he would listen to it.
ROBERT: I'd go with Tom, because say if William said 'Robert, do something', he might listen but I'd go with Tom. He'll listen to what we'll say.
GLEN: I'd go with Tom because William would always boss you about.
PR: Are you a bossy person, William?
WILLIAM: No, I don't think so.
SEVERAL;   Yes, he is!
PAUL: I'd like to be with Tom because he's nice and kind to me.
JANE: I'd be with Tom 'cos he does nice things.
JOHN: I think William would talk too much.
PR: People seem to think, William, that you are a bossy person. Are you bossy?
WILLIAM: Yes, I'm bossy at home.
PR: What would you do if you had a good idea and your group wouldn't accept it?
WILLIAM: All I'd do is ask them if they had a better idea. And then it doesn't matter — we'd just carry on with mine.
PR: If there was nobody in charge, how would you decide what to do?
PAUL: We'd just try out the good ideas.
WILLIAM: I don't think that's a good idea because if people had silly ideas, what would you do then? What if everybody didn't have good ideas? If everybody didn't agree with each other, what would you do then? What would you do without a boss? Suppose you didn't have one, all you'd be able to do is everybody would be arguing. Everybody would think they had better ideas than everybody else. They'd always be arguing.
●   I agree with you there.
PAUL: There would be no one to help you if you needed help.
WILLIAM: That's why I think you should have bosses because then everybody else wouldn't be arguing.
DAVID: William, I think your idea on voting was good.
WILLIAM: I know. If you voted, then that person would get to try out their idea. It's only to help you decide who is going to try their idea first and try it out.
PAUL: I don't agree with having a boss because I wouldn't like to be a boss. I'd just let everyone do their idea and then we'd see if they are any good.
WILLIAM: Paul, I think it's better to let people help you if the job's quite big. Otherwise people would be arguing.
PAUL: What happens if it's a small thing?
WILLIAM: If it was small, you could just go off and do it and see if it works or if it doesn't.
PAUL: What I would do is I would see if another person could do it first, to see if it would work.
PR: William thinks you would argue. Do you think you would argue?
SEVERAL: No.
STEPHEN: You would and no wonder — they'd be bossing you around. Like William, like

he was saying to his group and they didn't believe him, and they could say: 'William, we don't believe you'. Because if we was in groups, and there was a boss there, we shouldn't have a boss.

JANE: I don't think we would be arguing because we would be worrying about getting back to land.

NEIL: I quite agree with you there.

WILLIAM: I think I know what you're going to say. They can't boss the other group around because the other bosses will keep them in control.

PR: Suppose your leader asked you to do something silly like swim home from the island. What would you do if you didn't agree with them?

JANE: I wouldn't go swimming because some people might not be able to swim without armbands. Some people might not be able to swim at all.

PR: Suppose I said 'Jane, you are going to swim for home whether you like it or not', what would you say then?

JANE: I'd say it was a bit too dangerous.

(ibid., pp. 58–62)

I have quoted a long extract from this discussion because I think it is remarkable in several ways. First, for the ways in which the children listen to each other. This enables them gradually to clarify different positions and make decisions according to how they see the overall picture of life on the island. Secondly, for the ways in which they are able to listen and *build* on each other's points. A good example is when William takes up a point made by Samantha:

PR: Would you like to be in charge?

SAMANTHA: I don't think it would be fair on other people.

WILLIAM: Samantha, I want to say something there. Even though your idea was quite good, I don't agree with what you've just said. Because when your group goes off, they won't be able to know what to do. They need to have someone to show them where to go and lead them.

PAUL: Well I quite agree with Samantha, because if I was the boss of a team I wouldn't like to be organising because they would all get fed up.

(ibid., p. 59)

William and Paul's comments build on Samantha's point in interesting ways. The 'idea' that William is referring to is one that Samantha expressed earlier − that if there was somebody in charge, the other people might get fed up. William addresses what he perceives to be a problem in the implementation of Samantha's idea, whereas Paul supports Samantha. This occasions a turning of the critical spotlight by William from Samantha to Paul. This time he is more challenging:

WILLIAM: So, Paul, how come you're not getting fed up because you're in David's group and you've got a boss?
[Long silence]

WILLIAM: Don't explain what you're saying, Paul, because I don't think you knew what you were saying and if you don't have a reason . . .

PR: Paul, why did you choose to go into David's group?

PAUL: Because I thought it was an important thing to look for food and shelter for the night.

PR: Would you have gone into that group if you had thought that David was not a very good leader?

PAUL: I know he can do things very well and he's never bossy. He never gets cross.

(ibid., p. 60)

Paul suffers what borders on a personal challenge from William – a challenge, as it happens, that Paul is able to deal with when he provides the reasoning that he is happy in David's group because of the nature of David as a leader. David appears to be a leader who can lead without being bossy, and this point is at the heart of the whole discussion. In discussing whether a group (1) needs a leader; (2) operates best with a number of leaders; or (3) works best without any leaders, the class is not only demonstrating that it can argue well by sifting out one possible course of action from another, it is also discussing a topic – leadership in a democracy – that is intimately tied up with notions of argument and the purposes of argument in society. The whole discussion takes place in an imagined situation, and requires a leap of the imagination for everyone in the class to participate in it.

It has been argued that it is in role play that pupils might well be able to operate in the zone of proximal development – the potential area identified by Vygotsky as that in which teaching might best be directed in the development of children's learning. In the above extract from Appleton School it seems that arguing in role has liberated the children to say more, respond more fully and sustain the argument more satisfactorily than is usual at this age. Why is this? One possible explanation is that the children share a common locus for the argument that ensues. They have been presented with a fictional situation – shipwreck and survival on a desert island – in which they all have to support each other in order to survive. The parameters of the fictional situation can be checked and monitored, so that definitions of the terms of the discussion can be kept to a minimum. Another possible explanation is less procedural than psychological: in having to argue about themselves in role, the children are already taking a different perspective on their own views. They are stepping beyond themselves for the purposes of the shared fiction, but that stepping out also enables them to argue more effectively because they are not personally involved to the same extent as if the situation were real.

Argument through fiction

My third example from the infant years develops further the potential of improving the quality of argument through working with fiction. At Neasden Primary School, Deborah Dalton used Janet and Allan Ahlberg's *Burglar Bill* (1977) as the basis for a unit of work, the aims of which were to encourage children to express themselves in an articulate way, to listen to the opinions of others before making their own judgements, to express opinions and give weight to them, and to encourage written argument. Children discussed moral questions posed by the story, including whether it was good or bad to steal, and whether they thought Burglar Bill himself was good or bad. Scenes from the story were re-enacted, and again in-role voices were used to express arguments: with one child taking the part of Burglar Bill, one child being the policeman and one being Burglar Betty, the characters were asked to put forward their opinions as to why Bill should or should not be arrested. A further advantage on in-role work in argument seems to be that more than two points of view can be represented.[2]

ARGUMENT AT JUNIOR (7–11) LEVEL

Most of the work at primary/elemetary school level took place with 7- to 11-year-olds. There were some common strands between the ten schools that participated in the Esmée Fairbairn research: the prevention of bullying via discussion, movements from the antagonistic to the collaborative (with reference to disciplinary matters within the school), work on the language of argument, and an examination of bias in documents. In this section I will concentrate on three of the research projects.[3]

Detecting bias

At All Saints Junior School, two teachers (Margot McAlindon and Heather Grayson) focused their project on the detection of bias in historical documents, and on children's capacity to use appropriate language to demonstrate an awareness of such bias. In this school, the work on argument was integrated closely into the topic, and provides a good example of how argumentative language can develop in such a context. The topic in this case was 'The Victorians' and work included group discussions on Victorian advertisements and on aspects of Victorian life, like child labour; a computer task in which, given specific criteria, children worked in groups to plan a dinner party, a resort and a town; the designing of a poster to present a point of view on Victorian life; and a group discussion on *The Secret Garden*.

One of the spin-offs from the argument project at this and other schools was the improvement in group relationships and in speaking and listening skills – something we have already seen in the transcripts from Minster and Appleton schools. It follows that if argument is slowed down and formalized a little – if consideration is taken of others' points of view – then the habit of speaking over each other or of only pursuing one's own line of thinking will change. There is thus even more integration between the management of the classroom and the management of talk in the classroom.[4] A concomitant of the improvement in listening skills is that individuals who tend to take a back seat in talk can gain in confidence. Here are the accounts of two children from the class:

> When I came into Mrs Mac's class the first topic we did was Victorian. I enjoyed doing the Victorians but I found some of it a bit hard ... I found it hard because Mrs. Mac kept saying what do you think? and I was too embarrassed to say anything because I thought it was wrong. Now I know I can say something not minding if it's right or wrong. I found working in Groups was hard because nobody would listen but now I think I'm better in Group Discussion but I am still a bit shy about saying what I think. I'm a bit more confident inside my head.

> Our topic last term was the Victorians. We looked at Letters, diaries, Headmasters' logs, newspapers, Photographs, and artefacts. I think that the ads were not true and the letters seemed true. The ads were largely exaggerated because the people who made the ads had to make the ads interesting. Before I came into this class I hadn't done much discussion work. Some times I didn't like saying my point of view but I get more confident as we do more discussion work. My group work very well together, we can reason with each other. And everyone has a turn to speak and put forward ideas we can argue but sensibly. I enjoyed doing this topic.

> (Andrews *et al.*, 1993, p. 70)

The project at this school took place in two classes, one of fairly confident and able children and the other consisting of children who were more teacher dependent. Margot McAlindon describes the class and its approach to the work:

> My class ... was unusual in its number of easily distressed children and included four statemented pupils who needed continuous classroom support. Relationships within the class were problematic and the children were initially rather passive and unresponsive in class discussion. The children initially professed a preference for working individually from text-books/work sheets. They claimed that they were not used to discussing their work 'like you do it'. This was not actually the case. They had participated in discussion in various curriculum areas but seemed unused to planning and organising activities themselves. They were very good at finding information but did not seem to have any idea what could be done with it. They also seemed unaware of the process of listening and responding to each other. In written evaluations most indicated that they felt self-conscious and a little uncomfortable with the demands of more expressive classroom language.
>
> (ibid., p. 71)

Another unforeseen benefit of the project was that it was possible to link other curriculum areas. Open-ended science and maths activities which encouraged small-group discussion were very useful in providing a context for pupils to express opinions, think logically and 'argue' their case when offering explanation/proof. Such cross-curricular approaches were more feasible in the primary/elementary schools than in the secondary/high schools, and they reinforced the cross-curricular nature of the argumentative skills that were being developed.

Part of the work on this project took place in the spring term of 1992, in the run-up to the British general election in April of that year. The fact that argument was taking place at a national level inspired the children to develop their argument work yet further:

> When the General Election was announced the class decided that they would like to organize a school election and to this end classroom work related to 'argument' focused on this topic. Four parties were chosen and children allied themselves to one of their choice. Speakers were chosen by the class after each child presented his/her ideas and opinions to the class. The children listened critically to each other. Ideas, points of view and arguments were pooled, party manifestos were produced and distributed in the playground, and eventually four representatives were chosen to present a whole-school party political broadcast. Every child present in the school voted and results were posted. A videotape is the result. Among the party representatives were children who had been among the least confident in the previous term.
>
> The preparatory work concentrated on such issues as organization and presentation of material, tone, delivery, pace and diction. The children were able to voice their opinions and ideas clearly and confidently.
>
> (ibid., pp. 71–2)

A third term's work involved the children collaborating with the local high school to produce a cross-phase (Key Stage 2/Key stage 3) newspaper, with particular attention paid to the identification of bias in local and national newspapers. The major advance of the year's work on argument, according to the teachers, was in the quality of talk:

We think that there has been an improvement in interactive listening. The quality of talk or discussion seemed to depend on the ability of all the participants and the children gradually became more responsive, critical and constructive in their ability to communicate. Initially the purpose of talk was to build up and improve poor relationships. Some children could not take an active part in classroom talk and some obviously did not value the contributions of others. They tended to state opinions and give information rather than elicit it from others in the group. Talk did not flow. At best it was a series of self-conscious responses to whoever dominated the activity. In time however, conversation became relaxed and purposeful, and the children took on an active participative role showing that they had mastered the skills of discussion, being able to take turns, listen, and respond to others who took the initiative.

(ibid., p. 73)

A whole-school approach

Another school in the Esmée Fairbairn research project, St Faith and St Martin Junior School, took the link between behaviour and argument and applied it to interactions across the whole school, inspired by a headteacher who wanted to improve the way in which staff and children dealt with disputes. From the outset, then, the aims of this project were not only to improve discussion but also to improve sensitivity in handling interpersonal disputes, to promote moral dialogue in studying the incidence of bullying in the school and to help children resist peer pressure, persuasion and threats. Meetings took place every Friday lunchtime between the headteacher and children aged 7–11, and the gatherings became known as 'Friday Club'. The work centred on conflicts between individuals or groups over disagreements during break, and took into account the feelings, emotions, problems and frustrations of the children. There was the opportunity for social interaction, operating as a group, the clarification of ideas through reasoning, judgements of the accuracy of information, the bringing of differences into the open and discussion as to how to resolve them, an increased emphasis on listening to others' points of view and the development of personal responsibility for one's own actions.

This particular school's project bears comparison with some of the most successful schools in the DEFT[5] project which took place two years previously, in which attempts to move English beyond the confines of the classroom walls into the 'real world' proved most manageable when they operated upon the structures of the school as a whole, and within the limits of the school as an institution (see Brown *et al.*, 1990). What both approaches have in common is that communication and power relations within the school are transformed. The institution becomes more democratic, more responsibility is taken on by the pupils, and argument moves from the antagonistic to the collaborative. I discuss the relationship between democracy and argument further in the final chapter.

Important gains in understanding on the part of the pupils in schemes like the one described above are that there is an exchange of ideas and increase in argumentative discourse; children think explicitly about their ideas and reflect on their own and others' thoughts; and they also realize that questions do not always have answers or that they might have more than one possible answer. The children's own evaluations stress the benefits of being able to take decisions and have some say in the way the school is run; they also reveal the liberating effect of addressing issues like bullying and school uniform:

> I think that I have enjoyed nearly every bit of it especially the writing afterwards. The bit I liked the least was when people kept interrupting our discussions in the library. I think in fact I know I have learnt a lot, I have learnt how to stand up for what I believe, I have learnt to express myself better through argument, I have learnt to listen to other people's opinions and ideas without shouting them down and I have learnt the skill of communicating through discussions. The other thing I liked was having the freedom of speech I could say anything that I thought was right without somebody saying sit down and be quiet. I personally totally disagree with the saying 'children should be seen and not heard' as I'm a child and I'm not going to let an adult shout me down. I think or know that discussions should be included in our work schedule as it is no fun discussing something with yourself, you want other people's points of view to help you. Mrs Morris ought to give the rest of the teachers lessons on discussing as she is so good at it. These sessions are a real benefit to me and it helps bring shy people out their shell so they can put their points of view up for discussion as some people are very shy but they have excellent ideas. I have learnt and enjoyed so many things that it is impossible.
>
> (Andrews *et al.*, 1993 p. 119)

The development of written argument

A third project that focused more on the development of written skills in argument built on earlier work with a different class. It involved the teacher Gloria Reid whose work was mentioned earlier (see pp. 46–7).

In the work undertaken as part of the Esmée Fairbairn project, two years later, her aims were to give children an 'argument vocabulary' in oral discussion and debate and to transfer this vocabulary to written argument, in order to develop cohesion in their writing. One of the approaches taken was to look critically at examples of argument in the media, and again the British general election campaigns provided material for analysis. Other approaches included a mock election with invented parties, manifestos and publicity material, as well as the devising of an argument game in which children came up with controversial statements written on cards which were debated, using cues from the 'argument vocabulary'. Here is one example of the writing (ibid., p. 124) that emerged from the debate on whether to hold mock elections in school. I have italicized what seem to me the pivotal phrases in terms of argument:

> *I think that there should be* mock elections *because* it helps us understand what the real MPs feel like when they say their Manifesto. *Other people, though, might think that* the mock election is stupid and spoil it by voting for anybody and most usually vote for their friends. *Another reason why I think there should be* mock elections is that I think children should have a say in what happens in the world. *Other people, however, might say* that children never get a say in the happenings in the world *because* we are too young, and *therefore there is no point for us* to have mock elections. *I would then say that what if you wanted to be in politics when you grew up, you wouldn't know what it felt like* if you didn't have mock elections. *They would then probably say that* not many people wanted to be in politics and if they were they were stupid. *I would then say 'do you think helping your country and your world being stupid?' and I would wait for his answer.*

The toing and froing between what 'other people' might say and what the speaker/writer would say in return is the basic structuring device informing the writing of this piece, which ends with the striking challenge, 'and I would wait for his answer'. In another example (ibid., p. 125), the writer makes even more explicit the informing structure, and yet at the same time retains the liveliness of speech in the writing. This time the topic is whether children in the primary school should be allowed to go on residential weekends away from their parents. Again, I have highlighted the argumentative strategies used:

> *This is an argument which could swing either way. For instance someone could say that* younger children are too young to stay away from their parents for a week. *Someone could then say that yes,* the younger children are quite young to go for a week by themselves *but what about the older children, surely they are old enough* to be able to go for a week by themselves. *Someone could then say that 'fair enough they are old enough but are they sensible enough'.* Then someone could say that okay some would be a bit silly but they have to feel their independence don't they. 'Okay', someone would say 'they do need their independence but just think about the little ones, they would cry all trip if they weren't with their parents'. *Finally I think that* just Y6 should spend a week away from their parents, not because I don't trust the Y5 and the other years I just think that everyone should have a fair amount of times and it would cost too much money for the little ones to go every year.

This topic, along with the question of whether to have mock elections in school, and others debated during the year (like whether to have a leavers' concert rather than a leavers' disco, or complaints about the space available within school) seemed to generate interest and motivation among the pupils. As with comments made earlier with regard to the whole-school approach to bullying, the children are involved in decision-making within the school. Even if their views are not always put into action, at least they are being expressed, and when they see their aspirations argued about and either enacted or refused, they see argument and democracy in action.

Gloria Reid (ibid., p. 124) offered the following evaluation of her project:

> The children very much enjoyed this work. They kept asking when the next session was going to be. I feel that their knowledge of the vocabulary used in argument was extended by playing the Argument Game (which proved very popular). Their oral argument improved. This improvement transferred to their written argument. They wrote more, and their writing was less list-like and stilted. When asked, the children claimed that they could argue better at the end of the project. They said it would be 'useful for them at South Hunsley' [the local secondary school] and that they felt treated as 'more grown-up'. They also said it would help them 'when they had jobs, and to stick up for themselves'.

A close look at one example of written argument

One of the schools in the project devised an imaginative approach to developing argument, involving role play, tape-recorded group discussion, campaign speeches and written argument. Often, role play was used to explore a topic before written argument was attempted. In the following case, in work based on the Second World War, pupils had acted in role before committing themselves to writing. This is not an exemplary piece of written argument, but it is in many ways typical of what can be produced in the junior years and gives us the opportunity to reflect on how teachers can help pupils to improve.

War. The Right to Fight or Not.

I think you should be allowed the right to choose if you want to fight or you don't want to fight. Because if you are Forced to Fight you Might start a big argument. Some people saying I am not going in the army because I have a wife and children and I might get killed, and other people saying you have got to go in because we need you to Fight For the country. Women should have the right if they want to go in the army as well. But some women should go in the army because a woman's place is not necessarily at home Ironing and a Man's place is not necessarily at work. They should mix up. Women should sometimes do Men's Work and Men should sometimes do Ladies' work.

(ibid., p. 81)

What happens in this argument? It opens with a proposition that 'you should be allowed to choose' whether to fight or not. The consequences of not being able to choose are then presented: 'you Might start a big argument'. This consequential line of argument is then abandoned in favour of presenting a general picture: 'Some people saying ... other people saying'. In other words, the writer is recognizing that there is a range of opinion on this question, and that such a range should be respected. He then opts for an example to illustrate his general point: *women* should have the right to go into the army if they wish. In my reading of this piece, this is where the writing moves off the point, because the illustration distracts the writer from his main drift. The secondary thesis generated is that 'Women should sometimes do Men's Work and Men should sometimes do Ladies' work'. It is as if the illustration or example has been erected to become the main thesis.

What are the best strategies for helping the pupil to improve this piece of writing? They will not be particular to argument writing, I would suggest, but to any writing, and would include questions like 'What is your main intention in this piece?', 'Could you structure it [e.g. by breaking it into paragraphs] to make the line of the argument clearer?' and 'How would you continue this piece?' While not wanting to determine the structure of the piece oneself, as a teacher, one would want to help the pupil improve his command of the expression of argument in writing. If the response was in writing, it could take the form of a request for clarification: 'Which of the two points − the right to choose whether one wants to fight or the idea that men and women should do each other's work − is the more important to you in this piece of writing?'

OTHER APPROACHES

Various initiatives have taken place at junior level which share common ground with the three projects in the Esmée Fairbairn research and which add further to it. The Oxfordshire − Buckinghamshire Oracy Project, part of the National Oracy Project,[6] looked at speaking and listening as a means to learning, and more specifically at how children's ability in argument and reasoning could be developed through talk (see Lalljee *et al.*, 1991). Working within a curriculum development model of 'Plan − Do − Review', this project has reported case studies of teachers working to highlight the reasoning and argumentative skills of pupils through collaborative learning. As with the teachers at Appleton and Minster schools (and many others across the country), teachers in this project made a strong connection between reasoning, argument and collaboration; in short, between the process of argumentation and effective class management. Reasoning involves clarification, challenge, justification, different kinds of verification, hypothesizing, decentring, deduction, summarizing and generalization. Argument involves moving from the particular to the general and from the general to the particular, 'showing that the "world" is arguable' and finding the state of doubt tolerable, considering alternative points of view (as suggested by decentring) and finding a logical structure in which individual points relate to each other around a central thesis. Collaborative talk involves individual members of the group scaffolding each other in the development of argument and reasoning by introducing new ideas and stimulating ideas in others, giving support to each other's ideas, providing a pool of shared experience, providing a visible audience which prompts explicitness, organizing a discussion both structurally and socially, acting as critics in questioning and challenging, and making thoughts public, enabling distance and reflection.

The range of oral strategies here shows what is possible in the classroom. It has often been observed (e.g. Phillips, 1985, 1992) that small-group discussion in primary and secondary classrooms is consensual rather than 'argumentative'. The presentation of such a range of possible ways of arguing, however, makes it possible to see consensual and adversarial argument taking place in the same classroom, perhaps even in the same discussion.

Another regional initiative, this time under the aegis of the Language in the National Curriculum (LINC) project[7] took place in Shropshire and led to the publication of *Developing Argument* (Lancaster *et al.,* 1992). It involved teachers from the advisory service working with those from a secondary school and its feeder primary schools to develop argumentative talk and writing. In what has been one of the most distinctively successful in-service projects, teachers identified characteristics of argument and also examined the language of argument. In addition to points already mentioned in this chapter, the project identified the use of supporting evidence (for example fact, personal experience, reference and quotation), the weighing and evaluation of evidence (see further discussion of this point in the next chapter), qualifying, explaining the context, acknowledging others' points of view and being assertive but not aggressive as characteristic of argument. In terms of the language most commonly associated with argument, the project identified verbs that convey speculation and hypothesis, like 'I wonder …', 'It seems …' and 'I don't think …'; a range of modal auxiliaries such as 'could', 'might', 'should' and 'would', important in that they convey the tentativeness of positions taken in argument; adverbials used as reinforcement, like 'exactly', 'fundamentally', 'at the same time'; and a range of connectives like 'if', 'because' and 'though'.

Projects undertaken by individual schools included the use of picture books as a basis for developing argument with nursery school children, and the use of novels with illustrations to explore the points of view of books and the issues raised by them. This was not a project confined to children aged 7–11, but brought together teachers of children from nursery age to 16. As with the Esmée Fairbairn project, the very fact that teachers from a wide range of schools could come together to discuss a specific topic such as the teaching of argument had many benefits. What the projects had in common, too, was a clear sense that although as teachers it was useful to analyse the characteristics of argument, it was felt inappropriate to *teach* these characteristics to children, at least in the first instance. A better way to start was to create situations and contexts in which argument would take place, and then to develop it. This approach will be discussed further in the final chapter.

This is an appropriate moment at which to discuss a very different approach to the development of argumentative skills: one based on the identification of specific sub-skills in argument. Clark (1985) explored the effects of training fourth-graders (nine-year-olds) 'to construct persuasive arguments and to compromise in situations in which their interests conflict with those of the other interactant' (p. 331). This was a formal experiment in which researchers interviewed children twice, with a training session between the two interviews designed to provide the children with strategies for accommodating the views of others in constructing persuasive messages. It is thus no surprise that the researchers found that 'even very limited instruction can produce improvements in some forms of children's performance'. Whereas only 60 per cent of the sample of 41 children used compromising strategies prior to training, 'every child was capable of doing so after training' (p. 340). Little can be concluded from the experiment, I would suggest, other than the fact that the children responded well to a specific training programme. It is not known whether the specific skill of compromising was integrated into the children's repertoire of argumentative strategies, or whether the programme had any lasting effect.

More classroom based is the work of Frowe (1989), who describes work undertaken with a class of 10- to 11-year-olds in developing their argumentative abilities. Exercises included imagining an event and then evaluating the reasons given to explain why the event had occurred. Evaluations were arrayed on a four-point scale of 'impossible' (this could never be the reason), 'possible' (this could be the reason but is unlikely), 'probable' (this could be a reason and seems likely) and 'conclusive' (this *is* the reason). Frowe found these initial approaches useful in that they gave an insight into the argumentative abilities within the class, provided children with the opportunity to clarify their own ideas 'by examining the principles and presuppositions they employ in their own thinking' (p. 57) and laid the groundwork for the framing of coherent arguments.

As an example of the exploration of the relationship between possibility and probability, I can provide evidence from work with young children undertaken on teaching practice and in the first years of teaching. As preparation for reading and writing poems like the traditional 'I saw a pig riding to town ... I'll have the whetstone if I may[8] I introduced statements like 'Pigs can fly' and asked the children whether that was possible or impossible. You can imagine the answers. They ranged from 'Yes, they can fly in aeroplanes' to imagined contraptions that would indeed enable pigs to take off and fly through the air, to imaginary flights themselves. In short, nothing was deemed impossible, other than verbal impossibilities like 'A bird is not a bird'.

Frowe explains too how the repertoire of reasoning strategies was extended through work on making inferences, contradictions, *ad hominem* and *reductio ad absurdum* arguments[9] and the application of these devices in classroom discussion and debate. He concludes with the observation that however much children enjoy these approaches, and however much we have neglected the development of critical thinking and analytical powers in children, we must be aware that some of those in authority may be wary of the development of such powers.

SUMMARY

This chapter started out by trying to establish that argument could stand alongside narrative as a 'primary act of mind' and was evident in the talk of pre-school children. Through dialogue in particular, with the teacher or parent taking a responsive role both in speech and writing, argumentative skills and strategies could be developed.

With specific regard to what can be done in the primary/elementary school, accounts have been given of the following approaches to developing argument:

- tapping expressive sources in children, such as locating sources of anger and irritation and using them to drive argument;
- using fiction as a basis for exploring points of view and the moral issues presented by stories;
- breaking down the distinction between narrative and argumentative genres in order to create blends and mixes that are responsive to the communicative requirements of particular rhetorical situations;
- using role play to imagine oneself into the shoes of others;
- using dialogue writing as a stepping stone to more independent argumentative writing;
- discussion of the language of argument, particularly of pivotal terms around which arguments are constructed, but also of verbs and adverbs which help define the positions taken on issues;
- the creation or discovery of situations and contexts in which argument might flourish. This approach would include the identification of specific audiences to speak or write to;
- techniques of verbal reasoning which extend the repertoire of reasoning strategies;
- the use of small-group discussion for the development of consensual and adversarial argument, by recognizing the skills that are there and building upon them;
- looking for ways to make connections in terms of argument between different subject areas such as science and maths.

One of the main implications of an increased attention to what can be done in terms of argument is that the way talk is conducted in the classroom is closely connected with the development of argument, which requires formal turn-taking and careful listening to others' points of view. In the following chapter we turn to the secondary/high school years, where the problems to be overcome are somewhat different.

NOTES

1 A full transcript of the discussion appears on pp. 78–80 of the final report of the research project (Andrews *et al.,* 1993). Again, it is worth tracing the movement away from and back to the main topic in the light of Kaufer and Geisler's thesis (see final chapter, p. 165).

2 In *Language of Argument in the Writing of Young Children* (n.d.) Jenny Monk gives an account of a classroom research study in which 5- to 7-year-olds were asked to write in different genres for different purposes and audiences. For their topic work, the children were divided into two groups: one to research the argument against, and the other for the killing of elephants. The children chose roles – craftsmen, lorry drivers, governments, elephants – and

researched their arguments accordingly. She cites a fairly well developed written text that grew from interchange between the writer and teacher/other pupils, and another in which an opposing view to the writer's is embryonic, but not developed. In INSET work following the research, Monk reports that 'we have suggested to teachers working with very young children that it may be helpful to spend time developing this genre (argument) in the oral mode only. However, it is clear that a subsequent interim stage between a spoken argument and a free standing written one is the shared construction of a text with a teacher or another pupil acting as scribe. Working together can help to shape a text which approximates more closely to the structure of the genre than one written without benefit of support. For example, an introductory paragraph to the subject could be jointly written and then groups might add their differing points of view. Such a procedure allows teachers to demonstrate that argument is a dynamic process in which positions are successively explored and evaluated in the light of feedback and reflection' (p. 11).

3 Full accounts of all ten projects are to be found in the final report of the research (Andrews *et al.*, 1993).

4 The management of talk in the classroom was identified by the Elton Report, *Discipline in Schools* (DES, 1988) as the key area of concern for most teachers.

5 The Developing English for TVEI (Technical and Vocational Education Initiative) project ran at the University of Leeds from 1989 to 1990, involving ten schools in the north of England. TVEI was a large-scale government-funded project whose aim was to encourage enterprise in schools. The DEFT project was the first scheme within it to aim to bring English (as a subject) into the fold. DEFT was directed by Peter Medway and Stephen Clarke.

6 The National Oracy Project ran in England and Wales from 1988 to 1993 in a number of education authorities, coordinated in due course by the National Curriculum Council.

7 The LINC project was set up in the wake of the Kingman Report (DES, 1988a) which focused on what children needed to know *about* language in order to use it well. The LINC project ran from 1989 to 1992 under the direction of Professor Ronald Carter of the University of Nottingham. Publication of its materials and recommendations was suppressed by the Secretary of State for Education, but 'bootleg' copies were circulated widely.

8 This poem appears in Geoffrey Summerfield's *Voices* (1968).

9 *Ad hominem* arguments challenge the consistency of the speaker's beliefs and practices; *reductio ad absurdum* arguments accept for the sake of argument a particular premiss and then draw out its implications to an unacceptable conclusion.

Chapter 5

Argument, 11 – 16

'I have to be in an angry mood to do things like [write argument]. I hate having to write a letter of complaint over a packet of crisps so I usually just leave it, but I did enjoy writing about "Birds should not be allowed on the Earth" because it's a bit comical.' (Simon)

Whereas in the primary/elementary school, argument is relatively novel and has the benefit of being able to be developed across the curriculum, in the secondary/high school context there is already a conventional approach within English. This approach has the effect of limiting the scope of what can be done in secondary school English as far as the development of argument is concerned. Rarely, for example, do subject areas combine to look at the types of writing they are setting their pupils. Despite the potential of the National Curriculum in this respect, with argumentation being given a high profile in subjects like geography and maths, there has been little cross over between subjects. In English, argument is still seen largely in terms of the 'persuasive essay' or the literary essay.

In this chapter, in trying to offer alternative models for argument in the secondary school, I want to relate and discuss two research projects. The first, my doctoral research, was undertaken with 12- to 13-year-old pupils in three comprehensive schools between 1987 and 1992, and focused on the structures and composing processes in narrative and argumentative writing. The second involved ten such schools and was concerned with improving the quality of argument from 11 to 16. It was part of the same Esmée Fairbairn project referred to in the last chapter, and ran from 1991 to 1993 (see Appendix 1).

ON THE STRUCTURES OF ARGUMENT WRITING

I set out on the first research project[1] with the hypothesis that, if children at 11 and 12 were competent in the handling of narrative structures, then they might be able to use these structures to provide a foundation for the improvement of their argument writing. I accounted for the narratives in terms of 'episodes' and the arguments in terms of 'stages', and looked for patterns in the narrative writing that might be repeated or developed in argument writing. The periods for writing the narrative (most children chose to write a story) and the argument (most chose the essay as the 'default' genre) were tightly controlled: both pieces of writing, including their planning, were allocated one hour.

What I found, by analysing the plans and finished compositions in both modes for all 150 children in the sample, surprised me. The narratives ranged from three to seventeen episodes with a mean of 7.9 episodes. The arguments ranged from two to twelve stages with a mean of 6.1 stages per composition. First, then, there was a much greater range of structures than I had anticipated, and a much more varied range than even the two- to seven-part structures we discussed in relation to classical rhetoric in Chapter 1, or the clichéd 'beginning, middle and end' pattern.

What surprised me further was that of the 150 narratives, only two were alike in structure[2]; of the 150 arguments, no two were alike in structure. It was thus not possible to begin to look for correspondences between narrative and argumentative structures. Within each mode there was wide variation, and it was even possible that my own consistent analyses of the structures might be different from another reader's view, as the perception of structure is partly in the reader's mind. The hypothesis that argument structures could build upon existing working knowledge of narrative structures was unfounded, other than at the most general level where 'setting + event structure' in narrative could be paralleled with 'statement + proof' in argument.

As our concern in this book is principally with argument, let us look at some of the structures composed by the pupils in their essays. There were no essays consisting of one stage. This was also the case with the narratives, where the minimum number of episodes must be three. In the case of arguments, a two-stage essay is possible (statement + proof). There were six such essays in the total sample.

Of the seven essays consisting of *three* parts, each had a different structure:

Paul	Statement + 'nevertheless' + 'on the other hand'
Malcolm	Statement + reason + expression of opinion
Philip	Statement + reason + 'when' (instance)
Stephen	Supposition ('if') + example + example
Kathryn	Statement + credo + anti-credo ('I don't think')
Melanie	Statement + reason + statement
Sarah	Example + example + example

Two general points can be made: one is that most of these arguments fall into the 'statement + proof' pattern outlined by Aristotle ('A speech has two parts. It is necessary to state the subject, and then to prove it': Aristotle, 1926, p. 425), as did most of the arguments in the sample as a whole. Only 19 of the 144 (13.19 per cent) of the essays did not begin with a clear statement, and two of these began with exordia followed by a statement. Of the remaining 17, nine began with questions, two with examples (micro-stories), two with suppositions, and one each with a definition, a reason, a story and a setting respectively.

The second point is that no two structures in this range of three-part structures are the same. The first one begins with a statement and then proceeds to undermine itself: 'nevertheless' followed by 'on the other hand' makes for a redefinition of the basis of the statement itself. Perhaps the closest to each other in structure are the essays by Malcolm and Melanie: statement + reason + credo or further statement, But a credo has a different status and function from a statement. A statement needs proof in this context, whereas a credo can stand on its own. The relationship of a credo (or anti-credo, like 'I don't believe ...') to the other stages in an argument is much more tenuous than that of a statement.

Let us look in more detail at one of the seven essays that took a three-part structure:

Murder in our own homes and streets

I have nothing against London but I just decided to use it as an example, especially east is a main drug area. Because there are lots of homeless people so the drug dealers tend to stick to cities where the police can't get them.

Also in cities there is a lot of football hooliganism in places like Liverpool, London, Hull and Manchester. People just get out of control, injuring people for no reason.

In big cities as well as towns the pollution rises as there's more factories, people are just getting to know the dangers of the ozone layer as it's got large holes in it. But now more and more people are aware of the dangers.

(Andrews, 1992a, p. 243)

It is perhaps unfair to treat this as a finished essay. The plan indicates a seven-part structure, with paragraphs devoted to rape, drunk driving and stabbing as well as murder. But as an actual or potential structure, this work exhibits an and-type structure, giving the effect of inconsequentiality. What is particularly interesting about this essay, however, is the way it argues without stating its premiss. The premiss is assumed.

Emerging from the analysis of these and other essays in the sample are new kinds of stage that might be added to an emergent taxonomy:

solutions
amplification
second statement
restatement
analogy
homily
question
rhetorical question
coda

It is worth looking at some of the five-part compositions in order to illustrate the range and variety of their structures. Caroline, for example, had the following structure:

Statement ('Bull fighting is awful') + exhortation ('Just imagine someone sticking an arrow into you ...') + consequence ('Bulls could become extinct') + restatement ('It is not necessary and it is mean') + further restatement ('It's mean and horrible').

Stephen on the other hand, produces five separate statements, each of the 'I don't think it's right' kind, thus falling somewhere between credo (unsupported belief) and statement (in need of 'proof'). Three essays which use questions in various ways are those by Jane R., Jane M. and Zoe:

Statement + personal dilemma + restatement + rhetorical question + restatement

> Questions + examples + restatement of questions + further questions + however.

> Statement + evidence + 'I don't really see why ...' + question + tentative conclusion ('Maybe ... but ...').

In each of these structures, a question or questions plays an important part in the development of the argument. In the first essay, the question is merely a token – a rhetorical question – designed to reinforce the main exploratory thrust of the argument. The second essay poses questions to the audience and is much more of an oration than the first essay, which is more contemplative. The third essay falls somewhere in between these two styles and asks a genuine question on which speaker/writer and audience may ponder.

One of the essays in the sample consisted of eleven parts, and is worth looking at in order to determine how such a lengthy structure is built:

> Statement + supposition + conditional + rhetorical question + credo + evidence (to support statement) + supposition + 'Put yourself in this position ...' + conditional + consequences + directive ('Don't ...').

This shows a wide range of rhetorical devices, used with confidence and flexibility. It is probably fair to say that for these children there are no pre-packaged structures that could be imported to shape their compositions. Discourse units are defined relative to each other as well as to the informing function(s) of the discourse.

One last point: although it was true that the structure of the arguments followed the paragraph structure of the compositions more closely than occurred in narrative writing, it was not a case of absolute correspondence between paragraphing and argument structure. There are two ways of looking at this less than perfect correspondence. One is to suggest that those pupils whose paragraphing does not match their argument structure are deficient in paragraphing skill (paragraphing being a lower-order skill than structuring an argument). The other is to suggest that paragraph structure is not directly related to argument or narrative structure. My inclination is to the latter view, and I feel that it is up to us as teachers to (1) recognize this complexity; and (2) devise ways of teaching paragraphing that will help pupils to gain command of the complex relationship between composition structure and the placing of paragraphs. One of the best instances of such teaching I have seen was by a student who took a three-stage approach to the teaching of paragraphing. First, she explored the notion of journeys with her pupils, asking them to describe a number of journeys they had taken. These were depicted on the board, and each one fell into different stages which she represented in different colours and different lengths. These many-staged journeys were then used as metaphors to describe the composition of stories and essays in paragraphs. Next she asked the pupils to reconstruct a text that had been cut up into its constituent paragraphs. Finally she asked them to continue the text in their own writing, paying attention to the deployment of paragraphs as they 'completed the journey'.

The journey metaphor, mentioned in Chapter 1, is explored further in Chapter 7.

REARRANGING THE ARGUMENTS

Although the hypothesis on which the research was based was not proved, there were several positive results of the empirical study. One of the most interesting was that rearrangement of episodes in a narrative or of stages in an argument was possible, was different in the two modes and was also an aid in composition at the macro-level.

Again, the results of the empirical study were somewhat surprising. Whereas it might have been assumed that students would be more open to revision at the macro-level in narrative writing because they 'preferred' that mode and were more used to it, in fact the students in this sample were more ready to change the order of their compositions in argument than in narrative: over 62 per cent were able to conceive of changes to the order of their arguments, while 26.5 per cent could envisage such changes in their narratives. Of those who could envisage changes in their arguments, 49 per cent offered specific alternatives, 26.5 per cent suggested that the arguments could appear 'in any order' and 10.5 per cent argued that their first point must come first. Only 5 per cent claimed that only limited changes were possible.

In general, then, the students on the whole perceived that it was easier to change the order of their arguments than of their narratives. Some thought this was because the very nature of narrative is built around sequence, and that if the sequence of a story is disturbed then the story itself has to change; it is no longer the same story. Argument, on the other hand, is not predicated so heavily upon sequence. It may be just as effective, if not more so, to change the order of the argument. Changes of this kind in both narrative and argument are more readily effected at the planning stage. Furthermore the units of argumentative discourse are more discrete, more easily movable than those of narrative. All these findings seem to run against those of narratologists like Holloway (1979) and Goodman (1981), who suggest respectively that rearrangement may improve literary forms but that 'this could not be so of logical form' where such a changing of the order might be seen as a 'dis-arrangement' rather than a re-arrangement; and that 'a narrative reordered in any way at all is still a narrative'. In the first case, however, there is a distinction to be made between logical and rhetorical form. A sequence may be fixed in logical form but movable in rhetorical form. In the second case, while it is generally true that a narrative reordered is still a narrative, it has to be added that it was only the same narrative for a minority of the students sampled in the present study.

The pupils made many revealing and incisive comments in response to a question on whether it was possible to change the order in which things are said in narrative and argument. Several students felt that the order in which a statement occurred 'does not really matter' and that 'it is the same in the end whatever you put' (Simon). Others were less sure, and wanted to qualify their statements:

> It is alright changing the order of a piece of argument writing, though to start and finish off you have to have your own point of view. In a letter of complaint I don't really think it is possible to change much. (R.W.)

> It is possible sometimes because whichever order you put it in, you get the same result. But other times you can't because it will change what you're trying to say or express. (Clive)

One student went further in trying to define when a change of order was desirable in argument and in narrative:

> It is easier, I think, to change the order in arguments, because it doesn't usually matter except you have to get people interested first. For narrative you can change the order if more than one thing happens at a time. (Ruth)

The perception that the order is changeable in narrative 'if more than one thing happens at a time' seems to rely on an understanding about the nature of narrative: that the 'logic' of narrative development – *post hoc propter hoc* – is suspendable if the chronological drive of the narrative is suspended or transcended. So a section of narrative beginning 'Meanwhile' or with an equivalent construction may be placed in a different sequence in relation to the rest of the story. Another student makes a distinction between different kinds of argument:

> It depends what subject it is, and what points I've made. For example, I find it easier to swop points on science-fictional arguments. (Angela)

Science-fictional arguments are, we must assume, arguments that float free of terrestrial logic; arguments that are more like fictional constructs.

Concern about different sequences and arrangements was seen by some to be of little interest. This attitude serves as a reminder that *dispositio* is less important than *inventio* in the hierarchy of compositional skills. Furthermore, for some students, what goes down on paper first – whether the mode be argument or narrative – has a freshness and immediacy that is worth preserving, and no amount of revising and redrafting will affect that:

> I think the first thing you think up is always the best. (Baljit)

THE FUNCTION AND NATURE OF PLANNING IN ARGUMENT

Planning proved to be so different for narratives in relation to plans for arguments that it is worth describing the differences in some detail. Given the choice, 49 per cent of the students in the sample planned their narratives on paper. There is no possibility of statistical comparison with the composition of argument in this respect, as the planning of argument was compulsory. However, it is possible to compare the kinds of plan used for the two kinds of writing.

Of those who planned their narratives, 30 per cent did so in draft form, 24 per cent in the form of sequences of notes, 53 per cent used some kind of notation and 12 per cent wrote summaries (or abstracts) of the stories they were going to write. In the argument writing, only 2 per cent of the plans took polar form (for/against, yes/no, good/bad). Drafts accounted for 10.5 per cent of the plans, 'spider diagrams' for 29 per cent, numbered notes (implying a sequence) 46.1 per cent and sequential boxes 28 per cent. In both cases, the total exceeds 100 per cent because some students used more than one kind of planning for each kind of writing.

The most commonly used form of planning in each case was the series of notes, usually numbered to indicate the intended sequence. Differences occur when we look at the other kinds of planning used. Thirty per cent of the narratives used a first draft as the plan as opposed to 10.5 per cent of the arguments. It has been suggested that this relatively high use of the draft in narrative writing accords with the process of composing narrative: that 'getting started' is more difficult in narrative than argument and hence a first draft is needed for an initial breakthrough to be made into the narrative type of discourse; that structuring and the development of narratives occurs by accretion rather than by design; that it is more important to map the course of an argument before the writing starts than it is in the case of narrative. Planning in narrative seemed to fulfil five functions, acting as rehearsal for the main composition, as initial guide, as an orientation device, as a springboard and as a general map of the area to be traversed. In argument writing, the planning was more likely to act as an initial guide, as a blueprint for the final composition and as a map of the route to be taken.

Accounts by individuals in the questionnaire and interviews tended to support this point. One student described the process of writing narrative as like 'going into a series of caverns'; another as a matter of merely 'adding things' as opposed to the writing of argument in which one could 'add things and rearrange things'. There were no accounts of the relationship being the other way round. Many students said that they only began to think of the ending to a narrative 'in the middle' or 'three-quarters' of the way through the writing of it, and one student described having to read through an emerging story before 'doing the ending': 'I read it again and then think about my ending and then jot it down.'

All this points to the situation of more planning going on *during* the writing of narrative than during argument writing, where the composition tends to be pre-planned. Structures in narrative writing, then, are not always evident at planning stage, and there is less coincidence between plan and final composition in narrative than in argument. It is as if, in narrative writing, each stage of the process is there to act as a springboard to the next stage; once the next stage is achieved, the previous planning is jettisoned. Or to use a metaphor from building (one that we have seen is common in the description of argumentation), narrative is constructed 'as you go along' with a more general idea of what the finished product will look like than is the case in argument writing. In argument, on the other hand, there are fewer transformations from stage to stage. The components are more identifiable. At each stage the planning is reflected in the composition, and the surface indicators of structure – like paragraphing and discourse markers – are more closely allied to the structural coherence of the composition than is the case in narrative writing.

Of the 143 plans written for the arguments, only three (2 per cent) were in polar form. Fifteen (10.5 per cent) took the form of drafts, 42 (29 per cent) took the form of spider diagrams, 66 (46.1 per cent) were shaped into numbered notes and 40 (28 per cent) used a series of boxes supplied at the foot of the planning sheet. A further four took the form of pictures, a title, a route map/diagram and a Socratic dialogue.

It may be a surprise that only 2 per cent of the sample chose to plan in polar/binary form. This is a well-tried method for the teaching of planning essays, and yet given a free choice in planning method as well as in the topics of argument, very few students chose this technique. Indeed, the three plans which did take this form found three different variations: for/against, bad/good and yes/no. It is possible that the students, on being offered the chance to argue, chose to forgo the dispassionate presentation of both sides of an argument characteristic of this kind of essay.

Drafting as a planning strategy was used far less in the writing of argument than in narrative. A typical example of this kind of planning is found in the work of Melissa:

> My strong point is about abortion. I think it's wrong people get pregnant then they decide they do not want the baby so they have an abortion and it is killing the baby. I think it is murder. People get pregnant by a mistake sometimes they want them if they have got pregnant because fell [feel] the same way as me. Some people are cruel to have abortion. If they want to make love they should use a condom then it will not be a mistake. Abortion is murder, abortion is caused by under age sex under 16 years. They should not have sex so abortions will be veiwer [fewer] adoption is better the child lives.

This seems unstructured, but gave rise to an essay that was both well structured and well paragraphed; indeed, although the plan contains neither sections nor numbers to indicate stages in the argument, it is possible to identify such stages within the single paragraph of the draft.

It must be said that many of the essays emerging from drafts were minimal or non-existent (in the sense that the initial draft was all that the student managed). While a much-used approach in the writing of narratives, the practice of drafting-as-planning seems, on the whole, unsuited to the writing of argument. This does not mean to say that drafting *per se* is unsuited to argumentative writing.

By far the majority of students chose to plan in spider-diagram form, or in a list of numbered notes and in a series of boxes. Essentially these forms of planning are similar; they differ only in degree. The spider diagram identifies the question or topic to be addressed and places it at the centre of the plan: the spider's body. From the body the various legs (points) extend, sometimes branching into sub-points. When the legs are numbered in sequence, the plan takes on a similar function to that of the list or boxes, in that a linear direction has been established for the essay.

Lists or numbered notes seem to take the process of planning one stage further. There is already a commitment to a sequence, though it may be changed by arrows being drawn from one part of the plan to another, and by connections being made between points. The sequencing is visually vertical, moving from point one at the head of the page to point six, seven or whatever at the foot of the page. In this respect, the list is most like the draft in nature. The essays with the highest number of stages tended to be prefaced by this kind of planning.

Whereas the spider diagram is circular in shape and the list takes a vertical dimension, the boxes suggest a horizontal direction. There is a movement from left to right, rather like the illusion created by the reading of a book. The boxes indicate clear stages in the development of the argument and the sense of a journey from A to B.

Figure 5.1 (overleaf) shows an example of planning in box form, complete with arrows used to reorder the sequence of the argument:

And here is the final essay, in its two-voice mode:

> I think that people shouldn't eat meat firstly because it lessens the number of animals and secondly because of the cruel way they are killed.
>
> I want to take up your first point, the animals are not endangered in the slightest they are especially bred to be slaughtered ...
>
> ... but that is just the point they are literally slaughtered. If this large scale killing does have to be done they why can't they be put to sleep quietly instead of being brutally attacked, and brought slowly to death?
>
> I'd just like to say that they are not brought brutally to death, they are killed up to regulation. To your point about killing them by simply putting them to sleep well firstly this system would cost too much, secondly it would take too long, and thirdly you need experience to inject them.

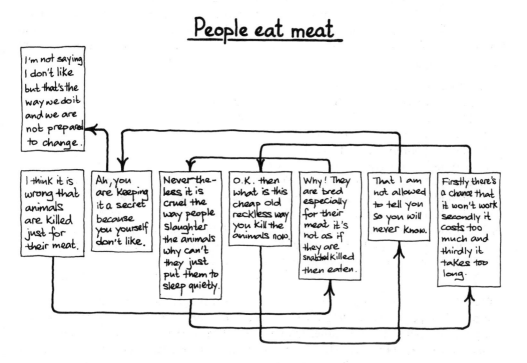

People eat meat

> I'm not saying I don't like but that's the way we do it and we are not prepared to change.

> I think it is wrong that animals are killed just for their meat.

> Ah, you are keeping it a secret because you yourself don't like.

> Nevertheless it is cruel the way people slaughter the animals why can't they just put them to sleep quietly.

> O.K. then what is this cheap old reckless way you kill the animals now.

> Why! They are bred especially for their meat it's not as if they are snatched killed then eaten.

> That I am not allowed to tell you so you will never know.

> Firstly there's a chance that it won't work secondly it costs too much and thirdly it takes too long.

Figure 5.1 *An example of a 'boxed' plan.*

Nevertheless you take in loads of money every year possibly as much as five million pounds a year. You have enough to hire experienced men and to buy the injection and you will still be making profits of each cow.

I agree with you we get enough money, but is simply not practical to have as many men around or else it will simply be too much hasal [hassle]. But I will put all the points to our management, it's been nice talking to you.

ARGUMENT THROUGH FICTION 2

In the previous chapter we looked at examples of the teaching of argument through fictional texts in the primary school; this chapter considers the potential of fiction for eliciting and developing argument in the secondary/high school context.

At Andrew Marvell School in Hull, two projects were undertaken as part of the Esmée Fairbairn research, both of which addressed the role of fiction in developing argument.

The first of these, with 12- to 13-year-olds, used Joan Lingard's novel *The Twelfth Day of July* − part of her series on relationships in Northern Ireland − and the second with 14- to 15-year-olds, used *Of Mice and Men* and various short stories.

One of the strategies used with the Joan Lingard novel was to ask the class to identify 'should' questions, i.e. questions with moral significance arising from the novel. Groups of pupils jotted down as many different issues as they could find, and then identified one issue about which they wanted to argue a case, either from a single point of view or from a range of points of view. One group (Kerry, Lee, Graham and Natalie) came up with the following questions:

1. Should we paint the wall, Sadie?
2. Should we [Kevin and Brede] give her [Sadie] a cup of tea?
3. Should Kevin and Brian destroy King Billy?
4. Should Tommy have come in late?
5. Should Tommy have left Sadie?
6. Should Kevin have walked Sadie home?
7. Should Tommy and Sadie have left the house without their mam and dad knowing?
8. Should Kevin and Brian have tipped the paint on the front door step?
9. Should Tommy and Brian have chased after them?
10. Should Tommy and Sadie get their own back on Kevin, Brian and Brede?
11. Should Kevin and Brede's parents have left when they knew it was nearly 12th July and there would be a lot of arguments in the city?

(Andrews *et al.*, 1993, p. 165)

The first question is asked as if it comes from one of the characters in the book, as is the second. It appears that as the students start on the framing of 'should' questions, they respond in participant role rather than as spectators to the action of the novel. As we move down the list there is a shift from involvement to detachment (and this movement is continued in the generalization of moral issues from particulars). There was intense sifting through the text as the pupils undertook this work, and argument over the formulation of the 'should' questions as they were written down.

When it came to the categorizing of questions and the selecting of the most important 'should' question for further discussion, this particular group first chose question 2, which seemed to be concerned with trust. Later they switched to question 5, which is more to do with loyalty. Thus they explored some of the themes of the novel by themselves, framing questions as well as attempting to answer them, all without the direct guidance of the teacher. They were also defining and redefining terms throughout their discussion, sometimes in oral discussion and at other times in order to get the wording of a written question right.

At the end of the lesson, the teacher fielded the various main 'should' questions and undertook the process of categorization herself, thus demonstrating to the pupils how a complete map of the themes and issues in the novel might be reached. This map was to be the subject of further refinement with the pupils in the following lesson.

The groups traced their chosen moral issue through the book, presenting it as a diagram. They then wrote a commentary on the diagram, relating their issue to the novel and to their own opinions. By this stage, the pupils had a great deal of evidence to support their views of particular strands in the novel. This evidence was used to good effect in fully-fledged essays on the chosen issues. For Year 8 pupils, these seemed a considerable achievement. A 700-word essay by Suzanne, for example, under the title 'How is the issue Obedience explored in the book *The Twelfth Day of July?*' ends with the conclusion:

> Should you always obey the law? Should you always obey your teachers? These are two questions which you should ask yourself. If a teacher asked you to write on a desk, would you? If a policeman said pay no poll tax, because you won't get into trouble this year, would you? Sometimes, where obeying is concerned, disobeying could take its place. I certainly know that I wouldn't obey either of these.

(ibid., p. 165)

In groups, pupils devised plays exploring their chosen issue, and acted them for another group. They then produced questionnaires for their audience, and wrote an evaluation of the plays and of their experiences in devising and performing them.

Teachers not connected with the project commented on the pupils' exceptional ability to handle issues and to work constructively in discussion groups. It can be seen, too, from the evidence of emergent essays, that these pupils had developed study skills that enabled them to explore fiction for its argumentative potential and to collect evidence that provided a solid basis for their writing and discussion about the novel. Similar results emerged from the work with 14- to 15-year-olds on *Of Mice and Men* in which pupils were asked to consider what they understood by the concept 'murder' before reading the book, and in particular the ending of the book where George shoots Lenny. The teacher – Kevin Fitzsimmons – estimated that about a third of the pupils in his class identified the moral dilemma at the end of the novel, but that grounding an abstract moral question – 'What is murder?' – in a fictional text was an excellent way to address such a question. In a fuller reflection on the issues raised by this project, Kevin set out some of his thinking on the relationship between argument, morality and fiction:

> When I first started teaching in the early seventies I read a story called 'Late Night on Watling Street' by Bill Naughton (1969). In it a lorry driver called Jackson murders two policemen who have been persecuting him. For me the story illustrated the difficulty of making moral judgements; it is not presented in black-and-white but in shades of grey.
>
> The story is presented dramatically and at the end there was a shocked silence in my fourth year [14- to 15-year-old] class of boys ... The moral as I saw it was that violence provokes violence until it ends in murder [but one boy came out with the statement] 'Serves them right'.
>
> The boy at the back, the 'troublemaker', provided me with the chance to show how there is always a 'Jackson' who does not know when to stop.
>
> To my astonishment the rest of the group agreed with him. According to their set of values the police were the enemy to be attacked or hoodwinked, and certainly not to be trusted. To their way of thinking, the police in the story 'deserved' to die .... Here were fifteen year old boys using the arguments employed by terrorists.
>
> I tried 'reasoning' with them. I presented abstract arguments about right and wrong, but this was not how they thought. I had chosen the form of discourse by reading them a story and now I was shifting the ground.
>
> I could have decided that they were simply 'wrong' and told them, as the church used to tell me when I was young. ... Equally, I could have decided that I had no moral responsibility to impose my value system on them and left them to believe whatever it was they wanted to.
>
> The decision I made I still endorse. I did have a moral responsibility, not to impose a

meaning and thereby a judgement on the text but to explain or show that they had made an immature judgement based on a superficial interpretation of the text.

I changed the direction of the discussion back into 'fiction'. If the discourse was narrative then I would use it to illustrate my interpretation. 'Just suppose,' I began. I took them by the hand and led them through the paths of their imagination until we met on common ground.

I showed them that their failure to 'see' what Jackson had done was due to the same failure of imagination that had allowed Jackson to go so far. They were like Lady Macbeth – encouraging or approving behaviour that they would be incapable of themselves.

They began to see the skill with which the author manipulated their emotional response, allowing the reader to 'know' the drivers as people but only referring to the police indirectly and then only by nickname.

The quality of the argument which followed was of an incomparably higher standard than my pupils could have engaged in if we had chosen the more conventional discourse of 'abstract' argument. ... [This] anecdote, like the story, is more complex than the narrow conclusion I have elicited from it. Narrative is dynamic in existing in several states at the same time. Not only does it contain arguments but it is an argument in a form fundamentally different to other forms of argument and equal to them rather than inferior.

(ibid., pp. 160–61)

Part of the teacher's responsibility, then, is to explore the moral hinterland of a fictional text in order for the pupils to appreciate more fully the significances of the text, or 'what the text is arguing'. This is an important activity because, as Kevin notes elsewhere, there is a possibility that 'a great deal of literature contains implicit argument(s) which in some way influence our choice or rejection [as teachers] of the texts for study'.

This possibility was indeed explored in a discussion between Stephen Clarke and Kevin Fitzsimmons on 5 November 1991. One of the many points to emerge in that discussion is that literature acts (or should act) as a challenge to the reader, presenting him or her with a new moral world to subvert or compare with his or her own. It thus is an important responsibility of the English teacher to choose the texts which present moral challenges appropriate to the developmental stage of his or her pupils. If the teacher makes this choice explicit, the pupils are better able to 'argue with the book'.

DIALOGUING WITH THE TEACHER

In Chapter 3 I raised the question of what effects dialogic writing might have on a class, and how we might generate ideas to encourage such approaches. In Withernsea High School – also basing her work on a fictional text – the teacher planned to integrate the development of argument with an attempt to increase the awareness of her pupils about gender:

In October 1991, I began a small, six week school-based research project with a Year 9 group of 28 mixed ability students, my English group. ... My intentions were two-fold: to develop the students' oral and written skills in argument and to develop the students' awareness of gender stereotyping ....

My way into this project was to be through the novel I had already chosen for the term's work, *Equal Rites* by Terry Pratchett. The story revolves round the character of Esk, a small girl who has inherited magical powers, and who wishes to attend Unseen University, the college for aspiring wizards. Needless to say, she is at first denied access and advised instead to opt for witchcraft, a domestic kind of magic more suited to girls than the 'headology' magic of wizards with all their angles and 'jommetry'.

I felt that by taking on the character's fight for access and acceptance, the students would ... be allowed to retain a safe objectivity which would, in turn, permit them to explore their own ambivalence about roles and expectations, whilst devising arguments and a repertoire of [argumentative] strategies. I have noted in the past that when a mixed group of students discuss equal opportunities in relation to their lives, there is a tendency for discussion to generate into an angry exchange between the oppressed and their oppressors. Whilst I feel there should be space made within the school curriculum for such anger to be aired, it was felt that such an interchange was neither desirable nor fruitful with regard to the objectives of this particular project.

[Initially] I asked the students to write a letter to the Head Wizard requesting admission [to the university]. For the purposes of determining later whether their skills in written argument had improved, such a piece of writing could act as a point for comparison. We then moved on to the textual exploration which I hoped would form the basis for a more informed understanding of gender inequalities, upon which they could draw in later work. I also intended for this series of lessons to allow for a variety of spoken argument or debate, such as pairs, small groups, both mixed and single sex, and whole class. By varying the contexts in which they worked, I hoped to create a climate for the development of a repertoire of strategies, skills and possible 'solutions'.

(Andrews *et al.,* 1993, p. 129)

I quote in full the letters that were sent back and forth from teacher to pupil for several reasons: to demonstrate the principle of dialogue in writing, to show that teachers can respond to pupils' writing in other ways than simply by 'marking' them, and to show how one pupil's argument-writing improved as a result. Both pupil and teacher are writing in role:

Letter from Granny Weatherwax (Anne – the student)

Witch Cottage
Magic Lane
Bad Ass
Discworld
2nd April, 15 Owl

The Head Wizard
Unseen University
Bad Ass

Dear Sir,

Please let me introduce myself. I am Esmerelder Weatherwax and I am a highly-trained witch, but I need your help on quite a large problem I have. The problem is that I have a young student called Eskarina Smith who has been handed to power of the staff of Mr Drum Billet, a wizard who died about 8 years ago. His staff was to be passed on to the eighth son, but he failed to check the sex of the new-born baby Eskarina, thus bringing the first female Wizard into the world. I hoped the magic wouldn't find her but it has. Just today I gave Eskarina the staff and she created a huge fireball in my fireplace making it melt like wax. I was hoping if there was a place for her in your university because if she wasn't taught how to use the magic, she would be very dangerous. If you do have a place for her I will be very pleased and will send money with her for her lessons. Eskarina learns very fast and she is a very clever young lady.

Thank you and good wishes,
Esmerelder Weatherwax

Letter from Chief Wizard (Jan Sargeant − the teacher)

Unseen University
Magic Avenue
Bas Ass
Discworld
21st Nov, 2098

Mrs E. Weatherwax
Witch Cottage
Magic Lane
Bas Ass
Discworld

Dear Mrs Weatherwax,

Thank you for your recent letter. Although we appreciate your concern for your grand-daughter, we regret to inform you that we feel it is impossible to accept her into our university for the course in wizardry.

It is our policy that girls should not be accepted for this very demanding course for the following reasons:

1. We have always had a tradition that boys only are accepted.
2. Girls' minds work differently. They are not good at maths and geometry, both of which play a large role in the study of wizardry.
3. Girls will want to have babies in the future. How can they possibly combine having babies and looking after them with the demands of being a successful wizard?
4. Other people would think it very strange to see a woman wizard. The other students might tease her.

We do not want you to feel that we are not being fair so we would be prepared for you to write again to us, if you would like to appeal against this decision. If you do, please give us good reasons to consider your grand-daughter. We regret that having the staff is not a good reason, since, as you said, this was a mistake.

Witchcraft is a very good profession for girls. Although it does not, obviously, have the same status or level of pay, it can be very satisfying for girls and they can always be a part-time witch when they decide to have children. We think you should give this matter some serious consideration before you decide to appeal.

Yours sincerely,
Merlin
(Chief Wizard Professor)

Anne's preparation for the writing of the reply included listing the points made by the wizard and devising arguments to counter them.

Mrs Weatherwax's reply (Anne)

Dear Mr Merlin,

Thank you for the reply to [my] recent letter and after some consideration I would like to appeal against your policies.

I would like to know (if possible) why it has been traditional to only have boys accepted. Witchcraft was taken up by women because they had some spare time and someone had to cure the ill. In the past, if men wanted to become witches I don't think women would have stopped them.

You said in your letter that men's minds work differently to women's. That is probably true, but then you go on to say that girls/women will want to have babies in the future. How do you know? Some women can't have babies. Others don't want to have them. If they did want children in the future, haven't you heard of nannies or the father looking after them?

You also said that women are not very good at maths or geometry. You obviously haven't heard of planet Earth where they have women maths teachers and women astrologers. If women from that lowerhand planet can do it, we can certainly do it!

You then went on to say that people would think it strange to see a female wizard. People think a lot of things are strange, like how sometimes you don't want to go to bed but in the morning you are tired out. You also said Esk would be teased. Believe me Esk can handle that very well.

I don't think you have thought about the advantages of letting Esk go to the university, like setting good examples to other colleges and universities and getting young people more interested in wizardry. I think it would be a good idea to see Esk yourself to see what a mature young lady she is.

Yours sincerely,
E. Weatherwax

(ibid., pp. 133–5)

The second letter from the pupil shows considerable advances in argumentative skill. The first letter is less focused, partly because its function is to *request* a place at the university. Its argument is non-adversarial because the writer does not expect to be countered. It seems a letter not entirely sure of its ground. There is no reason why the writer should feel sure of her ground − writing in role as a highly trained witch on behalf of a young student to 'Unseen University', however strong the fictional context, is bound to cause some difficulties. The teacher's letter, written in role as the Chief Wizard professor of the university, galvanizes the writing relationship. Mrs Weatherwax's reply is not only focused, sharp in its arguments and well structured; it also adopts the register of the formal letter and falls into paragraphs. This is not teaching by modelling, but by direct dialogue with the language produced by the pupil. Once again, the in-role dimension gives both teacher and pupil the scope and freedom to choose the registers and functions they wish to explore. A final pedagogical and logistical point: there is no need for the teacher to write an individual letter to each pupil in the class. The activity was set up so that a single letter addressed to all the pupils in the class would have the desired effect. In order to make such an exchange productive, the teacher has to anticipate the direction of the dialogue.

THE POWER OF EVIDENCE

One of the schools in the Esmée Fairbairn project decided to concentrate on the nature and deployment of evidence in the forming of arguments.

The pupils in the class were set an essay with the title 'Can testing on animals for any kind of research ever be justified?' and wrote this essay without recourse to any research of their own. In other words, the attempt was to set a 'pre-test' assignment that would give an indication of how children of this age argued without input from the teacher or further work by themselves – and without research for supporting evidence. To quote Stephen Clarke, independent evaluator of the project:

> Contained in the thinking of the teachers concerned was the idea that in arguing you argue first for (with?) yourself, at which stage, if you are arguing well, you are keeping good faith with yourself in terms of the evidence you gather, the degree to which you sift it and develop your own thinking. My notes, at any rate, suggest the notion of a 'pure argument', utterly sincere but subjective, and closely linked to instinctively held positions and beliefs.
>
> (Andrews *et al.*, 1993, p. 185)

Following this assignment (an example of which we will examine shortly) the pupils had discussed what they saw to be four main kinds of evidence used to support arguments. These were:

- 'gut reaction' (or instinctive positioning on an issue)
- anecdote
- facts (which could be validated)
- statistics

Conventionally, we can see this list in hierarchical terms. 'Gut reaction' – hardly evidence at all – and anecdote are considered 'soft' evidence, whereas 'facts' and statistics are considered 'hard'. But we know from court cases that anecdote ('testimony') has an important part to play in the weighing of arguments, and it may be that 'gut reaction' is related to the notion of 'character' (an aspect of persuasiveness that the Greek rhetoricians were aware of) and perhaps even conscience. The questions an arguer has to ask from this perspective are, 'Am I happy with the position I've taken on this issue? Can I justify my position in terms of my own conscience and integrity?'

The class was then exposed to two films: one was against vivisection and the other argued for testing on animals. The pupils also collected their own evidence in the form of pamphlets from pressure groups (which included much statistical evidence) and other material which they sifted and categorized. The teachers in this project worked out a sequence of stages in the collecting and sifting of evidence – stages in the preparation of arguments that are often overlooked:

1. First impressions: the ability to express a spontaneous opinion and to assert a position on an issue.
2. Information retrieval: the ability to find evidence for and against a statement. Independent research, using libraries and other sources of information. (The teachers found that supplying evidence for the pupils was not as motivating as having the pupils seek it out for themselves.)
3. Determining the nature of the evidence; and establishing the different shades of opinion informing the evidence.

4. Positioning evidence in relation to a given statement of opinion: this is where the arrangement of evidence moved beyond the 'for-and-against' pattern. Evidence was written on index cards which were moved around on a table until a 'map' of the field was drawn.
5. Prioritizing evidence: so that the spatial mapping of the argument could be translated into linear form for the writing of the argument, pupils then prioritized the available evidence, deciding on how they would use it in the writing.
6. Interpreting evidence: exploring the different comments and opinions that could arise from the evidence. This is a way of anticipating objections as well as making the most of the evidence collected.
7. Planning the direction of the argument: 'That's the rhythm I want' was a phrase used by a teacher to describe the emergence for a pupil of a line of argument.
8. Producing a first draft.
9. Offering the draft for comment (and argument) from peers or from the teacher.
10. Producing the final argument.

Stephen Clarke notes that after viewing the pro-vivisection video — evidence that seriously challenged the prevailing view of most of the pupils in the class — the interaction of teacher and pupils was particularly interesting as regards the development of argument:

> The video-viewing finished at 9.42am, and when it was over LD told her class to write down their instant reactions to the video, which they did, in total silence. After two minutes, she told everyone an anecdote about how her father had told her to look at the opposite side of a political question, of the need to test out another point of view from the prior one. She then asked if anyone had a particular question. Paul did, wondering why so many mice were used in an experiment .... LD formally put the question to the class. Something like the following dialogue (not exact words) ensued:

BOY: Get a better result?
LD: Can you explain?
STEPHEN: One of them might be wrong — so they'd have to use a lot (of mice) to get the test right.
LD: You're all on the right lines. We did a survey of reading habits — we couldn't have got a fair picture from one class. That's a very good point ...

> In this dialogue (verbally far richer than the recorded notes suggest) argumentative statements between teacher and class construct the idea of empirical researchers requiring a large sample of subjects in order to obtain valid results. This idea might be an important one in learning to argue, since it has to do with evidence, logic, systematic thinking and the necessity to do empirical work in order to answer some types of question: medical questions on the one hand and reading habits on the other.

(ibid., p. 185–6)

The important point here is that the teacher, though seeming to intervene at the content level, is also making a procedural point to the class about the nature and conduct of arguments and the role of evidence within them. As Stephen Clarke says, 'Her move, in referring to her father's reminder, was a neutral procedural move, and it led to a question right at the heart of the prior concern about the use of evidence.'

Managing class discussion of this kind is difficult. The range of viewpoints expressed in a lesson can hardly be expected to shape themselves into an argument; it takes a great deal of skill on the part of teachers to find a balance between encouraging expression of views, including as many pupils in the class as possible, keeping to the topic in question and engineering some kind of progression in the discussion. Teachers' agendas are often different from pupils' in this respect. There is a difference between the process of discussion and arguing on the one hand, and the product (words in the air, a transcript, a decision) on the other.

In the lesson described here, the issue was too full of unresolved positions for any clear-cut conclusion to be reached. The teacher suggested at the end of the lesson that the pupils spend time 'consolidating all these ideas in your minds' via a journal entry, thus asking for an interim appraisal of each child's position.

Let us look more closely now at one pupil's writing on the topic. This is the beginning of Katy's initial essay:

> It is not fair that animals should be used for testing. They cannot fight back – they are defenceless, unlike us. We wouldn't like it if we were tested on – used – for other people's benefit. It should be against the law, and I'm positive that the majority of people asked would agree as most of us care for animals due to having pets of our own . . . .
>
> (ibid., p. 186)

The essay continues in this way, adamant in its argument against testing and providing a good deal of evidence in the form of programmes seen on TV, material read, and hearsay. Sentences are underlined for emphasis, and the essay ends:

> I was told once that cosmetics and medication etc can be tested some other way without using defenceless animals. If this is so, animals should definitely not be used.
>
> (ibid.)

Several weeks later, after the work on evidence in class, Katy wrote:

> My feelings on testing on animals are very mixed up. At first, before I knew much about testing, I was very much against it, which I explained in my first essay. But now that I know about its importance in medication, I feel slightly different (and confused).
>
> (ibid.)

This is the beginning of a 1,500-word-plus essay under the same title used for the first essay. The second one includes many 'facts' and statistics: 'There are 442 places which are licensed to perform animal testing in Britiain . . . 20,000 people are licensed to conduct these experiments'; 'Economic considerations are a major factor in the use of laboratory animals: a laboratory mouse costs approx. £1.40, a cat approx. £100 and a beagle dog approx. £200–300. Animals are bred for particular qualities relevant to research needs'; and 'in 1990, 3.2 million animals were used.'

My general impression of the essay is that it moves some way from the position of the first essay; that it is an accomplished piece of writing for a Year 8 pupil; that she has managed to integrate the demands of a more fully researched essay well; that the interim work of the project has had considerable effect on the way she argues. At the same time, you can't help but notice, along with her teachers, a sense of confusion and disturbance as the initial position is affected by the evidence that has been discovered.

One of her teachers commented:

> Katy's folder is interesting as an example of the successful appreciation of new evidence but also resultant confusion. The essay becomes an attempt to find comfort somewhere.

The confusion seems more apparent when founded on 'gut reaction' material ('my pet rabbit') of a personal/empathetic type. Does the conventional neutral voice [of the essay] facilitate a clearer argument by reducing its place?

(ibid., p. 187)

The effects (and affects) of argument cannot be underestimated. If we are to promote argument in schools, we must accept that seeing other points of view and changing one's own position can be a painful business, especially for younger children. And yet we would not want to forgo the chance to argue different positions and create a climate of tolerance and understanding. The potential dilemma is a real one.

There are also dangers in sending pupils to find evidence without the kind of discussion of the nature and deployment of evidence that I have just described. Take the following essay, for example. It was written by a 13- to 14-year-old pupil who had 'researched' the topic before writing the essay. I have italicized those phrases which seem to have imported undigested evidence from sources that are perhaps not entirely appropriate to the topic, and which also use evidence to 'prove' statements in short-circuited ways:

Do you feel that due to the increased levels of crime in Great Britain capital punishment should be reintroduced?

Many people nowadays feel that murderers do not receive an acceptable sentence for the terrible crime which they have committed. Most murder sentences are life which is about twenty five years in prison. This would perhaps be suitable were it not for the fact that *prisons today do not really teach people a lesson because of the seemingly endless list of facilities available in British jails. Many poor and homeless people commit murder because life in a modern prison is more promising than the life they were leading.*

Based on these facts and on other beliefs, I do feel that the death sentence is the best form of punishment for a crime as serious as murder is. At the start of this project I felt the same way and thought that the project might have changed my mind and although it did not, it gave me some insight into *how fair capital punishment could be in the past.* There was equipment with deliberately scary names and equally scary jobs. Equipment such as: *the iron maiden, a coffin shaped object with spikes attached to the inside of the door and the guillotine, a platform with a head rest cut in to it and a sharpened blade above, ready to fall.* These are only two examples of former methods used to lay the condemned to rest, many are far more horrifying.

There are only two forms of execution which I am aware of today, those being the electric chair and the gas chamber *although I am led to believe that the method of standing a blindfolded man against a wall* is still used in the army. *As these are not particularly gruesome and only one rarely used method leaves blood, I do not see any reason why the sentence of death should not be reintroduced* to Britain. I do believe that the condemned man should have the right to a second trial before his execution and also I believe he should have the right to choose the form of execution which he must face. *Some people may choose to get it over with quickly (electric chair), while others may choose to live slightly longer (gas chamber).*

If someone takes another person's life (outside of the law) no matter what the other person has done, he has stolen the one thing which is more valuable than any amount of money or possessions and therefore his life should be taken as well. As it says in the Bible:

Do unto the man as he would do unto you.

Whatever happens I will always hope that the death sentence is reintroduced in Britain so the country is a much safer place for us to live in.

From the italicized phrases, I think it is fair to say that the pupil has probably read a book on medieval torture to argue *for* the reintroduction of capital punishment in Britain. By selecting evidence at an extreme end of the spectrum of views, his own fairly right-wing views look more moderate and 'reasonable'. A look at the logic of the argument, too, reveals some loose thinking.

However critical I might be as a teacher of writing like this – partly because I, personally, don't subscribe to the same viewpoint as the writer – it is salutary to remember that positions that I might be more inclined to agree with should receive the same kind of critical attention. I would be doing a disservice to pupils who put forward views I was in general agreement with if I didn't criticize their arguments; they are more likely to become better arguers if they have to grapple with my criticisms than if their views go unchallenged.

ARGUING IN THE 'REAL' WORLD

What happens when argument in schools moves beyond the boundaries of simulation and academic exercise? I will describe two projects, each lasting about six weeks. The first took place with a class of 13- to 14-year-olds and the second with 14- to 15-year-olds. The first is a story of becoming aware of boundaries and limitations; the second of using the boundaries to create an effective outcome.

The first project intended to address a local issue: whether a nearby village should have a bypass to relieve it of heavy summer traffic. Some of the problems to be addressed were:

In what ways can the parties to a dispute best influence public opinion?
How can parties overcome self-interest and achieve objectivity?

The initial objectives of the project were:

- to evaluate media reporting of the issue;
- to learn how both (or all) sides presented their cases;
- to produce – in tape, video and written form – arguments to represent differing points of view;
- to conduct a 'public inquiry' into the issue;
- to help pupils understand the differences between fact and opinion;
- to help pupils recognize when a talk or piece of writing is attempting to persuade;
- to make pupils more aware of ways in which speakers and writers can try to persuade listeners and readers;
- to give pupils a chance to put into practice what they have learned from the above.

Following initial research work on newspaper reports of the controversy and a visit from a protagonist in the pro-bypass campaign, the pupils became so committed to the argument *for* a bypass that the teacher felt compromised. As the anti-bypass lobby was the local council – who also funded the school – would it be appropriate for a class of 13- to 14-year-old children to become involved in the politics of the issue? As a result, the teacher switched the project to a simulated one in which pupils addressed a similar issue more indirectly. There was a resultant tailing off in motivation, though pupils did complete the simulated project and produced good work from it, exploring ironies in the relationship between fact and opinion. Lack of conviction about position, however, made for uncertainty about the bases of their arguments; procedurally they were competent and learnt much about the technical side of arguing. Politically, the arguments took place in a relative vacuum.

The school and the teacher are not untypical in the way the issue of arguments was handled, and the case is an important one to discuss. What happens when the walls of the classroom and the school are bypassed in the interests of exploring real arguments? First, the variables increase and it is much more difficult to control the flow and nature of material that the pupils encounter. Logistical problems can ensue: how long do we have to wait for an answer from the council? What do we do while we are waiting for an answer? How can we get time off school to visit that library? Is it possible to arrange for bus fares to visit a local company to interview the project manager? Will parental permission be necessary to undertake the project? Do we need to copy the results of our findings to the parties concerned before publication? Who speaks to the press? Secondly, the real political issues that are discovered might be too hot to handle. Should a class of 13- to 14-year-olds become involved? What are the relationships with parents and school staff over this issue? What if the pupils' views go against those of school governors or staff?

I would argue that these potential difficulties are worth facing in the interests of making argument 'real' and in teaching pupils the nature and limits of argument in society. A line has to be taken, however, between over-commitment to one side of a divisive topic on the one hand, and too dry and academic an approach on the other. The line is a thin one, and treading it is a delicate matter. Nevertheless, it is an important one to tread because understanding the nature of arguments in society is not only valuable – perhaps necessary – in a democracy; it is also a motivating factor in learning and an opportunity to witness and use language in a precise and effective way. By that I mean that language used in arguments has results *in action*.

Perhaps the best approach to take in the first instance is the taking on of a project that operates within the boundaries of the school itself. The school is a community that is part of the real world, and yet is one step removed from the world. It is framed within institutional assumptions shared by society and operates as a community in its own right as well as in relation to the wider world. A particular project I am thinking of involved a commission from the school librarian to a class of 14- to 15-year-olds[3]. She was concerned about the lack of interest in the periodicals to which the school library subscribed, and commissioned a report on the matter, pledging to act upon the recommendations of the report. The class decided how it would go about the research necessary for the writing of the report. It decided to issue a questionnaire to pupils in the school, visit local libraries to see the range of periodicals used, and interview people to find out what the patterns of periodical use were in the school library.

Such a project involves a great deal of cooperation and planning, and such collaboration requires meetings for all groups in the class to keep up with developments and coordinate progress. This is the only class I have seen in any school in which not only a meeting was taking place to discuss progress, but in which minutes were being taken by the pupils to record the discussion and to inform all involved of the progress to date. At the end of the six-week period, a 60-plus-page report was delivered to the librarian on time. She acted upon its recommendations and the library was transformed as a result. One of the benefits for the whole school was that the periodicals in the library were used a good deal more after the project.

These two projects indicate the problems and achievements of taking argument beyond the confines of simulation and the classroom into a relatively wider world. In that wider world, arguments have consequences. The question of the functions of argument in school in relation to those in the wider world are discussed more fully in the final chapter.

ARGUMENT USING WORD PROCESSORS

In a study undertaken in Australia by Snyder (1991, 1992, 1993), the effect of word processors on the contexts, processes and products of writing in different genres was explored. One of these 'genres' was argument; the other two were narrative and report. The pupils – two classes of 13-year-old girls – remained intact and became a 'pen group' and a 'computer group'. Over an eight-month period, the pen group did all its writing with pens; the second group on word processors. One of the findings of the research was that the computer group made fewer errors in producing argument and report texts than the pen goup. This may be partly due to the fact that pupils in the Melbourne study came to enjoy writing arguments and reports on word processors, and generally preferred the pen for composing narrative.

The examination of the writing processes in this study comes to a similar conclusion to my own research: that pupils plan less for narrative than they do for argument. This is because the leap from oral competences in argument is greater than in the composition of narrative, and so more scaffolding, more preparation, is required. So too, as far as revision is concerned: pupils revise less in narrative writing, and tend to make surface changes. In argument writing they are more likely to make substantial changes.

Snyder reasons that it was partly the change in learning environment in the computer classroom that accounted for the higher grades awarded the writing that took place there – in particular the writing of argument and report. In the computer classroom the students were more task oriented and independent, and there was more collaboration. How is this more conducive to argument? Perhaps it is the sense that the writing act is less of a ritual, and has more audience and purpose than usual. I argued in Chapter 3 that a dialogic classroom is likely to be more conducive to the development of argument: a classroom in which the teacher is freed from the conventional mixing of roles (classroom manager/setting of writing tasks) to be able to work alongside pupils and engage in the kind of response – both oral and written – demonstrated by Jan Sargeant earlier in this chapter.

Not only the environment and dynamic set up in the classroom by word processors, but also the word-processing programs themselves contribute to the increased facility with revision in argumentative texts. Word processors enable the writer to revise an emergent text with ease. Most importantly, it is possible to move around paragraphs or chunks of text, thus effecting more easily what was taking place in the doctoral research quoted at the beginning of this chapter, and providing pupils in classrooms with the missing ingredient in revision: the arrangement and rearrangement of the large-scale structures of composition, the inclusion of *dispositio*. Because word processors make this part of the writing act more manageable, they may well enhance the kind of writing – argument – that depends on such flexibility at this level.

At the same time, it may be that the discovery in the Melbourne study that the pen is a better medium for the writing of narrative is an interesting one. Is it because for student writers the composition of narrative is basically linear and additive that the pen is mightier than the word processor in the composition of this kind of writing; and that the pen moves across paper in a relatively more linear and additive way? Or is it that the pen is a more intimate tool than the word processor, thus acting more readily as a conduit for expression and feeling? Negatively speaking, is pen's difficulty with major revisions (in that you have to write the whole piece out again if you are making large-scale structural changes) in tune with the resistance of pupils to revision of narrative?

Another point to bear in mind is that on word processors the page scrolls from top to bottom rather than the left to right movement we find in books or in writing on paper. This difference may have a significant effect on the act of composition. I would suggest that the way writing appears on the page on a screen is more conducive to *listing* than to linearity,[4] because lists tend to appear in vertical shape. Linearity, on the other hand, suggests the left-to-right movement and the horizontal plane. Because we think of stories and novels in book form, we associate the experience of reading (and therefore writing) with turning pages and with the horizontal. Arguments are less bound by the book, as we have already seen, and are therefore less likely to be associated with the left-to-right movement. I would argue that arguments tend to be thought of *spatially* rather than in linear terms, and that the word-processing screen goes some way towards assisting that conception (see Selfe, 1989).

Not all the way, though. One of the limitations of the computer screen is that however much it tries to simulate a desktop, it is usually smaller than the top of a desk. The composing of argument and report – perhaps to some degree more than the composing of narrative – requires space because there are often other texts to lay out on the table: sources to refer to, data, other arguments that one wants to use as a starting point or to fight against, and so on. The image of composition in argument that I have is very like the photograph of Stravinsky working on a large table with a large score spread in front of him in which no doubt he is 'composing' or bringing together the different 'voices' of the instruments.[5]

On the computer screen, however much a large screen can accommodate annotations (in voices as well as in print) or commentary alongside text, the very size of the screen acts as a limitation on what the mind can see at any one time. By its very nature the screen is no more than a window through which one looks at myriad possibilities in terms of composition. One can imagine a much bigger screen – already available to typesetters and designers – on which pupils could compose and have more than one text on the screen at the same time. They would thus have the facility to splice texts or parts of texts together, to annotate and comment with ease, to begin to see the whole of an emergent text at the same time. The screen would become more and more like a large desktop, and begin to approximate the physical pleasures and possibilities of composing and recomposing text, of moving bits of texts around on the table until one had the right arrangement. As hinted earlier in this chapter, finding the right rhythm to translate a spatial arrangement into a linear one is a crucial moment in the act of composing an argumentative text, and a difficulty that is not fully recognized. Just as moving from a concert (or discordant set) of voices to a written text has been identified as one of the problems of composing written argument, so too the move from the spatial to the linear is problematic.

Let's follow this line of argument a little further. Imagine, for a moment, that written texts did not have to take linear shape; that the book no longer defined the format in which argumentative texts presented themselves for consideration. Would it be possible to conceive of new, less linear, formats in which arguments could be framed? To a certain extent, arguments already feel happiest in shapes other than those defined by the conventional book: articles, chapters, monographs and so on. They appear in column format in newspapers, as letters, as multimedia texts, in magazines and on television and increasingly in dialogic format as print races to match speech in its variety and shape – and in hypertext.[6]

If pupils make fewer errors in argument writing when composing on a computer screen than with pen on paper, we can assume that they are gaining more time for the large-scale compositional demands, and that the computer is indeed facilitating the composition of argument. This is an important finding, and one which invites further research into the effect of word processing on composition in different modes and genres.

SUMMARY

In this chapter I wanted to explore the ways in which the quality of argument-writing might be improved in the secondary/high school context. I have suggested that the conservative tendencies of the teaching of argument at this level – with the drive towards assessment at the end of compulsory schooling, the long tradition of the 'opinion' and literary essays, the hold of the 'for-and-against' model and the largely unconscious generic constraints upon writing in the classroom – have limited what is possible in terms of the writing of argument. New approaches to the process and range of argumentative writing need to be taken. These include:

● increased flexibility to the structuring of arguments in order to free writers from the classical and quasi-classical formulations about arrangement;
● a closer coincidence between the purpose and functions of a piece of writing and the structures and media used to fulfil those purposes and functions;
● diversity in planning arguments, so that the important stage of planning in the composition of arguments can be given higher profile and more range;
● the breaking down of the polarity of narrative fiction and argument, so that fiction can be seen in argumentative terms and can also provide texts from which arguments can be generated;
● transformations in the role of the teacher, who can respond to written work more as an interlocutor than as a judge, and who can frame his or her evaluations about pupils' work through the medium of direct, dialogic response to what is said and written by pupils;
● more sensitive consideration of the nature and power of evidence, and of how it is best deployed in the construction of arguments;
● a movement beyond the walls of the classroom to argument within and beyond the school itself; looking for real audiences to enhance the dialogic aspect of argumentation;
● using word processors to experiment with composition in argument, and becoming aware of the advantages and disadvantages of computers in relation to different modes and genres of writing;

● continuing to give pupils the choice of topic, so that hypotheses can be formed and tested, titles tried, and the formulation of arguments made part of the business of learning to argue well.

NOTES

1 This section draws on the doctoral research which is described in more detail in Appendix 1 (see p. 173). The full title of the research thesis is 'An exploration of structural relationships in narrative and argumentative writing, with particular reference to the work of Year 8 students' (Andrews, 1992a).

2 I defined episodes by following van Dijk (1981) and the relationships between episodes in terms of 'and', 'then' and 'cause' relations, as described by Stein and Glenn (1979).

3 This project was part of the DEFT (Developing English for TVEI) research.

4 In an article entitled 'Mapping the world' Myra Barrs (1987) discusses the importance of listing in the writing development of young children. Her arguments accord with the line being argued here: that listing is essentially a non-narrative action that is not only a spontaneous activity practised by children, but one which forms a foundation for later work in classification and conceptual block-building.

5 The photograph, by Sanford H. Roth, appears on the cover of the paperback edition of Roman Vlad's biography of Stravinsky (1960).

6 The advent of hypertext and hypermedia adds a new dimension to the possibilities of structuring and framing arguments. In conventionally written argument, the paradigmatic classification and logical tendencies of argument sometimes struggle against the linear, syntagmatic notion of print. But because hypertext allows texts to stand alongside each other or 'behind' and 'in front of' each other, contiguity comes much more into play. For example, double-column writing is easier and there is also the opportunity for the reader to interact with the text by inserting evidence or arguments to complement or argue against the text.

Chapter 6

Argument, 16−19 and Beyond

> Essay: a taste, or first taste, of food or drink presented to a great personage.
>
> *(Oxford English Dictionary)*

In England and Wales, at least, the context for argument in education is one in which, increasingly, argumentation becomes embedded in particular disciplines. In extreme cases, like philosophy and politics, the discipline is almost constituted around argument. Because education 16−19[1] and further and higher education for students are still generally characterized by immersion in a small number of disciplines, the forms of argumentation in those disciplines becomes more and more a matter of concern for students and teachers alike, particularly as assessment often takes the form of argumentation and success in the discipline at university level depends on command of the discourses of the subject.

The picture, then, is different from that at primary or secondary levels. At primary, we saw argument operating across the curriculum, relatively free of subject boundaries. At secondary level we saw increasing specialization, with the curriculum based around 'subjects', each with elements of argumentation embedded into its practices and required of students at different levels within each subject. At tertiary level we see yet further integration of argumentative practices within distinct disciplines, so that the way a scientist might argue a case becomes increasingly different from the way a lawyer or English student might argue a case.

At the same time, there are contrary movements in education. Primary schooling, as I write, is becoming increasingly subject oriented with certain times of the week being allocated to certain subjects. The secondary curriculum remains much the way it has been for several decades, with the National Curriculum reinforcing subject boundaries that evolved in the second half of the nineteenth century. The tertiary picture, if anything, is becoming more diverse, with more subjects on offer and blends and mixes possible, especially at further and higher education levels.[2] Contrary to the general picture I drew in the first two papagraphs is a movement in the other direction, with implications for the framing of argument at each level and indeed for the practice of argument. It is no longer possible to state categorically that the drift is towards increasing specialization, or from the concrete to the abstract, or from 'lower-order thinking skills' to 'higher-order skills' within an education.

Nevertheless, it is with the nature of argumentation in different disciplines that this chapter is principally concerned because that way of thinking about education 16–19 and beyond is still prevalent, and because it was the way that the main research project which informs this chapter was framed.[3] The first half of the chapter deals with A-level education in a range of subjects with regard to both spoken and written argument; the second half looks at the shift to university undergraduate work, with a brief look at postgraduate writing.

THE USE OF QUESTIONS

Any reflection on the use of questions by teachers and students in classrooms needs to refer back to the seminal chapter by Douglas Barnes in *Language, the Learner and the School* (1990). In that chapter, Barnes categorized the questions he and his team had collected in a range of subjects. These categories were 'factual' ('what?' questions concerned with naming and information); 'reasoning' ('how?' and 'why?' questions, further subdivided as 'closed' reasoning, 'open' reasoning and observation); 'open' questions not calling for reasoning; and 'social' questions, including those of control and appeal.[4]

It is not so much the pure categorization of questions and what it tells us about the nature of questions asked in a number of subjects that is of interest in this chapter, as the relations between questions in a sequence and the questions asked by students. Such is the suggestiveness of Barnes's analysis that, a generation later, classrooms have changed and the territory is now different. In the following extract from a transcript of exchanges in an A-level history lesson, the students (Robert and Neil) are talking with the teachers about posters used in the First World War. Source 103, which Neil refers to, is a poster about the value of working on the land as part of the war effort. The discussion revolves around the overall question of propaganda – a question raised by one of the students.

ROBERT:	They're obviously blatant propaganda aren't they?
TEACHER:	Why are they blatant propaganda?
ROBERT:	Because the message seems so obvious.
NEIL:	Why's that propaganda?
TEACHER:	Well, propaganda in itself has taken on as a word – it's an important word really. [*Boys: 'but . . .' – protesting mumble*] What do you understand by propaganda? It's taken on a very sinister meaning – propaganda. Particularly with regard to Goebbels in the Second World War.
NEIL:	Goebbels?
TEACHER:	Goebbels was the German Propaganda Minister in the Second World War. [*Inaudible interchange*] But what is propaganda anyway? What do we understand by it as a term? It's one that you'll probably use for certain in your historical writing.
NEIL:	Y'see I don't count source 103 as propaganda.
TEACHER:	Why not?
NEIL:	Because, although it's to do with war, I see propaganda as like events in the real world, sort o'like bent.

At times the discussion borders on the defensive on the part of the students, and through-out the full six-minute exchange (of which the first minute or so is printed here) they have to fight to keep the teacher on the point. He has a different agenda (what he wants to 'get through' in the lesson) whereas the students' is driven by what they want to learn. In this case, the definition of propaganda requires clarification for them. And so the transcript opens with what appears to be a rhetorical question on the part of Robert in referring to the sources ('They're obviously blatant propaganda aren't they?') but is, within the context of the power relations in the classroom and of the subject, a challenge to the teacher. The teacher's response is to throw back the question to the student: 'Why are they blatant propaganda?' The answer, 'Because the message seems so obvious' is seen as inadequate by the other student and the teacher, who uses the second student's question as a chance to make a point about propaganda. The interesting thing about the way the teacher makes his point is that he stops himself short of giving the explanation, and again sends the ball back into the student's court with 'What do you understand by propaganda?', finishing his lengthier turn with a reference to Goebbels, which in turn provokes a question as to the identity and significance of Goebbels from the second student. The teacher provides a partial answer and then reverts to a more teacherly style of questioning with 'What do we understand by [propaganda] as a term?' Still the students – with the second one, Neil, taking up the point – persist with their view that source 103 is not propaganda. The teacher then asks what might be called a genuine question, addressing the students' needs directly for perhaps the first time in this extract: 'Why not?' This moment, at which the teacher fully engages with the questions of the students, marks a shift into total concentration on the question of the definition of propaganda. By the end of the six-minute diversion from the overall direction of the lesson, teacher and students have hammered out a working definition of propaganda to cover all their different views on it: from propaganda as 'blatant' to propaganda as insidious or subtle (and possibly deployed in peace – as well as wartime).[5]

In this very ordinary exchange, it is the nature and sequence of the questions which mark turning points in the argument. The teacher's questions can be categorized as first, open and not calling for reasoning ('Any other comments . . . ?'); and then open with a call for reasoning ('Why are they blatant propaganda?'). The third set of questions ('But what is propaganda anyway? What do we understand by it as a term?') is, as I have suggested above, more 'teacherly' in that its function is more to demonstrate than to argue. Like many teacherly questions, its aim is to create in the air, using students' voices, an exposition in words of the knowledge to be covered. It is not argument as such, but more Socratic in its style and – I would argue – less valuable and certainly less economical than a combination of direct exposition and direct questioning from the students or between teacher and students. The teacher's last question in this extract, 'Why not?', in response to Neil's resistance, is of a different nature altogether. With this question, the teacher is directly engaging with the student's difficulty and hence the long exploration of the word in question. There is a true dialogue taking place as a result, but one for which the students had to fight. To the teacher's credit, he put aside his plan for the lesson to deal with this genuine difficulty on the part of the students – and the fact that they felt they could take up the question is further credit to the existing dynamics of the classroom. But, interestingly, the transcript ends with Neil's point not being fully resolved and with a return to the teacher's agenda: 'Ah, we'll probably find time to explore [the question again] later. Anyway, let's turn back to source 89 . . . .'

Three further points about this interlude in a history lesson. One is that the teacher's interpretation – we could almost say his *authority* – has been challenged, and challenged to good effect. This particular teacher allows a six-minute 'diversion' and addresses the question seriously, but at the same time is anxious to get on with the main substance of the lesson. Managing the demands of the syllabus while at the same time responding to and following up students' questions is a perennial balancing act for all teachers. And thus my second point: is this kind of exchange one that happens only in history lessons, or is it typical of exchanges in a range of subjects? Is the function and nature of questioning, and its relation to argument, more to do with teaching style than with the nature of the discipline? Finally, how can we, as teachers, use students' doubts to promote productive argument in the classroom?

ARGUMENT IN THREE SUBJECTS AT A LEVEL

It is perhaps premature to assume that school subjects at 16–19 have attained the status of a discipline; or, for that matter, to assume that any discipline has set procedures or 'discourses' and that these are not subject to change and interpretation by individual teachers. In short, it might be presumptuous to proceed at this point as though all the subjects available at 16–19 were discrete. Furthermore, the relationship between the language of the subjects – in the broadest sense, from the diction of textbooks in the subject to the nature of interaction in the classroom – and the subjects themselves (however defined) is complex. Without claiming any absolutes, however, it *is* possible to make comparisons between subjects in terms of the degree of argumentation present in the following of a syllabus. The three subjects I will take for the purposes of this section are sociology, physics and English.

According to our research in sixth-form classrooms, one of the principal aims of sociology at this level is to encourage students to think sociologically. In other words, the accent is on process and on understanding sociology as an approach, rather than on, say, a particular text or writer in the field. This means that students of sociology have to become adept at handling ideas, and aware of different perspectives and critical approaches to topics. Often, access to these ideas is via example, but students are expected to be able to quote different perspectives, and this sometimes means summing up a particular perspective with a name for example 'Marxist' or 'Darwinian'.

The handling of ideas, the interpretation of social phenomena from different points of view and the lack of absolutes and scepticism about fact all suggest that thinking sociologically is thinking argumentatively. There is scope for challenge of the teacher's and other pupils' points of view – indeed, a good sociologist at this level will be required to challenge different points of view, especially the ideology of the status quo and received opinion.

The teacher's role within this subject is to present different points of view for discussion and/or explication by the class, and to foster argument. It may be that from the perspective of other subjects, the move from description to interpretation to criticism in sociology is too fast, and that students race to generalizations without a 'proper grounding' in description and observation. Sociologist would argue, I think, that discussion of the phenomena of society is impossible without access to the theories that inform our explanations of these phenomena. Furthermore, they would see it as part of their role as teachers of sociology to enable students to move beyond personal feelings and perspectives to a more reasoned and academic appraisal of the 'facts', while at the same time becoming more aware of how their own opinions and values are constructed sociologically.

Because there are no absolute theories of society there is always room for argument, and rhetoric thrives. There is a need for persuasion and debate, for multiple perspectives as well as for the presentation and defence of a particular point of view. Language is important in sociology at this level because it is a way of framing points of view; and so too are questions, many of which can be hypothetical. Whereas in the transcript discussed in the previous section, the history teacher was keen to 'get on' with the syllabus – because in history there is a 'lot to get through' in terms of content – the sociology teacher is more likely to see such an exchange as central to the discipline, rather than as a means to an end. Like politics, argument in sociology is almost the *sine qua non* of the subject, and any reading that takes place, whether of source material or of theoretical texts (or secondary theoretical texts) is designed to act as grist to the mill of argumentative discourse in the classroom.

In physics at A level, the picture is different in many respects. First, it should be said that physics, of the three main sciences (chemistry and biology being the other two) is ostensibly the most argumentative, because of its tendency to generalize more quickly from data, its more theoretical nature at this level, and its dependence upon mathematical reasoning. Biology is at the other extreme, and is discussed in Mitchell (1992a). Often argument in physics takes the form of problem-solving, with small groups of students working on a particular problem and then presenting their solutions and thinking to the wider group, to which the teacher also contributes. From the outset, then, physics differs from sociology in that students generate their own hypotheses rather than play with the hypotheses and theses of others. These hypotheses are generated from observation; the action of the lesson is more inductive than deductive.

In written work arising from such experiments and speculations, the emphasis is not so much on the writing of an essay – as it is in sociology, English and history – as on answers to questions set by the teacher or the examining board. Questions ask students to discuss reasons for the behaviour of phenomena, to list advantages and disadvantages of a particular explanation, to select the best explanation, and to justify and test a decision. All these are argumentative skills, and they are broken down into discrete units in this subject rather than employed in a substantial discourse like an essay or report. This does not mean that the different skills are not related. On the contrary, the sequence of operation is often tightly controlled. It is as if the structure of thinking is provided, and is seen by the 'gatekeepers' of the discipline as a necessary induction into the nature of the subject, a kind of training for procedures to be used at a higher level. The emphasis on demonstration in this subject – both by the teacher and by the students – perhaps leads to the entrenchment of points of view, because demonstration *per se* does not lend itself to challenge as readily as provisional statement or hypothesis. In other words, physics seems relatively conservative compared to sociology; rarely are underlying assumptions about the way experiments are set up or the methods for working towards conclusions questioned.

English, too, seems more conservative than I had imagined. Whereas sociology works in the classroom through the consideration of different points of view on social phenomena, the nature of the subject 'English Literature' at A level requires a different alignment. The data for analysis is usually a fictional text. There is no doubting, then, what the 'evidence' for argument is, because the evidence is already processed and exists at one stage removed from the 'real world' in which sociological data exists. To put it another way, the evidence in English is already framed more tightly than the evidence in sociology. Because the evidence in English exists in a fictional world, it is decontextualized to a greater extent than evidence in sociology. Interpretation is more open to different points of view, within the limits of the words that make up the text.[6]

The fact that interpretation is wide open in English leads, ironically, to a counter-movement within lessons to establish a common ground for discussion. That is why discussion in English often sounds more like exegesis than argument. Any argument that does take place tends towards the consensual as students, with the help of the teacher, work towards a common reading of the text in question. Only when there is some common ground can criticism and analysis of where the text stands in relation to other texts be undertaken. To return to the nature and function of questions in the discourse in English lessons, it may come as a surprise that many of the questions in English (just as Barnes found in the late 1960s) are closed. Their function is to recall elements of the action and to help students weave a web of interconnections in the text. We will see this richness of texture demonstrated when we come on to look at examples of written argument in English later in the chapter. But richness of texture – the most prized quality in much A-level writing in English, enmeshed with a personally argued viewpoint – is not fully-fledged argument but rather interpretation and 'appreciation'. It still stands in awe of the text it is discussing.

In a sense, much more so than in sociology or physics – or for that matter, any of the subjects discussed here – the ground against which the texts are judged is personal rather than public. Classes work towards a collective subjectivity so that, for some of the time, in the words of one English student, 'we all end up thinking the same'. That this sameness is but a stage on the road to diversity of opinion and viewpoint has to be recognized. Nevertheless, it is a dominant stage at A level. While there are no right answers as such to a text that is discussed, ther *are* wrong ones. This, I take it, is what makes English frustrating to many students, but it is part of the role of the English teacher to act as gatekeeper to interpretation and to make sure that no student leads him or herself down a path towards an untenable position on a text.

The nature of English as a subject which encourages interpretation rather than criticism, and appreciation rather than argument, is understandable when we consider that reading in the subject tends to be only of the text in question and rarely of criticism surrounding the text. With modern texts like Amy Tan's *The Joy Luck Club*, Graham Swift's *Waterland* or J. G. Farrell's *The Siege of Khrishnapur,* there is little available criticism. Students are thrown back upon their own interpretations and operate largely on the levels between the 'facts' of the text – the particularities of wording and event – and interpretation. Students rarely see the text with enough perspective to read it as an argument for a specific point of view; not until they are able to compare it to other texts can such a perspective be gained.

In summary, argument in subjects at A level requires the student to stand back from the facts of the case and apply different theories to the evidence. This happens more readily in subjects like sociology which deal with points of view in an explicit way, and in which the various points of view are the primary focus of attention in the subject. In physics, set procedures for framing discoveries made by problem-solving tend to direct the argument into particular channels, once initial speculation and reasoning have taken place. There is less scope for debating the rights and wrongs of the case and more emphasis on procedure and method. In English, the situation is different. Because English at this level operates between observation and criticism, attempting to create sensitive readers who can interpret and respond to texts, it tends to forgo 'higher' deliberations for interpretive ones in which the personal viewpoint, the web of feelings and thoughts generated by a text, is retained. This level of operation is driven by the assumption that the text is the primary authority.

One could say that each subject limits as well as frames the kind of arguing that goes on within its boundaries; that setting limits to argument is a way of controlling it and making it permissible within civilized discourse. At the same time, there is considerable freedom to play with argument in different ways within each subject. Perhaps the different kinds of interaction are what attract students to particular subjects? In the next section, I look across the curriculum 16–19 in more breadth, reporting the results of a questionnaire administered to students in two sixth forms about their attitudes to argument.

ATTITUDES TO ARGUMENT ACROSS THE CURRICULUM

A questionnaire was administered to sixth-form students in two institutions in Hull in the second half of 1992, in order to provide futher evidence of attitudes towards argument amongst students at this level. In total, the sample consisted of 522 students with 1,535 cases of A level and AS level recorded.[7] The questionnaire, which consisted of ten principal areas of questioning, each divided into between one and nine sub-questions, is included in this book as Appendix 2.

I will focus first on the subjects we have just discussed, sociology, physics and English, to see if the answers to the questionnaire confirmed or shed new light on the observations already made about the subjects. I will then report on findings in other subjects in the 16–19 curriculum.

The first three questions dealt with the perceived importance of argument to the subject, dealing separately with the forms of argument used, the factors of argumentation important to success in the subject, and the importance (or otherwise) of participation in spoken argument to success in the subject. As far as the first question was concerned, the average for the six sub-questions on the argumentative forms used in the subject was 86.6 per cent for sociology (sample = 32), 69.3 per cent for English (sample = 114) and 41 per cent for physics (sample = 85), confirming the relative importance of argumentative procedures in the three subjects that has already been suggested. When we break those results down into their constituent parts, we see that the most important aspects of argument in sociology are considered to be seeing both sides of an issue or question followed by raising questions, supplying evidence as proof and weighing up the arguments of others, with making points related to previous points following hard behind (all these scoring more than 88 per cent). The least important feature was seen to be 'persuading someone of your point of view' (56 per cent of respondents), perhaps because persuading others in the class of your position is not necessary in sociology, as long as a range of views is expressed and explored.

The lack of a need to persuade others of a point of view was much more marked in physics, as one would expect in a subject in which interaction was more restrained. Only 15 per cent of the physics sample recorded that such activity took place in their subject, a low figure matched only by their perception that 'weighing up the arguments of others' was even less prevalent (14 per cent).[8] In English, the persuasion of others was seen to be practised more than in sociology, but only marginally (60 per cent).

Forms of argument used do not necessarily correlate with the students' perception of how important aspects of argument are to success in the subject, and so the second question shed a different light on the three subjects. Sociology still came out on top, but less emphatically so, with an average of 74 per cent across the seven sub-questions as opposed to 67 per cent for physics and 64.8 per cent for English. In many ways, these questions were indicative of the argumentativeness of the subject, though generalizations ar difficult because of the diverse nature of the ingredients that were seen to make up 'argumentativeness'. For example, 'knowledge of facts' and 'memory' were seen to be crucial to physics, but so was 'making logical connections'. In sociology, the first two factors were similarly important, but rather less emphasis was put on making logical connections (81 per cent as opposed to physics' 95 per cent). Predictably, English scored relatively low on these factors, but was far higher than physics (9 per cent) or sociology (31 per cent) on the importance of sensitivity to success in the subject.

On the question of the importance of spoken argument to success in the subject, the hierarchy was similar to that in our observations and in the first question discussed, with spoken argumentation seen to be important by 84 per cent of sociology students, 78 per cent of English students and only 27 per cent of physics students.

These results do not tell us anything surprising, or anything that we had not intuited or observed about the differences between the three subjects; but they do confirm our perceptions and do so, importantly, from the students' point of view.

The second half of the questionnaire was concerned not so much with spoken argument as with written, and in particular it tried to gauge the kinds of essay that formed part of studying the subject. Looking more widely across the curriculum, the following picture emerged of those subjects in which it was felt that essays were 'often' written:

Politics	100%
Theatre studies	100%
English	99%
Sociology	97%
History	95%
Biology	79%
Communication studies	74%
General studies	61%
Design	43%
Art	18%
Chemistry	18%
Physics	4%
Maths	0%

It is important to remember as we interpret these figures that the frequent writing of essays may not mean that the incidence or quality of argument is high. Essays can be used for exposition as well as argument. What the figures do show is that within the assessment and curricular practices of 16–19 education, essays are prevalent in the humanities and not often used in the sciences, with the exception of biology.

What kinds of essay are these? The categories offered as part of this question were 'the presentation of a line of reasoning', 'an exploration of my personal opinion', 'a way of demonstrating what I have learnt', 'a discussion of more than one point of view' and 'a way of working out what I think'. I line with responses outlined above, sociology students saw essays as primarily a discussion of more than one point of view (*all* the sociology students felt this to be true) with 91 per cent of them seeing the essay as 'a way of demonstrating what I have learnt'. The more personal aspects of essay-writing were firmly in the background with these students. The same was the case with physics students, half of whom saw essays as a way of demonstrating what they had learnt. For both sociology and physics students, the essay does not offer a place where thinking may be undertaken. These students do not write to discover what they know or to discover what they don't know; they write to demonstrate what they already know. In English, on the other hand, students saw essays as primarily to do with 'an exploration of my personal opinion' followed by its function as a place to discuss more than one point of view. The presentation of a line of reasoning was seen by English students to be the least important aspect of essay-writing.

In history and politics, however, using the essay for reasoning was a common practice, though second to the discussion of more than one point of view in both cases.

In general, students see essays as having to be well structured, clear in their expression and showing a reasonable amount of logical development. The demonstration of knowledge of the subject is considered an important function; more so than either the provision of data, examples and illustrative material, or originality — which for most subjects, scored lowest in a question designed to determine the features essential to a good essay. There is little sense that students come to a new position via argument. Rather the drive is to see which of existing positions is 'right'. These views would seem to suggest that students see the essay as a place for exposition rather than argument.[9]

TWO ENGLISH ESSAYS COMPARED

In this section I will consider two styles of essay-writing from an English literature A level course and reflect on how each of them contains argument. Both are on the poetry of Sylvia Plath, and the students have chosen their own titles. These are 'Plath's treatment of women' and 'Sylvia Plath: illness and death in her poetry'. Here I will focus on beginnings and endings, and give an indication of what comes in between.

The first essay, 'Plath's treatment of women', begins with an epigraph: 'Her emotional life came straight out of a glossy magazine.' Then comes the first paragraph:

> It seems we are all to be subjected to various images of perfection, various roles of women, as Plath was. It also seems we are all to be disappointed with ourselves, for not being beautifully feminine, dashing, practical etc. Instead of exploring the options for women, Plath attacks the roles present, and in this way, through a narrator, we can grasp many of Plath's emotions. In fact because the poems are so assertive, so extreme, it is difficult not to feel that these relate to her own life, that these poems are Plath's experiences.
>   'A ring of gold with the sun in it?
>   Lies. Lies and a grief.'[10]

Marriage was perhaps the real disillusionment for Plath, I think. She married with dreams, set about to adore her handsome, intelligent husband and found the reality – that it brought her mostly pain.

It must be said at the outset that the title invites exposition rather than argument. There is no point of view expressed in the title – nothing to agree with or fight against, but rather a thematic heading under which a good deal might find its place. The epigraph sets the tone for the fine command of language that the essay exhibits: it's a neat, acerbic statement that also happens to sound Plath-like (emotional life/glossy magazine). As with most epigraphs, its relation to what follows is oblique. Then begins the body of the essay itself, with two general opening statements, couched in the careful and rhetorically useful 'it seems . . .' mode, and setting up propositions against which the poetry of Plath will be weighed. There's a defensiveness about the opening statement: 'It seems we are all to be subjected . . .' A philosopher might want to question the 'all'. Does the writer mean the 'we' to be all women? That does seem to be the case. If it 'seems' that all women are to be subjected to various images of perfection, is it in fact the case or not? 'Seems' is used, not in opposition to 'is', but sardonically: 'so this is what they [men?] are doing to us'.

The essay, then, opens with clear positional moves, identifying itself with the point of view of subjected women and deploying a sharp critical intelligence on notions of the ideal, manifested in precise, acerbic (but not aggressive) language. Rhetorically, it skilfully uses repetition to build up pattern: a pattern against which the poetry of Plath is discussed. The setting up of straw targets at the beginning of an argument, especially targets of such generality that they are difficult to disprove, is a useful device in arguing. It gets the audience on your side from the start and allows you the tacit support to go ahead and make your case in detail, safe in the knowledge that you have general agreement with your direction.

What happens next? The conflation of Sylvia Plath the woman with Plath the poet is complete in the lines that follow, and like many sixth-form students, the writer assumes the two to be the same. The connection is admitted – 'it is difficult not to feel that these relate to her own life, that these poems are Plath's experiences' – but nonetheless little attempt is made at the beginning, or indeed throughout the essay as a whole, to disentangle the two. As a result, the writer makes generalizations about Plath the woman on the evidence of the poems, almost like a barrister putting Plath the woman in the dock and using the poems as 'evidence against her'. Although the generalizations are phrased tentatively at times – 'Marriage was perhaps the real disillusionment for Plath, I think' – these qualifications might be seen as rhetorical in the less noble sense of the word. The tentative statement just quoted is followed by 'She married with dreams, set about to adore her handsome, intelligent husband, and found the reality – that it brought her mostly pain'.

Many sixth-form English literature essays show these qualities. The tendency to paraphrase, to explain, to generalize from the evidence of the text about life in general, and specifically about the life of the author, is typical of the genre. What is not so typical, and what is distinctive about this essay is that it integrates quotations from Plath's poems into the 'narrative' or rather the 'exposition' of the writer. Sometimes these quotations are so subtly integrated that they seem to be part of the writer's own voice. She (for the writer is a woman) has almost appropriated Plath's voice into her own and has woven a commentary around these quotations. The texture of the commentary is therefore rich, and although the prevailing mode is expository, the closeness to the studied text is much valued by assessors of this kind of writing.

The main body of the essay runs for some 800 words and discusses eight or nine of Plath's poems. 'Discusses' is hardly the right word, however. The poems are used to 'prove' the general proposition that marriage causes pain/we are all to be disappointed for not being perfect. The poems tell us about Plath's emotions in these respects. The first five poems ('Daddy', 'The Applicant', 'Tulips', 'Stings' and another, the title of which is not mentioned)[11] are all used in this way and no substantial new theme is introduced. Then the essay moves from women's relationship with men to women's search for self-identity. The shift is made by using a poem ('Stings') as a pivot in the essay. To refer back to the mathematical definition of argument, it is as if we have taken a new direction, a new angle in the course of the essay. This line is pursued through another three poems ('Lady Lazarus', 'Letter in November' and 'Cut') and then again the last poem is used as a pivot or turning point to move the essay on to the theme of birth, domesticity and self-identity, explored through 'Balloons' and 'You're'.

The essay ends with two short paragraphs:

> Plath's poems could be a way to break free of the black boot that suffocates her. Maybe she's trying to assess the alternatives for women, although she does not approach it with an open mind, the poems are too full of bitterness about past occurrences and observations.
>
> I think what Plath is declaring is that women are abused by men, but she also recognises the magnificence of womanhood, of birth, of love even. She is still, after all, as we all are, transfixed with the idea of being loved.

The first of these paragraphs is full of slippages: from metaphor to metaphor ('the black boot that suffocates her'); from plural subject to single subject ('she's trying to assess the *alternatives* for women, although she does not approach *it* with an open mind'); from sentence to sentence ('with an open mind, the poems are too full . . .'); and most importantly, from idea to idea (the whole paragraph in its movement from breaking free to alternatives to bitterness). The last paragraph takes us back to the generalizations about womanhood that were evident in the first paragraph of the essay, but also reveals a sense of complexity ('women are abused by men, but she also recognises the magnificence of womanhood'). And then the nicely weighted coda: 'She is still, after all, *as we all are,* transfixed with the idea of being loved.'

Overall, what is the structure and nature of this essay? It has a static quality, because rather than develop an argument about Plath's poems, it states a proposition at the beginning, finds evidence to support that proposition, and then restates the proposition at the end. There has been a move beyond the original proposition, however. The writer perceives that it is not simply a question of disillusion in the poetry but that there is also the sense of alternatives, of 'magnificence'. That this is found in women's own self-identity rather than in relation to men is indeed a new idea in the essay. The ability to handle more than one idea at a time, and to find more than one idea in the poems, begins to move the essay beyond paraphrase and towards an awareness of ambiguity and multiple meanings. This quality, and the close interweaving of commentary and quotation, are signs that the writer is on the way to becoming a successful student of English – as indeed she did become, attaining a grade A at A level and going on to read English at university.

I will deal with the second essay on Plath rather more briefly. Its title is 'Illness and death in her poetry' and it begins with the following sentences:

> Many of Sylvia Plath's poems explore the theme of illness and death, yet this does not make all these particular poems the same. Plath treats these two subjects in several ways; she considers the aspects of illness and death being welcome, in the sense that it allows for relaxation and genuine recuperation.... Contrasting pieces of her work let her vulnerability show through, and her sense of insecurity with the prospect of facing death or a long illness. It had been said that Plath was almost schizophrenic, and the varying ways she approaches writing about illness could well suggest this....

This opening suggests that the writer is going to use contrast and comparison to build the essay: first, the comparison between illness and death; second, that between illness and death as a chance to revitalize oneself, and illness and death as an indication of insecurity. This sense of duality is then transposed to Sylvia Plath the woman: 'It has been said that Plath was almost schizophrenic ....'

Already we can see parallels and differences with the first essay. The major parallel is that both students aim to compare the poems to Plath's own life. The difficulty – not perceived by either student, and one that would have to be explored if they were to make progress in the subject – is that they see Plath's own life as represented in the poems in an unproblematic way. There is no reference to biographies or *Letters Home* (1978), i.e. to evidence of her life. Assumptions are made: Plath was almost schizophrenic. There is no real need felt by the students to test their hypotheses and assumptions, because the poems 'prove' the assumptions to be the case. The students' writing cannot therefore be *critical* of the poems, because it does not have sufficient perspective on them. No ideas are put forward against which they can test their reaction to the poems, other than 'the poems represent certain aspects of Plath's life'.

This essay is different from the first one, in that it proceeds in even more of a paraphrase-like way, incorporating snippets from the poems in an expository narrative which demonstrates the themes signalled. What is implicit in the first essay in terms of the complexity of Plath's 'position' on love and disillusion is explicit in the second essay as far as death and illness go. There is even more appropriation in the second essay of Plath's words, and less of a sense of a subtle interweaving of poems and commentary. The direction is clearer in the second essay, but the expression less oblique and less attention is paid to the actual words chosen by the poet. This sense that the poems are transparent windows on to Plath's own psychological state, rather than consciously crafted works, makes for a simplifying of complexity. This is how the essay ends:

> Throughout her poetry, it is obvious *that Plath did not fear death.* Apart from the fact that she tried to commit suicide several times before succeeding, *lines from her poems suggest she was ready to accept it.* (my italics)

References are then made to 'Fever 103°' and 'Lady Lazarus' to drive home the point.[12]

Despite the differences in approach, both students show a reverence for the texts which leaves their critical gearbox in neutral. To use Scholes's (1985) terminology, they are operating *with* and *upon* the text, but not *against* it. In other words, they are reading and interpreting, but not criticizing the text in question. Reading *against* the text is something the best of A-level students will do by the end of the course, and which university courses in English will encourage them to develop.[13]

TRANSITION FROM SCHOOL/COLLEGE TO UNIVERSITY

Induction into the practices and 'ground rules' (see Sheeran and Barnes, 1991) of undergraduate courses is a serious business for university departments. Students come from a wide variety of backgrounds, and perhaps because A level is still the most unreformed and conservative examination 'gate' through which students have to pass, it is a poor indicator of success at undergraduate level, just as success at undergraduate level is a poor indicator of success on postgraduate academic and/or professional courses. One of the reasons for the unpredictability of success at each new stage is that each course has its own ground rules.

Ground rules are beginning to be made more explicit to students, often in the form of criteria against which performance will be evaluated and 'competences' to be attained during and at the end of the course in question. Rather than take in too wide a range of these new developments, I will focus here on two elements of the conveying of ground rules: induction programmes and guides to the writing of essays.

Induction programmes tend to assume uncritically that certain skills necessary for success in the subject can be imparted prior to engagement with the subject in the course itself. Instead, I would see induction programmes as warm-ups or exercises before the actual participation in the game or race. The skills of argument in English or history, for example, can only be gained in actual use. In one carefully designed induction programme for a communication studies course (Mitchell and Kenyon, 1993), the aims were to make sense of the complexity of the issue of press regulation and the arguments which surrounded it in 1992–93, to practise basic study skills which are of use in lectures and academic writing, to analyse and be critical of these arguments, and to use the above processes to arrive at a considered and perhaps original contribution to the debate of press regulation.

The induction module consisted of two sessions. The first presented the basic facts about the Calcutt Report on press regulation (Calcutt, 1993) in the form of an article from the *Guardian,* asking students to jot down ideas on the subject and to listen to a recording of a programme relating to the report. Students had to *summarize* speakers' positions, then check their summaries against a transcript of the radio programme, revising where necessary. From this information, common themes were identified and speakers' positions mapped in relation to these themes. An account of the different positions on the common points was then requested from the students. The second session involved a sharing of these accounts, with reflection on the processes of reaching such summaries. Then further views were provided from a second radio programme, and these views fitted to the existing template (with the possibility of new categories being created).

After the two sessions, students were required to find evidence to support or refute the views expressed, and an 800 to 1,000-word essay was then required on the issue of press regulation.[14] The essays were analysed by the module authors and diagnostic notes sent to students. Students were also asked to write an account of not more than 200 words on the problems encountered in completing the exercise, and to complete a questionnaire on the module.

Another form of induction to the ground rules of disciplines (or, it has to be said, as preparation for success in coursework assessment and/or examinations) is the provision of notes on the submission of essays. These can vary from advice which pertains solely to the surface features required in the submission of essays, like:

Writing   Some people write illegibly. This disease, though it can prove mortal in the examination room, is not incurable.

Clichés   Avoid.

through to extensive advice on the preparation, planning, content and format of essays. Neither of the two guides I have in front of me as I write – one from a department of education and one from a department of economic and social history – addresses the large-scale structuration of the essay. Just as stylistics had ignored this level of composition, forcing a divide between content and style (a division discussed in Chapter 3 and in relation to the demise of rhetoric), so too these guides assume that structuration will have no influence on content. The prescription for essays is therefore conservative in formal terms. First it is assumed that the essay is an unproblematic form; secondly that the student will want to write an essay to express his or her understanding of the topic. The sense of demonstration for assessment that we encountered in the sixth-formers' attitudes towards the essay is reinforced in one of these guides:

> An essay should be a considered opinion submitted to a tutor for criticism; the essay which you hand in is *not* the place to work out your basic ideas.

There is institutional pressure to conform, and little guidance as to what forms might be suitable for the working out of ideas. Otherwise, the notes of guidance for history essays are very much like the A-level criteria and priorities discussed in relation to the Cambridge History Project (CHP, 1992): analysis and criticism are the most important qualities looked for; narrative and description must always be secondary to analysis.[15] Fundamentals of argument are also important to the historian:

> Show that you are thinking as an historian: distinguish between opinion and fact, event and viewpoint, contemporaries and historians, direct and indirect causes and consequences. If you prefer one argument show why you think another is inadequate. Deal with the positive and negative aspects of a question.

The homiletic advice on 'beginnings, middles and ends' is also evident in one of these guides, despite the suggestion of D'Angelo (1975) and others that such advice is almost useless. What the three-part structure suggested by the homily is really about is *framing*. How essays or other text-types are framed is a rhetorical issue, to do with the mediation between audience, writer and material. A student sitting down to start a piece of writing for a specific occasion should, I think, first consider what material he or she has available for the job and whether this material is adequate to the task. Secondly, he or she should consider who the writing is for, and what the purpose of the writing is; thirdly, and crucially, what the best form for the material, purpose and audience might be. This will not necessarily be the essay, as I will go on to discuss in the rest of this chapter. Fourthly, the large-scale *possibilities* within the broad text-type chosen should be considered – possibilities of mixes and blends with other text-types, or arrangements and rearrangements within the text-type chosen. Fifthly, what stylistic features are best employed in the writing of the assignment? Finally what further features of layout are necessary to a successful completion of the communicative act? As I have argued above, stages two to four are often ignored, often resulting in sterility of expression or a mismatch between what is produced and what is expected to be produced.

One of the practical offshotts of the Leverhulme project on the examination of argument in sixth forms and universities has been a guide for writing essays in philosophy (Burwood, 1993). This introduction to the topic – both a reflection on essay-writing in philosophy and a practical guide – aims to *elucidate the expectations* philosophy tutors have of students' essays in this discipline.

Rather than start with content or form, Burwood's text looks at the essay in context. The context turns out to be not a single identifiable context, but a matrix of interrelated contexts within which the student has to find a voice (or number of voices):

> Firstly, you are now working in an **academic context** and, more specifically, within the context of a **particular discipline** (in this case Philosophy). You also have to take into account that within these more general contexts you will be writing essays as **tutorial assignments,** for **examinations,** and as **assessed work** [or 'coursework']. Each of these contexts has its own implications for, and imposes its own constraints on, the purpose and style of your essay.
>
> (Burwood, 1993, p. 5)

There are yet further considerations to take into account in what becomes for the student a balancing act between the various demands and influences. Students, as we saw earlier in this chapter, view the essay as primarily a vehicle for *demonstrating* what they know. At the same time, the other functions of the essay do not go away: essays are places where ideas might be worked out; where learning takes place in the act of writing. The essay may well be a demonstration, but the act of making that demonstration brings to some sort of other existence the knowledge that might be tacit, unformulated and latent. The different functions of the essay partly depend on the occasion for which the essay is written, and the nature of the audience in each case. This is not as simple as first might appear. If an essay is written as an exploratory, provisional piece in order to generate discussion in a tutorial, it can consciously take a particular stance, present questions for discussion and be written (if not prepared) over a longer period of time than is afforded an examination essay. A coursework essay – or, more extremely, a dissertation or thesis – can be prepared over an even longer period. In each case, the audience may be the same person, but the nature of his or her reading of the essay will be different: a position paper will be 'read' differently from a coursework assignment, and these in turn will be read differently from an examination essay or from a dissertation. I have given each of these a different name, but often they are grouped under the generic term 'essay'. Such variation of context, form and audience, however, ought to alert us to the fact that the phrase 'essay as genre' (by which is usually meant 'essay as text-type') is too crude to account for what really takes place in the act of communication in a social context. One of the confusions experienced by students at sixth-form, undergraduate and postgraduate level is to see the essay as always a definitive, polished work, even if its function is that of a position paper or even as a stimulant to discussion, at the informal end of the scale.

For me, the second key point in Burwood's guide is that to engage in philosophical argumentation is to engage in 'an essentially dialogic enterprise' (p. 13). It is worth rehearsing here what Burwood says about the role of dialogue in philosophical investigation, and in particular – as my concerns are with manifestations of argumentation in speech and writing – in relation to the essay. The reasoning goes like this: philosophers (and student philosophers, because they are being inducted into a discipline's way of thinking and discoursing) take up the arguments of others, using them in the production of new arguments. These new arguments, in turn, can provide the starting point for further arguments. Philosophical writing and discussion thus conforms to a general dialogic principle. The *principle* is not always manifested in written texts: Platonic dialogue is one version of philosophical dialogue, but as I suggested earlier, a rhetorical form in which the dice is weighted in Socrates' favour. Cartesian meditation, on the other hand, however monologic it looks on the surface, may embody dialogic principles. The contrast between the two texts 'is really only a difference between alternative forms of presentation' (ibid.) and so just as a monologic meditation might be informed by dialogic principles, so too an ostensible dialogue might be relatively monologic in principle. To be genuinely argumentative, though, a text should be dialogic at its core.

Following from the point about the dialogic basis of argumentation in philosophy is an important point for learning and teaching in any discipline: improvement comes from engaging in a dialogue yourself. This may take the form not only of presenting your thoughts to a tutorial or seminar group and listening critically to the feedback you receive; but also of your reading, in which you will move backwards and forwards between complicity with the text, 'obedience' to it or a suspension of disbelief on the one hand (the passive mode of reading) and suspicion of the text, interrogation of it and critical positioning in relation to it on the other.

The rest of Burwood's introduction to essay-writing in philosophy deals with formal requirements and the processes of writing – the subject, in fact, of most of the guides produced for courses in the UK. What is distinctive and important about *Essay Writing: An Introduction* is that most of it is devoted to the links between essay-writing and the practices of the discipline. It is, almost despite itself, an essentially rhetorical work.

PROBLEMS WITH THE ESSAY, AND SOME ALTERNATIVES TO IT

We have looked at the problematic nature of the essay – the written form of argument that is asked to do too much. The limitations of the essay include the potential confusion between explication and argument; the difficulty of distinguishing points of view; the difficulty of including multiple points of view in a basic adversarial structure; the tendency of students to use critical sources 'safely', i.e. in support of the student's views rather than to develop alternative positions; the tendency for the student's views to be neutralized, or couched in a rhetorical impersonal voice, so that she refers to herself as 'I' only in the conclusion; the tendency to avoid doubt and speculative thought; and the avoidance of questions.

In Chapters 3, 4 and 5 I set out the principles of a dialogic approach to writing and presented some examples of such work. Moving on from the points laid out in the previous section in relation to philosophy, I now want to re-address the question of the essay and its alternatives in the context of sixth-form and higher education.

The essay represents a broad church. And yet the assumption in many disciplines – or perhaps we should say in some departments – is that the particular essay form *they know* as the essay *is* for them the text-type 'essay'. I have tried to argue that it is better to think of the essay as a broad text-type in which there can be many variations; that the monologic surface form of the essay hides what is the true nature of the essay – either as a response to an existing point of view or as the incorporation of two or more voices in a monologic blend. Departments, disciplines and subjects need to think of what the essay means to them as a form of expression. Why is it used? What are its advantages and disadvantages? Is this the only way in which expression can take place? How does it change in different contexts within the teaching and learning of the subject?

When these questions are addressed, alternative forms of practice suggest themselves.[16] Much of what takes place in tutorials and seminars in speech is not seen as directly useful in the writing of essays, so that tutors are often disappointed that a rich discussion fails to manifest itself in the students' essays. Here are some ways to diversify the spoken and written discourses in sixth-form and university English classes, and also to build bridges between speech and writing:

- Note-taking and talk are often seen as initial generative procedures prior to writing, but writing can take place prior to discussion, as in the preparation of position papers which do not work toward formal closure (as in the 'conclusion' to the conventional essay) but rather to opening up discussion.
- Writing tasks can be tailored to address specific aspects of approach to the study of a text or theme. Reports, for example, can be distinguished from arguments rather than conflated with them.
- Students can play a part in devising essay questions as an outcome of shared discussions. We have already seen that devising a question is an important stage in formulating an argument; a loosely thematic question (or statement) may result in a similarly undirected essay.
- Students can reflect on the processes in which they have been engaged. Many tutorials are rich in argumentative and literary critical strategy: the gathering of textual evidence, the identification and juxtaposition of themes, the analysis and categorization of imagery. These tutorials are often led by the tutor while the students participate at a level of exemplification. This in turn leads to unsatisfactory essays at a low level of critical analysis. A more productive alternative is for students to review the process of learning, and to end such a reflective exercise by considering any questions left unanswered by the tutorial.

(adapted from Mitchell, 1993b, p. 8)

In short, these approaches are geared more towards learning than teaching, but they have implications for the planning and execution of teaching occasions. They do not all lead to alternatives to the essay; indeed, many of them are intended to enhance the quality of essay-writing by giving students access to the workings of the essay. As Mitchell writes,

> behind these considerations is the sense that students can be actively involved in choosing, developing and critiquing the forms in which they write. It seems to me to be particularly appropriate that students of language and literary form should do this. The present rhetorical and formal emphasis on the essay privileges normative ways of thinking in a subject [English] which in other ways is seeking to move beyond narrow cultural limits and to promote the values of difference and diversity.

(ibid.)

One of these 'alternative forms' is the journal, often associated with work in the 11 to 16 phase and underused in the 16 to 19 and higher education phase. The journal incorporates dialogue in that it allows the writer to speak to herself, without the pressure of an outside (public) audience. Journals can include lesson notes, reflections on lessons, fleeting thoughts and feelings about a topic or text, connections between texts and ideas (cf. E.M. Forster's 'Only connect'), questions raised that may or may not be answered, drafts, revisions, scribblings and reflections on progress. There is no formal requirement in terms of length of statement, tone or style; and no propriety to observe. Structure is a feature that comes later, with the need to shape thoughts for presentation to an audience. And so writing of the quality of the following, from an A-level student of history and English, can ensue:

> In the next week I have to do two essays: one for English and one for History. For both, both teachers have suggested that the first step should be to write down any ideas at random. Both used the word 'brainstorm' for this process. It shows what a strong relation there is between writing an analysis of historical events and writing an analysis of events which are fictional. The only difference is that one set of events is totally imaginary. It is interesting that man can do this: it must be necessary for him to break away from history and reality and to imagine what he likes; to put himself in another age, another personality and act as he would have liked. Even more interesting is that in this breaking away from history, man, in his fiction, bases his actions on his feelings about the present eg a political or social situation. He is relieving himself from history ... for however long it takes to solve the problems he would like to solve. It is fantastic that novelists and playwrights can do this and pass it on to readers so that they in their turn can relieve themselves.
>
> (in Andrews, 1987, pp. 45–6)

Putting aside the unfortunate phrasing at the end, this is typical of the high quality of reflection in this particular journal, kept over a year at the beginning of an A-level course. It indicates the value of writing that is close to talk, expressive, provisional, tentative and exploratory.[17]

If a diary of this sort represents dialogue with oneself, other forms make the dialogue more explicit and closer to the spoken voice. Take the following essay title, for example:

> 'These novels [*Tess of the d'Urbervilles* and *Jude the Obscure*] seem to me to be an expressive, irrefutable criticism of society's debilitating version of womanhood.' (P. Stubbs, *Women and Fiction: Feminism and the Novel, 1880–1920)* Do you agree?

This is typical of many essay titles in English at A level and on undergraduate courses in that it invites a response. It is *as if* the quotation from the critic has been spoken and within the terms of polite, civilized discourse, the student is invited to reply. The reply, however, is to be written; and written at length. An alternative way of framing the question would be as follows:

> Take a critical essay or essays on Hardy and use it/them to write a dialogue between yourself and the critic(s).

or

> Write a conversation between Hardy, a nineteenth-century feminist and yourself.

What are the implications of such reformulations? These 'dialogic' invitations to write imply a situation in which there is opportunity to research the assignment. They may look less serious than the traditional essay questions, but in fact they are just as serious in that they require research and careful reading to do them justice. There is less scope for hiding what you don't know behind a cloud of rhetoric (in the negative sense of the word!). But research, in its turn, requires that such assignments are set for coursework assessment rather than in the examination context – if, indeed, they are to be assessed formally.

The essay used as a means of examination seems to be part of the problem, because many courses assume that if students are to be examined via the essay at the end of the course, they might as well start writing essays at the beginning. So little attention is paid to the potential cognitive development that might take place during the course, or indeed the personal development, in relation to the texts studied or the written assignments undertaken. It is assumed that the formal expression of understanding is static, that product is the sign of development rather than process, and that the essay is the default product.

Another alternative to the essay is the review. This is a common form with 7- to 14-year-olds, and sometimes with even younger children. It is also a common form in the adult world, where reviews appear frequently in newspapers, magazines and on television and radio, as well as in academic journals. Oddly, it appears very infrequently in the years from 14 to 19 and at university level. This is odd because it is at this stage that the appraisal of the work of authors and authorities takes place, more than at any other stage.

Asking students to write a review of a book puts the emphasis on point of view and analysis. There is a great deal of freedom in the writing of such a review. The student has complete choice as to where to stand in relation to the book, can draw on his/her wider reading to inform the review, and select evidence from the book to prove the points made. As with reviews of fictional texts at school level, the aim must be not simply to give an account of the book (though summarizing is an important foundational element of argument) but to select, critique, argue and give logical reasons and/or provide evidence to back up the view taken. As Sally Mitchell suggests,

> This exercise feeds into students' essay writing, but it could also give rise to spoken argument. Student could engage in debate about the relative merits of the books they had read; they could be involved in a process of selection for a list of essential course reading or for a prize (in role play). The advantage of this kind of spoken discussion is that it would follow serious consideration and research and would therefore be based upon strong and reasoned arguments.
>
> (1993d, p. 10)

There are other forms of writing that help students to bring the process of arguing and thinking closer to the speaking voice, as well as to sharpen and clarify these processes and – at the same time – make for engaging reading. The making of patterns, for example, by arranging and rearranging statements or images and thus rehearsing possible patterns for the writing of an essay; the non-linear collage-like argumentative presentation, either on a poster or in exhibition form (and generally using a range of media), the chronological or time-related argument which draws heavily on the power of narrative to make its point, and so on. None of these detracts from the conventional essay. Indeed, they can enhance essay-writing by drawing attention to the spoken and/or visual roots of argument, and by building bridges between these primary genres and the conventional forms, enliven the writing of essays. Such experimentation has to take place in a classroom or tutorial context that recognizes the rhetorical nature of communication, and in which students are aware of the ground rules operating in that context.

It is possible to break free of the conventions. The manacles restraining lecturers and students from such variation are mind-forged, supporting power structures and often too heavily driven by assessment concerns. Here is an extract from a postgraduate student's 5,000-word assignment, written for coursework assessement after a course on narrative and argument. She has decided to present the arguments in script form. This is not Socratic dialogue; there are two characters in the script, but they converse on a roughly equal footing, using each other to explore ideas together consensually as well as adversarially. After a lengthy and oblique exposition by Y of a point about the National Curriculum and argument, the conversation continues:

X: So what are you saying?

Y: I think I am saying that perhaps they (the writers of the National Curriculum) recognise the importance of argument in the development of critical thought, but they do not consider school the appropriate forum for real controversy. As soon as children approach an age where their arguments could be really effective, or influential in the world outside, they are expected to focus their energies on simulated situations, or academic essays. They are allowed to engage in sparring, but never the real full scale battle.

X: Ha! Do you see it as wholly a political issue then?

Y: It depends what we mean by political! No, I think the issue is one of educational priorities.

X: Well, you might be right to be suspicious of government influence in educational policy, but I think there is another influence at work: the community around the school. Don't you think that concern to balance the various interests served by the school can result in apparently defensive behaviour on the part of teaching staff and headteachers? Allowing the school to be a breeding ground for 'real' controversy can be too sensitive an issue for the toughest of heads.

Y: Isn't that the same thing as Andrews calls 'the political climate in schools — one in which real argument is not encouraged' (Andrews *et al.,* 1993). Clarke also made some observations about how schools are expected to conduct their curriculum outside the area of political exchange. (ibid., p. 193ff.)

Thus the dialogic form is one that is able to include references in the same way as the conventional essay, is able to include extensive continuous arguments by any of the characters, but also allows supportive or challenging moves from characters in order to ensure the development of clear, purposeful argument.

SUMMARY

This chapter has looked at argument in the tertiary context, tracing the changing functions of argument in different disciplines and from A level to undergraduate and postgraduate levels. The use of the essay at this level as a vehicle for the development of thought and as a means of assessment was discussed, and the following alternatives suggested:

- writing logs in which connections could be made and questions asked and explored without the pressure of having to make the writing public;
- dialogic or multi-voiced forms of writing in which two or more characters could explore and debate issues;
- reviews, in which students could find a point of view in relation to a text;
- rearrangements, both of statements and images, in order to find argumentative lines and directions;
- chronological, time-related and non-time-related arguments.

NOTES

1   I use the rather awkward term 'education 16–19' in preference to 'sixth form' for a number of reasons: to make comparison with systems in other countries a little easier; because the term 'sixth form' is becoming increasingly anachronistic ('sixth' refers to the sixth and seventh years of secondary schooling) in the light of the National Curriculum, in which compulsory schooling ends at 16 with Year 11; and because 16–19 education embraces vocational (General National Vocational Qualifications) courses as well as the traditional academic (advanced level) courses. Further education tends to be vocational and sub-degree level, whereas higher education covers degree and postgraduate courses at university level (many of which are now deemed vocational).

2   The move to modular degree programmes in higher education in Britain – pioneered largely by the 'new' universities (ex-polytechnics) – might mean that cross-disciplinary transferable argumentative skills grow to be more at a premium. The level at which the argument in this chapter is conducted, however, is one at which differences between disciplines are the emphasis rather than similarities between argumentative practices in different discplines.

3   'The Teaching and Learning of Argument in Sixth Forms and Higher Education' research project ran from 1991 to 1994 at the University of Hull. I am particularly indebted to Sally Mitchell, the research fellow on the project, for much of the research material used in this chapter.

4   Barnes notes in the 1990 edition of *Language, the Learner and the School* (p. 19) that it was not always easy to assign questions to a particular category: 'I discovered that in order to arrive at a satisfactory interpretation I had to look at succeeding utterances by teacher or pupils, and sometimes at preceding ones. . . . Meaning seemed not to be an adjunct of words alone but to be generated by teachers and pupils from the cultural resources they shared in the classroom.' For a further discussion of the issues raised by Barnes's chapter, see Mitchell (1992a, pp. 8–14).

5   A copy and discussion of the full transcript appears on pp. 53–61 of the interim report of the Leverhulme project (Mitchell, 1992b).

6   I am referring only to the study of texts at A level, which takes place largely in the New Critical tradition of seeing the text as a 'unity' and as a law unto itself, cut off from the wider ideological and social influences that become the concern more explicitly – though not exclusively – at undergraduate level.

7   Advanced-level courses are normally two years in duration and the general pattern has been that three A levels are required at good grades for entrance to university. Advanced Supplementary (AS) levels were introduced in the late 1980s and are at the same standard as A levels, though they contain about half the content of A levels and normally take one year to complete. Entrance to university is now possible with, say, two A levels and two AS levels. The new qualifications therefore have the effect of broadening the 16–19 curriculum.

8   Sally Mitchell notes that '70% of Physics students place reasoning as important, whilst only 39% of Maths students do. Both groups of students agree on the importance of logical connections, however (93% of Maths students and 95% of Physics students). Though this [is] at first glance surprising, reasoning and the ability to make logical connections are clearly perceived as quite different things. It may be that Maths students see themselves as following sequences and rules which have an unchanging pattern, whilst physicists make connections between actual situations and theoretical representations or abstractions of them; that is, they *apply* their knowledge' (unpublished source).

9   See Berrill (1990), who, in a doctoral study of the writing of 16-year-olds in Croydon and Norwich, found that when asked to write argument the students tended to write exposition. She concludes thus: 'Sixteen year olds demonstrate their ability to value alternative points of view and through their exposition they display an awareness of the importance of making those differences explicit. The teacher's role in this dimension is to make the pupils aware of the strengths of the exposition and then to give them strategies to use in condensing the exposition and in showing the relationship of the exposition to the central argument. The pupils need to gain the skills of using exposition as *part* of argument, elaborating or quantifying ideas, rather than letting the exposition substitute for the argument' (p. 88).

10 Sylvia Plath, 'The Couriers', from *Ariel*, published by Faber & Faber. Reprinted by permission of the publisher.
11 These and subsequent poems mentioned are collected in Plath (1981).
12 The Leverhulme research project has published extensively on other subjects at A level. Mitchell (1992a) discusses the function of questions in English, politics and biology; Mitchell and Andrews (1994) discuss essays in history A level against criteria set by the Cambridge Advanced Level History Project – criteria which are further discussed in the final chapter of the present book; Andrews and Mitchell (forthcoming) discuss differences between English literature and politics essays at this level; Mitchell and Reid (unpublished) look at the negotiations of genre in the A-level English language essay; and Mitchell (1994c) examines the transition from A-level to university English literature in the work of the first student discussed in this section.
13 This does not mean to say that reading against the text cannot be undertaken at primary and secondary school level; just that the tendency is for students to read with and upon the text at A level. See Scholes (1985) pp. 21–4 for further elucidation of these approaches to reading.
14 A topical issue at the time, with the tabloid press seeming to abuse on a regular basis the Royal Family's 'right to privacy'.
15 The assessment criteria for the Cambridge History Project in relation to the question of argument at sixth-form level are discussed fully in Mitchell and Andrews (1994).
16 One of the most inventive of books in this respect is Brown and Jackson (1984), a textbook for English 16–19 which contains a wide range of kinds of writing, from personal histories, travel writing, documentary and letters to various forms of journalism.
17 An issue of the *English Journal* (**82,** 6, October 1993) includes many articles which offer alternatives to the essay, each taking the personal, expressive momentum as their driving force and resisting the pressures of the formal academic essay. See especially Abrahamson (1993), Sitler (1993), House (1993), Sheridan (1993) Gillespie (1993), Burnett and Foster (1993) and Reissman (1993).

Chapter 7

Writing Argument – and Beyond

the gulf is wide between mastering the art of putting a viewpoint, and mastering the larger art of argument.

(George Myerson in *The Argumentative Imagination*, 1992, p. 9)

This chapter pulls together some of the strands that have been identified so far, but it does not claim to have the final word on learning to argue. It would be against the spirit of argument to claim such finality. Rather, the chapter revisits some of the topics or places we have touched on, addresses implications of what has been said as far as assessment is concerned, looks at wider issues like the relationship between argument and democracy and between argument and the imagination, and summarizes the case I have been trying to make so that rejoinders can be put, extensions followed and new angles calculated.

ANOTHER LOOK AT METAPHORS

In the first chapter I highlighted a picture of argument that had already been drawn by Lakoff and Johnson (1980) and developed further by Berrill (1991): that argument need not be thought of solely in terms of the metaphors of war and battle, but could also be conceived in terms of dance. I further added metaphor systems of construction and building, and of journeying, both in an attempt to diversify notions of argument and what it could achieve, and to accentuate the constructive, positive side of argument. For although I think Ricoeur (1970) is right to suggest that argument is a suspicious mode, its suspicious, critical nature is designed to enhance a situation and move it on in some way, however coruscating that criticism might be.[1]

The metaphors of dance suggest that argument is a place where two (or more) people might choreograph for themselves, and perform, a movement that is mutual and that moves them on to a new position. At times one might seem to move backwards while the other goes forwards; one might lead and the other follow. But the overall effect is harmonic. The dance metaphor is close to that of music: one which was used many times by the 12- to 13-year-old students I interviewed on the writing of argument:

> I believe argument is like a piece of music. You start off with the first note, and then you go on gradually bringing up the pieces but you can actually start off loud or you can start off quiet, and coming to the end you can have a crescendo (which is getting louder) or you can have a diminuendo (which is getting softer), and you can have an ending note which is in tune and a conclusion.
>
> (Andrews, 1992a, p. 294)

Whereas argument is conceived in terms of harmony, pitch and tone, the same student saw narrative in terms of the rhythmic relations in music:

> You start off with a beginning note, and you have bar lines, but the bar lines still flow on from each other, and you can have bar lines syncopated, and you can go on and you can repeat the bar lines and you can make them go on to another part.
>
> (ibid., p. 297)

In other words, argument is a place for the resolution of conflict and difference as well as for verbal conflict itself.

The construction metaphors afford insight to another aspect of argument: the processes of its composing. Architects and those in the construction industry lay out plans before they start building. These plans are not drafts or sketches of what might happen in the construction of the building; they are blueprints for the building, and although the final building may turn out to look somewhat different (for reasons we will discuss in a moment) the whole building has been imagined before the actual construction takes place. That the building has been imagined does not mean that all the constituent parts are in place before the construction starts. As I pointed out in the first chapter, this is not the case in the real world of putting up buildings, nor is it necessarily the case in written composition. Contingencies such as the unavailability of certain kinds of material (evidence) might change the course of the building, just as shifts in the ground might cause a radical reappraisal of the line of argument. Economies of scale also affect the outcome of the building (writing).

The metaphor of argument as a journey is a more generalized one but affords further insights. Argumentation is a process, considered by some (see later in this chapter) as a lower-order thinking skill (as opposed to critical thinking, a 'higher order' thinking skill with which it has much in common). The route which arguments take is rarely planned and executed precisely, even though the terrain may be mapped. Instead, because of the vagaries of situations, the fact that the dynamics of argument change according to the participants' moves and the nature of verbal language, the route taken is rarely a direct one. This is why it is inappropriate to discuss argumentation in terms only of the syllogistic patterns of logic: argument is more rhetorical than philosophical. This is also why the definition of argument that is used in mathematics and astronomy is richly suggestive as far as the composition and movement of argument is concerned. New angles, new directions are taken as a result of the preceding point or set of points. In this respect, argument is not much different from the process of composing and reading narrative as suggested by Holloway (1979). It has a horizontal, linear drive as well as a vertical, architectural one.

Looking at argument through the filters of different metaphors alerts us not only to the different forms argument might take, but also to its multiple functions.[2] Just as the war metaphor views argument mainly in terms of adversarial conflict, winning and losing, so too the functions of argument have been seen as being to do with winning —

or, more subtly, with persuasion. The next section explores the much wider range of functions that argument actually performs in society.

THE FUNCTIONS OF ARGUMENT

Why do we argue in everyday life? Here are some of the answers that teachers and students have come up with over the last years, and I want us to compare this list with the reasons for argument, the *functions of* argument in schooling. We argue in order to:

- **clarify**, as when issues and positions are clearer after they have been argued out. The clarification may be public, or it may be on the part of the audience (in which case persuasion will have come into it) or it may be on the part of the thinker/speaker. Clarification can also take written form. As Vygotsky (1986), Billig (1987), Rogoff (1990) and others have testified, clarifiction via argument is akin to critical thinking. The argument has simply given dialogic shape to half-formed thoughts and feelings, thus sharpening them for consideration – as in philosophical method.
- **persuade**, as when we want someone to do or feel or think something different from what they currently do, feel or think. Argumentative persuasion can take many forms, from book reviews and the arguing of specific points of view (e.g. against vivisection) to persuading someone to lend you money or not to leave home. It is often thought that all argument is persuasive – a scan of the present list makes it clear that this is not necessarily so.
- **win**, a more extreme form of persuasion. While persuasive argument may be working towards a compromise of some sort, arguments that aim to win and to defeat the other party are more absolute in nature. The metaphor of battle is more appropriate to this kind of argument, predicated as it is upon 'destroying' the other point of view, 'shooting down' others' arguments and 'establishing the supremacy' of one's own position.
- **entertain**, as in the letters of Groucho Marx to Warner Brothers, for instance (see Clarke and Sinker, 1992). While we don't consider the primary *initial* function of these letters as having been to entertain (Groucho's case against Warner Brothers over the use of the word 'Casablanca' in the film *A Night in Casablanca* having been a bona fide one that he wanted to win), the subsequent function has been primarily to entertain. Some arguments – like Punch and Judy shows, dialogues between comedians and even formal disputations between monks – have entertainment as their primary function.
- **unload**, as in a domestic row when the ostensible reason for the dispute is not the real reason for continuing the argument. This is interesting psychological territory. Suggestions have been made that arguments can be deliberately or unconsciously triggered in order to release pent-up and unresolved emotion. This release of tension is often brought about between two people who know that each will forgive the other; thus people argue with close family or intimate friends in ways in which they would not even consider with professional or more distant associates.
- **resolve**, or come to a consensus. Argument is not always combative or adversarial; rather than metaphors of war and battle, it can be conceived of in terms of dance

or negotiation. Naturally, this kind of argument requires the parties involved to move their positions to accommodate others' points of view. Without such listening and preparedness to move one's own position, resolution cannot take place. To draw on Gunther Kress's (1989) formulation and to move beyond it: argument both creates difference and is able to resolve it.

● **find identity,** as when adolescents argue against a position taken by their parents in order to assert their own position. This is an important function of argument, linking the process of argumentation to expressiveness, group identities and power. Although argument has often been assumed to be rational, distanced and public, its functions for the maturing individual is also to create space, to assert a position, to define oneself in relation to others.

There are no doubt other functions that argument fulfils in society, but I feel that even those listed here are more extensive than is usually assumed. Many of the above functions can be combined in a particular situation. Someone might be arguing to clarify, persuade *and* to find identity at the same time; sometimes one of these functions may be primary and the others secondary. At the very least, I hope in this list to have opened up the notion that argument can have multiple functions in society, and that the functions it does fulfil are important ones for the health of society and of the individuals within it. Compare this range with the functions of argument in schools, colleges and universities, which is largely to display competence in argument, and to offer up such display for judgement by the assessor. Less important are arguing to win, clarify and persuade. Rarely is argument used to entertain, resolve or unload – within the formal curriculum, that is. Part of the function of this book has been to extend the range of functions and forms available to emergent writers in educational institutions.

If we look more closely at argument in educational institutions, we can generate another set of functions that will help us define what goes on in schools and universities, and determine how we might improve the quality of argument in these contexts. Argument might be said to have a *social* function, to assist in the *learning process*, to provide a means of *containing and assessing* what is produced in schools and universities, and to have the functions of embodying the practices of a *discipline*.

Its social function is important, not only because being able to converse is a social skill that makes a range of discourses possible in the classroom, but also because the very act of sharing views, listening to others, expressing opinions and revising them in the light of further discussion is itself contributory to the development of argumentative skill. Argument, as I have been pointing out throughout this book, is essentially social. Furthermore, when students are encouraged to question and challenge they are being offered control over the content with which they are presented; this in turn implies a degree of control over their learning and a certain autonomous status within the institution of learning. In our experience on the Leverhulme project, argument functions in this social way more frequently in the arts and humanities than in the sciences, perhaps because 'proof' in the arts and humanities is less a matter of finding evidence to support hypotheses than of finding a voice within an orchestra of other voices (see the section on pp. 157–65 on problems with assessing argument).

Argument assists in the learning process by providing a tool for enhancing students' understanding of a topic or issue. Much of this process takes place in speech, with the toing and froing of classroom discussion – in pairs, small groups or as a whole class –

being the manifestation of the process. Talk often progresses through challenges and qualifications of propositions and statements. The talk is fast-moving, loosely structured and transitory, but what happens in the students' heads as they participate in such talk can be defined as the transforming moves we take to be 'learning'. As a sixth-form student said in an interview (Andrews, 1987) on learning processes at A level, 'if we want to remember something for life, we have to talk it through; if we think we're going to forget it, we write it down'. Writing that argues as part of the process of learning is more likely to be close to speech: informal, provisional and speculative rather than finished and demonstrative.

The third function identified for argument in educational contexts is, however, the evidencing of learning in demonstration, and this function is often closely allied – one might say, confused – with argument as part of a learning process. Where evidence of argumentative ability is required by an examiner its form and scope is usually already determined. Often, as we have seen in earlier chapters, in the humanities, this form is the essay: a conventionalized and standardized end-point for learning. Students, because they are the grist in the assessment mill, tend to see argument in these ritualized terms, cut off from the functions of argument in everyday life.

Finally (if there can ever be a 'finally' in argument), argument can be culturally determined by the discipline. In this aspect of the functions of argument, we are concerned with the *real* status of practices within the subject or discipline as they are represented in the teaching of the subject. At the highest levels in and at the cutting edge of all disciplines argument of this kind is engaged in as the disciplinary boundaries are reinforced or shifted. Argument at this level can be conceived of as the distribution, exchange and reception of information, insight, opinion and theory. The discipline becomes a community of dialogic exchanges.[3]

ARGUMENT AND DEMOCRACY

The extension of the range of functions and forms in argument is intimately linked with the notion of democracy, but conventional school and university practice narrows what is possible with students. I want to make three points in relation to this connection between argument and democracy: that such a range of functions of argument is essential in a democracy; that hitherto the range available in schools and colleges has been much narrower than that deployed in society, so that students are in effect disenfranchised from their own education; and that an extension of the range of forms and functions of argument might well have implications for class management and the structure of relationships in schools and colleges.

First, the range of discourses in a democracy. If different points of view are to be listened to, debated, used to reach a consensus or argued out until one point of view gains ascendancy, then argument is the principal means by which decisions are reached and democratic processes are seen to work. It is no good just 'telling our story'. Personal or group narratives may be effective ways of persuading another party that our case should be taken into account, but without dialogue or comeback they cannot hope to hold much sway. (Narrative isn't essentially monologic, but is often used that way by groups in weak positions and also as a power tool.)

Representative democracies are, on the whole, bureaucratic. As the *Oxford*

Companion to Classical Literature (Howatson, 1989, p. 178) notes, 'It was a feature of Athenian democracy that considerable power to influence decisions was wielded by skilful orators who held no official position and exercised this power with varying degrees of responsibility.'[4] Hence the importance of rhetoric in a democracy: being able to use language to persuade and convince and argue one's position as well as to be critical about other people's use of language to persuade and control (especially the language of those in power). The range of discourses needed in a representative democracy is great if (a) people are to express themselves; (b) the machinery of democracy is to work; (c) people are able to defend themselves against sophisticated techniques of persuasion; and (d) there is to be any commerce between what the people want to say and the system that represents them. This last point is an important one, because we are seeing ostensible democracies in the West, like those of the USA and Britain for example, suffering tension between notions of direct democracy (the voice or voices of the people) and representative democracy.

The Liberal Democrats, who occupy a position in British politics just to the left of centre, see the present structures of British politics as outmoded. 'Above all else,' they declared in a 1993 policy document, *Facing up to the Future,* 'we want to build a *reinvented democracy* . . . which provides government which is open, accountable and participatory — which belongs, in short, to its people' (Liberal Democrats, 1993, p. 3). Of course, each party says it will do something like that, because the diction of democracy has become essential to making its views palatable to the general populace and to the press. The terms differ slightly: the Conservatives use 'choice' and 'freedom' as their buzz words; Labour use 'community' and 'responsibility'. The caricatured problems presented by these two main parties — the Conservatives on the right and Labour on the left — are clear:

> Although the Conservatives have used the rhetoric of individual freedom, they have in reality constructed a state that is more powerful and authoritarian, and less participatory and democratic, than at almost any time in peacetime history.
>
> (Liberal Democrats, 1993, p. 4)

Labour is accused of putting the demands of society before those of individuals. The Liberal Democrat solution is to go for a form of government which is, in their terms, enabling, decentralized, reinvented and participatory.

What has all this got to do with what goes on in classrooms? The Conservative government has brought in a National Curriculum over the last few years, not without some major hiccups. One of the problems of the curriculum is that it sees children and their learning in terms of product, performance, grade levels and output — in other words, in terms of the language of business and industry, not that of choice or participation. In prescribing levels of attainment in each subject, its implications are that material will be *taught* so that it can be readily *assessed* and then tabulated in league tables. There's nothing very democratic about this, and it implies teaching by transmission rather than interpretation or negotiation.

By the same token, the range of writing prescribed to test the levels of attainment or competences of students is narrow. As we have seen, there is very heavy emphasis on the essay at the higher levels of schooling, as if all writing lower down has been contributory to it. There is even heavier emphasis at university level where, with some exceptions, we have found lecturers to be very conservative about the forms in which they ask their students to write. The form is understood as a vehicle for the disciplined free expression of thought, but rarely considered in terms of the thought it suppresses or excludes. The situation at university level is similar to that in schools with the National Curriculum in that both the essay and the National Curriculum announce their inclusiveness and sufficiency rather than what they leave out or disallow. Real argument, on the other hand, can question an ideology.

There are certain principles of this dialogic approach to remind ourselves of: writing must have a relatively more specific audience than in the past; there must be scope for dialogue and hence real communication. What does this mean for the classroom? It means that there will be clear *purposes* for writing. I stress purpos*es* to pick up what I said earlier about the multiple functions of arguing. Although in the past student teachers and perhaps even conscientious experienced teachers have outlined the purposes of a writing assignment to themselves, they have rarely – as far as I have seen – communicated these purposes to the children who are actually carrying out the assignment. 'Why are we doing this?' is often met by 'Because you have to. . .' at worst, and at best, 'Because it will help you to apply for a job' or 'Because it is the best way to write if you want to pass the exam'. There is an element of coercion and simulation about the whole enterprise, and of deferred pleasure. It's not real communication, but you have to do it. It's good for you.

So whereas in the 1970s, thinkers about the range of writing in schools, like James Britton and others were urging real audiences for *some* of the writing taking place, what I am urging is real audiences for most – if not all – of the writing that goes on in school. Those real audiences include public organizations, parents, industries of all kinds and, of course, the teacher and children in the class, as well as the other teachers, secretarial and support staff and other children in the school.

In Chapter 5 I referred to a classroom project on writing a report for a school librarian in which the audience and function of the writing was immediately public and clearly defined. To quote from the report on this and other projects:

> The students thought that this kind of work was more difficult than conventional group work which they enjoyed and were used to. One student explained that in literature groups there was the text before them and if someone came up with a reasonable idea then it was likely the rest would go along with it. But when groups formed for this kind of research they had nothing to start with except their aims. In class discussion, this type of group work was identified as being different because the students had to begin to collaborate on questions and procedures, searching for methods of working which would produce results. Often they did not feel any sense of achievement until something practical had occurred, such as the undertaking of interviews.
>
> (Brown *et al.*, 1990, p. 57)

Whereas students would be inclined to agree with each other, often for the sake of getting through an 'exercise', now they were arguing with each other in order to reach a consensus and thus put their collective resolution into action.

Classrooms like this, and others described earlier, are democratic classrooms. The freedoms of democracy imply responsibilities – to themselves, to each other, to their teacher and to whoever was commissioning their work – and the children involved in the projects were aware of that. Indeed, in the DEFT project, in which I acted as independent evaluator, increased responsibility of this kind was rated by all the students in the ten schools that took part as *the* most important advance that the project had offered, followed closely by being allowed to make decisions and initiatives and the brining about of equal opportunities for boys and girls. Three students (14-year-olds) in another school in Oldham confirmed the overall view:

YASMIN: I feel a lot better now that I've got some responsibility in school.
RA: And is this the first time you've felt like this?
JOHN-PAUL: It's the best thing that happened in school since we came here.
JOANNE: Yes, it's true, that.

NARRATIVE IS NOT ENOUGH

It is not enough for everyone to 'have their own voice', nor for us to 'tell our own stories'. There is a rhetoric of such expressiveness that has been current in the field of English teaching for some years. It is a wonderfully rich and varied vein that we must tap and celebrate, but if such a line is played too exclusively it can lead right into the powerbrokers' hands. At national levels, some things are allowed and some are not. It is important to look at the wider context when considering what can and cannot be argued. Democracies in which power is wielded by the few on behalf of the many, but in which that power is abused to impose upon the many forms of English which are neither enlightened nor ultimately usable and practical in that they don't take children's oracy and literacy needs into account – these democracies don't deserve the name of 'democracy'. Such governments and societies are quite pleased if individuals and groups of individuals are content to 'tell their own stories', because however powerful story is as a mode, it does not threaten or challenge the stories that the hegemonic powers tell. It is allowing people small spaces in which to operate, while denying them access to larger public space.

Take Reagan, for example. William F. Lewis (1987) argued that Reagan's preferred mode of discourse was narrative rather than argument. When asked a direct question about, say, the Irangate affair, Reagan would not answer directly but would tell a story about his childhood or about how wonderful America was. This web of stories built up a mythical representation of America and of the president's role as figurehead of the country: a story that people wanted to believe and that could not be dented by reality or argument. A story is a story – change any element in it and you change the story. It is also inviolate, unless a more powerful story comes along to supplant it.

The ideologies that support a narrative line in the learning and teaching of writing are set out in Martin (1985), a book we looked at in an earlier chapter. Martin suggests that these ideologies make us see children as individuals, as spontaneous learners, as cognitively immature, as creative, innocent, egocentric, imaginative, ignorant of the world and irresponsible (pp. 54–6). Martin pits contrary theories against each of these ideologies, arguing for example that children appear irresponsible mainly because adults tend to assume responsibility for them all the time. The comment from the students in Oldham reinforces the sense that students in school would indeed *like* to take on more responsibility, a preference based on the real audiences for their writing and talk during the projects undertaken. Although I agree with many of positions taken by Martin on this question, I can't accept all the solutions offered for remedying the situation. His argument goes like this: pupils in school (especially young children) are disenfranchised from power because it is assumed that they are as described above and incapable of exhortatory or analytical exposition. The over-dependence on narrative forms of expression is a result of this limiting of discursive range. The remedy is to teach the grammatical structures of 'factual' writing so that children's voices are given expression in this respect. If 'discriminatory' practices such as sexism and capitalism are to be 'erased', and the latent ideology underlying them to be challenged,

> then children need to be taught the writing of power as early as possible. The sooner they control factual writing of different kinds, the sooner they will be able to understand and challenge the world in which we live. And they need to be taught to write; only a few of them can learn it on their own.

> (Martin, 1985, p. 61)

Perhaps a better way to bring about more involvement in democratic processes and an engagement with expositional and argumentative writing would be to create situations in which exposition and argument were required; some of these situations may require narrative modes and forms of expression as well as argumentative.

What is needed as well as narrative is argument: argument between individuals that will accept or resolve difference; argument to arrive at a consensus; argument to clarify, expose, unload as well as argument for expressive purposes. This might mean forming groups to argue a case, and it certainly means that governments who claim to be standard-bearers of democracy, not only in their own country but to the rest of the world, must reach decisions by fair and open argument, at local, regional and national levels. Schools are microcosms of that larger society, and the classrooms in which we teach are even smaller versions of society at large. That is why the encouragement of argument in the classroom, not only in English but in other subjects as well, is something we should celebrate and shape to the positive. It is essential to thinking as well as to social harmony, and it is one small way in which our classrooms, and the lives of our students that are partly shaped there, can contribute to a healthy, active and real democracy in our own countries, and in the wider world that surrounds them.

ARGUMENT AND THE IMAGINATION

I have been assuming that argument has as much access to the imagination as does narrative. The generally held assumption, however, does not see argument as drawing on the imagination. I now want to draw out the links between argument and the imagination in order to enliven argument and to press for a new alignment in thinking about discourse in education.

It is generally held that narrative and lyrical expression are the most likely to use the imagination. Stories, novels, poems and plays inhabit a world, or create possible worlds that are delimited by the imagination. The 'worlds' of *Middlemarch* or *The Joy Luck Club* are not the 'real world', though they stand in critical relation to it. (At the same time, we have to accept that the 'real world' is only one of a possible number of worlds and that not only is it subject to constant change, but how it is perceived may differ from person to person, culture to culture.) Few people ask 'Why does fiction take narrative form?' or 'Why does the imagination seem to express itself most commonly in narrative or lyrical form?' These are questions about rhetoric.

Fiction − made-up stories, products of the imagination − takes narrative form for a number of reasons. First, in order to create a world which has no point of reference with the 'real world', the fiction has to be made from 'a mouthful of air'. To begin to delineate that world, one unit of potential narrative (in the 1970s, at the height of narratological structuralism, these were called 'narremes') has to be linked to another in a time-related (not necessarily chronological) way, so that the beginnings of a system are created. The novel, the story, even the play that takes narrative shape are self-referential in this respect. My second point is to do with the nature of framing in narrative fiction. Kress (1989) has suggested that narrative is a form whose fundamental characteristic is to produce closure, whereas argument is a form whose fundamental characteristic is to produce difference and hence openness.[5] If we accept this formulation for the moment, it suggests that the self-referential nature of narrative fiction has a purpose: to mark and guard the boundaries of the fiction. The very act of framing in this way highlights what is inside the frame, and thus makes it more 'imaginative'. To put it another way, the framing of an experience is seen as an act of the imagination. What is inside the frame is no longer completely subject to the laws and vagaries of the 'real world'. Thirdly, much narrative fiction is an answer to the question, 'What would happen if...?' To answer that question, the writer has to pursue a line of thinking, and as possibilities open up before her, she has to choose a route. At any moment in the fiction, the direction could change completely. There is nothing to stop it.

The second major question was, 'why does the imagination often take narrative or lyrical form?' The answer to this is much simpler. It has been *assumed* in the last two hundred years or so that the imagination must express itself in these forms. What we have witnessed is the appropriation of the imagination by these forms, so that we find it hard to dissociate the imagination from them. Imagination has been associated with the 'other', with expression, and with difference and alternatives.

Apart from the point about closure (which I will discuss below), there is nothing in narrative's claims for the imagination that cannot also be claimed for argument. Let us take the claims in turn. First, the need for coherence. This is as true for argument as for narrative. One points needs to be related to another and indeed to all the others in an argument in the same way as in narrative (see the Vygotsky/Applebee model of development in story and essay-writing in Chapter 2). Secondly, the framing of discourses. Arguments are socially framed rather than textually framed. This means that they take place in public (on the whole) and the emphasis is not so much on the cohesion of the text as on the action that takes place between two (or more) participants; they are more obviously dialogic. But arguments are still framed, and the act of framing changes the nature of what is inside the frame. The exchanges within the frame are bound by generic laws, and the relationship between the inside and outside of the frame takes on the character of other large-scale polarities, suggesting, for example, that reason operates inside the frame, and feeling and the imagination outside it. This is a rather sterile convention, however, because most arguments are resolved with the help of the imagination and with cooperation between feeling and reason. This brings me to my third point about argument and the imagination: just as narrative fiction asks 'What if...?' and then takes the consequences to the nth degree (thus maintaining a certain distance between the world of the fiction and the 'real world' – a long distance if the fiction is fantastic, a shorter distance if the style is 'realist'), so too argument asks 'What if...? In fact, suppositional questions are central to argument, and these imaginative questions are crucial to development in argument, and to play.

Imagine (*sic*) the following moves in an argument: 'If A was the case, would it follow that B would happen?', 'Let us suppose for a moment that...', 'If what you are saying is true, the consequences are as follows...', 'If you follow that line of argument...', 'Imagine a situation in which...' are analogies all involving the operation of the imagination. You can argue that argument is as much removed from the action of the real world as narrative fiction is. It acts as a rehearsal of issues that will be played out in action, but the verbal argument itself exists apart. Some arguments exist at a distance – for example, philosophical arguments – whereas others exist in close proximity to action.

The relationship between argument and the imagination in literary terms is explored in *The Argumentative Imagination* (1992, p. 1), in which George Myerson suggests that reading arguments can become a great experience of imagination:

> There are ... whole, poetic worlds which would not exist except through the representation of argument. Such worlds are arguable worlds, even when one of their voices has more authority than any other, even when one voice speaks much of that world's truth.

Myerson argues that it is the shift to seeing argument as dialogue – a shift engineered throughout most of the present book – that is essential to seeing arguments in narrative terms, and behind Myerson's own thinking on this issue is Bakhtin's *The Dialogic Imagination* (1981), the title of which should now be apparent as central to my argument in this section. For Myerson, the 'argumentative imagination' is the power of creating and re-creating the process of exchange between differing voices. He critiques Bakhtin, however, for failing to embrace poetry in a dialogic paradigm, and in a close look at *The Excursion, The Hind and the Panther, The Book of Job* and *The Bhagavad Gita* explicates the connection between narrative, the imagination and argument. Such explication holds on to the differences between narrative, argument and fiction for fear of straying into the 'no man's land' between them that Habermas (1987) has condemned.

ASSESSING ARGUMENT

Principles to consider

In attempting a framework for assessing written and spoken argument I have rejected one possible foundation: that afforded by Piagetian notions of development. A movement from the egocentric through 'cursory awareness of an alternative point of view', 'acknowledgement of an alternative point of view', 'appreciation of an alternative point of view', to 'accommodation of an alternative point of view' seems too heavily predicated on notions of an initial egocentricity in the junior-age child.

Preferable is a view that sees such a development as possible in adults as well as young children, in line with Donaldson (1978). In effect, Piaget's is a psycho-sociological model of development in argument. It offers a useful platform for our emerging model, but is inadequate when it comes to gauging improvement in written or spoken argument. It *is* useful in determining *where the writer stands in relation to his or her argument*, however.

Berrill (1992) suggests a thesis development scale running from 'no thesis' through 'loose focus', 'emerging thesis', 'restricted thesis', 'elaborated thesis' to 'hypothesizing thesis'. I find this useful as far as thesis development goes, but am more concerned to define a scale that can apply to argumentative writing that does not necessarily aim to present a thesis. Nevertheless, Berrill's proposal (see also Berrill, 1990) has the advantage of keying in closely to the Vygotsky/Applebee formulation (see pp. 34−6 of the present book).

A useful and unexpected source for a model for assessing progress in argument is the A Level Cambridge History Project. In its assessment scheme, a narrative or one-sided argument scores low (equivalent to an E grade at A level), a two-sided argument scores the equivalent of a C, and a two-sided argument in which the student is able to present his or her own opinion scores A. At this high level, it also seems possible for narrative to be reintegrated into the writing without suffering a penalty. This is because the narrative is transformed and serves an enlightened argument; the expression of opinion at this level might well be in the form of a narrative of events.

Even against these models for the development of argument, the National Curriculum formulations − in English, at least − look inadequate.

In the interim report of *Improving the Quality of Argument 7−16* (Andrews and Costello, 1992, pp. 56−9) we put forward a provisional model for gauging development in argument. This took the form of ten stages, from pre-verbal physical arguments (like fights) at one end of the spectrum, to an understanding of the process of argumentation in relation to context and different disciplines at the other end. We were aware at the time of the limitations of such a model. Subsequent experience in working with teachers and observing children arguing has led us to revise our original model and to incorporate further dimensions.

What elements or components might a model of assessment in argument include? A question that has to be asked regards fitness for purpose: what is the assessment for? With this question in mind, three components might be identified. First, a profile that can be used for formative purposes and for providing evidence of a pupil's strengths and weaknesses in argument. Secondly, a diagram that reveals the connection between concept development, narrative development and argumentative development (already discussed in Chapter 3). Thirdly, a description of stages of development that might form the basis of summative assessment of argumentative competence. Each of these elements has a different function.

Any contemporary assessment model looking for evidence of improvement in written and spoken argument must include the following:

- some notion that the length of an argumentative utterance is important; in other words, a criterion for assessing the ability to *sustain* an argument;
- sensitivity to other points of view: whether these are rejected by the arguer or incorporated within his or her argument does not affect the basic ability to appreciate another point of view. It is here that Berrill's account of the Piagetian notion of development is useful, though we should not see progress in argument as necessarily moving towards 'accommodation'. In some case, a writer might want to demolish the other point of view or use it (as in the Aristotelian 'refutation') to strengthen his or her position;
- an understanding of the diction of argument, i.e. terms like 'however',

'nevertheless', 'but' and 'despite the fact that' (see Reid's work with junior school children, described on pp. 93–4). These terms are surface manifestations of structural relationships in argument. We could compose a more complete list of these, but must distinguish in the assessment of progress in argument whether these terms are fully understood and applied accordingly, or whether they are merely being used on the surface. In other words, do they reflect thought structures or are they merely linguistic?

- an awareness of rhetorical possibility. What rhetorical strategies does the writer use to convey his or her message, or to frame his or her argument?
- an appreciation of propriety and strategy in arguing. When is it appropriate to argue, and what are the best methods for doing so?

An argument could fulfil all of the above criteria and yet still be 'illogical'. Logical coherence is therefore but one element in the formation of a good argument.

A possible model

Requests for such a profile came from within the 5 to 16 argument project from teachers involved in the research. The work of one of these teachers – John Adamson – provides the basis for the beginnings of the present model.

Many of the skills of argument apply to both writing and speaking, so the first part of the profile applies to both. I have fused John's original categories of 'processes of argument' and 'nature/form of argument' in an attempt to see this profile as a formative document concerned with processes and skills rather than with final products.

Formative: processes of argument

The pupil is able to:

1 express a point clearly
2 take a point of view, express an opinion
3 make a personal value statement
4 express a preference

5 give an example
6 give several examples
7 give appropriate examples

8 make a comparison
9 draw a contrast
10 use an analogy

11 use supposition
12 use persuasive language
13 give a reason
14 give a variety of reasons
15 give appropriate reasons

16 quote evidence

17 weigh up evidence
18 refer to own experience to support arguments
19 appeal to authority (of various kinds)

20 stick to the point, be relevant
21 show a degree of logic in the development of the argument

22 repeat an argument in another form

23 take into account others' points of view

Specific to oral argument

24 listen and respond to others' points of view
25 sum up the progress of a discussion or argument
26 speak at length, linking several points together
27 avoid diversion
28 speak with authority, and without hectoring or aggression

Specific to written argument

29 vary the structure of written argument
30 write in various forms (e.g. letter, dialogue, essay)
31 use appropriate connectives (e.g. although, nevertheless, on the other hand)
32 introduce and conclude well (if necessary)
33 write in a lively, readable way
34 be sensitive to the purpose of the argument, and to the audience

As well as a formative profile of argumentative development — a profile that simply describes what children can do in terms of argument — there needs to be a way of gauging progress on a more summative basis. For this purpose I have chosen a ten-point scale that is more detailed than that offered by the National Curriculum, where it has already been observed that argument gets short shrift and for which descriptors do not appear at every level.

Summative: the products

  I There are two pre-verbal stages of argument. One is purely physical and is evidenced in struggles or fights to make a point, defend a position or assert a right. This kind of 'argument' can be evidenced not only in explicitly combative situations, but also in negotiations over territory, possession and other kinds of behaviour in society from babyhood to adulthood.

 II The second stage of pre-verbal argument moves beyond the purely physical in that it is conveyed by voice, but does not attain the verbal level. It consists of utterances like crying and other proto-verbal ways of communicating. This is not necessarily a 'birth to adulthood' developmental model, so these kinds of behaviour may manifest themselves at any period in life.

III A child/student will be able to assert an opinion, but be able to go little further (e.g. 'I want...', 'I like...' or 'I think...'). Much television and perhaps also some 'discussion' in small or class groups can be at this level.

IV   A student will be able to assert an opinion and give a single reason to support this opinion. The quality of this reason will not be at issue at this level, simply the ability to supply a reason (e.g. 'I think hunting is wrong because it's bad for foxes and other wildlife').

V   A student will be able to assert an opinion or proposition which he or she can support with a number of reasons, or with some other kind of 'proof'. This is a step on from IV in that the student is able to support a proposition in a number of different ways − not in the same argument necessarily, but showing more of a repertoire than the simple equation 'I think ... because...'

VI   A student will be able to take on board opposing arguments and incorporate them into his or her own position; this is equivalent to the classical 'refutation' (*refutatio*) in which the opponent's argument or point is raised in order to demolish it, thereby strengthening the case for the protagonist. This might be done quite simply by saying, for instance, 'I don't think that the view that suggests A, B and C can be taken seriously...' or 'Some people say...'

VII   A student will be able to sustain an argumentative position at length, in speech or in writing. In dialogue or group discussion or debate, this will mean listening to others' arguments and reinforcing one's own position accordingly; in a speech or in written argument (which are, on the whole, more univocal) this will mean sustaining an argument by any of a number of different strategies (e.g. a variety of different kinds of 'proof', use of refutation, multiple propositions, use of logical consistency, etc.).

VIII   A student wil be able to consider both sides of an argument, weighing up the pros and cons of each side, judging the quality of reasons provided to support those cases. The nature of argument has moved to a kind of meta-level at this stage: it is more a question of weighing up arguments, and the role is more like that of a judge making a summary than of a barrister making a case. This is a different stage from...

IX   ... in which the student is not only able to weigh up two or more sides to an argument, but is able to make a judgement and find his or her own position in the light of such deliberation. This may be the position described by history teachers as seeing both sides of the question while at the same time establishing one's own position on the question in the light of the evidence. Narrative might re-enter at this stage as a way of representing a reinterpretation of the 'facts'.

X   At this stage, the student is aware that however carefully such a position had been established, it could still act as the thesis for an antithesis and future synthesis. In other words, no argument can be final; instead it serves as the basis for future arguments. At this stage we have not only an understanding of the nature of committed argument (characterized as meta-argument at stage VI), but an understanding of the whole process of argumentation and its relationship to the advancement of thought and knowledge.

Initial commentary upon the model

First, it has to be said that this is not intended as a developmental model, i.e. as if we all started at level I and progressed to level X in a natural developmental progression. Although pre-verbal argument (such as fights, wars) appears at level I, a situation can be imagined in which all attempts at verbal resolutions to differences had failed and in which fighting/war was necessary. The model could be said, however, to be one which incorporated increasingly sophisticated stages of *verbal* argument.

It follows from the first caveat that it is possible that a student will exhibit two or more stages of performance at any one time. It may be that a student shows fitful acquaintance with level VII while most of his or her discourse is at levels V and VI. In that case, VII represents a zone of proximal development for that student: the area in which teaching can be focused (though not exclusively).

This is intended as a working model. It does not correspond to National Curriculum levels, nor does it assume that progress will be steady from levels I to X. It is a provisional descriptive model, and will no doubt be further refined.

The model clearly assumes that a disinterested awareness of the operations of argumentation is the most 'advanced' level, and that the ability to maintain two or more sides of an argument at the same time and mediate between them is more 'developed' than being able to argue one side of an argument well (in order to make something happen/change things in the world). This very formulation is itself arguable.

Furthermore, the model attempts to embrace both speech and writing. Is this possible? Are there distinctly different ways in which we might gauge improvement in spoken argument as opposed to written argument?

Further problems with assessing argument

Argument implies collaboration as well as conflict, and it certainly usually involves more than one voice. How is such a mode to be assessed? Haworth (1992) points out a tension between the Programmes of Study and the statements of attainment in the 1990 National Curriculum for English in this respect.[6] The Programmes of Study – the syllabus, in effect – assume a collaborative model of learning. This model is currently assumed to be 'best practice', and in the mid-1990s, as I write, is still the best model for learning in the classroom. It is a model in which talk is seen as instrumental in the business of learning, in which the dynamic of the classroom is seen as central to learning, in which learning is the aim rather than teaching, and in which collaboration rather than competition is the keynote of what happens – both socially in the classroom and inside the student's head. This dynamic is close to what I have been outlining in this book about argument: it is social, interactive, collaborative as well as adversarial (competitive) and designed to bring about action through talk.

Haworth notes (p. 41) that the collaborative principle is well established, not only in English but in all the main subjects in the National Curriculum, but:

> when translated into the statements of attainment the language is more determinedly individualistic: pupils are required to 'give an account'; 'advocate a point of view'; 'use transactional language'; and participation is measured by 'performance' or 'presentation'. The interactive principle goes underground when assessment becomes the issue.

Collaboration does not translate well into the assessment context because the statements of attainment do not recognize the interactive nature of talk. Instead, they see 'product' as individually produced, thus emphasizing the performance dimension of talk at the expense of the compositional, interactive side. Furthermore, the National Curriculum makes a less than useful distinction between 'social' talk, which it sees as merely oiling the wheels of discourse in the classroom, and 'transactional' talk which gets things done. The hiving off of 'transactional' talk from its social context makes it more easily assessable, but at the same time cauterizes its source. There seems to be no understanding of the aesthetic potential of talk, nor of the importance of listening, nor of the contribution to the understanding of the function of talk in the social context of classrooms afforded by Barnes *et al.* (1990), Vygotsky (1986), Britton (1987) and others.

There are further ways in which the identification of the complexity of collaborative talk are relevant to the place of argument in the spoken and written curriculum. Haworth posited four styles of talk for her study of collaborative learning: *experiential*, in which pupils contribute ideas, anecdotes and stories from their own experience (see Phillips, 1985); *reciprocal*, in which pupils place their own contributions alongside those of others (see Halligan, 1988); *hypothetical* (see Barnes, 1976; Edwards and Mercer, 1987) as in the 'What if...?' mode discussed earlier in this chapter, in which pupils are able to see contributions to a discussion as propositions or hypotheses which might be tested against criteria; and *reflexive* (see Barnes and Todd, 1977; Bruner, 1985, Chang and Wells, 1988) in which pupils become conscious of the cognitive strategies at their disposal. We have already seen all four styles in operation in the transcription of the 6- to 7-year-olds discussing the pros and cons of playtimes, quoted in Chapter 4. What is distinctive about Haworth's contribution to the debate is that she has arrayed the four styles in a model of collaborative learning that links closely with the model proposed in the key pedagogical text cited earlier, *Small Group Learning in the Classroom* (Cook *et al.*, 1989), and also provides a rationale for the relationship between the four styles, helping teachers and pupils to see how collaborative learning can be developed and what its value is.

We have in Haworth's emergent model a fusion of what is best in current practice in collaborative talk: a recognition of the centrality of Vygotsky to the formulation of such a model; a range of styles of talk, linked closely together; a recognition of the reciprocity of individual and group in learning; and important questions asked about the suitability of current models of assessment for doing justice to the complexity of talk in such classrooms.

It is clear that what I have been arguing has much in common with Haworth's model. The informing of written argument by spoken principles; the dialogic and multi-voiced nature of argument, according with classrooms in which talk is valued and practised in its full range; the emphasis on process as well as product – these common elements suggest common difficulties. This is why, in my suggested model of the assessment of argument, I have opted for formative as well as summative descriptions of what pupils can do in this respect; and also why the summative scale of competence in argument is still inadequate – largely because it assumes that the highest degree of competence in argument is (a) individual and (b) a balancing of the various views on a particular case.

We thus face a dilemma in conventional forms of assessment, and this is highlighted when it comes to assessing argumentative competence. Assessment to date has been predicated on the assessment of individual performance and yet we know that performance in argument and in talk generally is the result of the processes that have gone on in the shaping of that argument. Are we to accept the limitations of assessment, accepting that we cannot truly gauge the extent of the whole iceberg by simply measuring the tip, or are we to look for more sensitive forms of assessment that look at the base of the iceberg as well?

I think it essential that we look at the whole iceberg. We know that schools teach to the test and that if we delimit what is learnt to what is tested we end up with an impoverished model of learning. We also know that coursework has enabled the production and presentation of a wider range of discourse types, both in speech and writing, than was the case in a primarily exam-based form of assessment. One-off examination papers in argument are bound to focus on decontextualized skills which may or may not transfer to other situations. I argued earlier in this chapter that such a framing of argument is inappropriate because argument depends on contexts and is subject to contingency. The same applies to narrative and other modes of writing. Examinations in writing may be neater and easier to administer, but they fail the basic principle of any form of assssment: fitness for purpose.

Take the recently formulated examinations in the Meno Thinking Skills Service (1993) provided by the University of Cambridge Local Examinations Syndicate.[7] This service, intended for use by institutions of higher education, by employers and by organizations concerned with professional training and vocational education, aims to teach six transferable skills. At the centre of the model is 'Communication' (understanding of material, relevant selection and re-presentation of material) surrounded by the 'lower skills', 'Understanding Argument' (recognizing arguments, identifying conclusions, identifying reasons), 'Literacy' (reading, writing and discrimination) and 'Numerical and Spatial Operations'. The 'higher skills' are identified as 'Critical Thinking' (assessing argument, critical evaluation and further argumentation) and 'Problem Solving' (selective encoding, selective comparison and selective combination) leading towards 'Academic and Professional Effectiveness'.

However radical or opportunistic this model and programme is as a means to improve thinking skills in practice (though one would want to critique its hierarchical notion of 'lower' and 'higher' skills) its forms of assessment are conservative. There are basically three forms of assessment: multiple-choice questions, 'objective' questions and essays to be written in 1−1.5 hours. The view of argument that informs the scheme is an impoverished one. It is defined as 'a piece of ordinary language in which **reasons** are put forward as grounds for a **conclusion**'. Argument is distilled as syllogism: 'Jill promised she would attend the meeting or send a substitute. We know she can't attend the meeting. So we are expecting a substitute.' Sometimes one of these elements is suppressed (an 'enthymeme' or rhetorical form of syllogism based on probability) and an assumption is made in order for the conclusion to follow. Assumptions are therefore identified as the third major feature of arguments.

Compare this definition with the one put forward in the first chapter of this book which attempts to take into account the rhetorical dimension of argument. The Meno definition is based in Aristotelian logic; mine is based on everyday discourse and on argumentative discourse in educational settings. The two are connected, but not in the way that the Meno scheme suggests, in hierarchical relation. Rather, I see argument as embodying thinking skills in social contexts, following Billig (1987) and Rogoff (1990), and being developed in those contexts rather than in isolation. If such skills are learnt in context and operate in context in the 'real world', then they must be assessed in context. The closest we can come to such contexts in educational settings is in coursework, in which students and teachers alike are able to take contingencies into account, develop interactive and dialogic forms of communication, and thereby vary the parameters of the communicative act.

There is another respect in which the Meno approach, based as it is on the syllogistic tradition, is not entirely suited to the *methods* needed in order to teach argument. 'Universal' or distilled forms of argumentation are not as helpful as guides on how to situate content and deploy/subvert conventions; abstraction needs to be tempered with the concrete. We need to know more than which structures to use; we need to know how to vary structure according to purpose. An insight into how sources are used in argument proves the point. The conventional advice is that students use sources to support their own position; these sources act as one form of evidence in the proof of the statement or proposition. But reflection on one's own practice in writing argument – for example the composition of this very book – and on the writing of students at advanced school/college levels and at university will soon lead to the recognition that sources (authorities, critics, etc.) can also be used to establish a position. Writers in academic contexts often establish their own position in relation to that of others in the field. They may wish to stand in opposition to a particular point of view, at an oblique angle to it, at a large distance from it or accept some of its tenets but not others; they may wish to concur with it and use it as the basis for further argumentation. To come back to the dance metaphor: the writing of argument is sometimes like finding your place on the dance floor in relation to other dancers, and moving from A to B in relation to those other dancers. The final configuration is a different one from the one in which you started.

Writing argument thus involves an orchestration of voices as well as the assertion of a particular voice. If the writing is close to dialogic principles, those voices will be near the surface and obvious. If the writing has embodied dialogic principles but transformed them into a relatively monologic voice, the voices will be submerged. But argument can hardly take place in a vacuum, or in the *individuum* of the single voice; in this, argument is at the opposite end of the spectrum from the lyrical. Kaufer and Geisler (1991) offer a model for writing argument that they describe as having a 'main path' and a 'faulty path' (thus drawing on the journey metaphor with which I began this chapter). The notion of the 'main path' coincides with the ordered set of assertions, points or claims advanced by the author; it has a strong narrative or at least sequential drive to it, and writers of argument conventionally end on this path. On the other hand, 'faulty paths' are presented by writers 'as claims that readers need to understand if only to avoid' (p. 114). When the main path gets hard to follow or to define, reference to faulty paths helps to keep writer and reader on the track, even if the method is 'negative'. This notion of using the negative to accentuate the positive – the role of the critic or of the critical intelligence – links the composition of argument as described here to the Ricoeurian notion of argument being 'suspicious'.

Although Kaufer and Geisler justify their use of the term 'faulty' to describe the divergent paths in the composition of argument, pointing out that 'faulty' does not mean logically fallacious (p. 115), it seems to me that the term is awkward as far as use in educational contexts is concerned. Students determined to avoid 'faults' in their writing may well not take these 'faulty paths', even if these paths might have offered them a useful perspective on the argument they were trying to establish. The notion of such paths is, however, useful. They might be better termed 'points of reference'.[8]

RECOMMENDATIONS

Such a long exposition and discussion of the field of argument in education may seem, at times, to have strayed from the 'main path' of this book, which has been to reflect upon the teaching and learning of argument from nursery to university. In the closing pages I want to draw out some of the implications of what has been said and to make some further practical suggestions for the development of written and spoken argument. I make these initial recommendations in the knowledge that all is not well in the state of argument in education and that changes in the way it is perceived and taught are necessary. At the same time, I hope I have indicated that many initiatives have been taken in this field over the last fifteen years. What I offer here builds upon those intiatives and contributes to the furtherance of developments in the field. I will set out the recommendations under a number of headings; these also serve as a summary of the thinking evidenced in the book.

Argument begins early

The assumption that argument is not possible until the early teens was perhaps the biggest obstacle to the development of argument in education in the earlier years. Now that alternatives to the Piagetian model are well established, it is possible to link argument to cognitive, emotional and linguistic development from an early age. Not only is it becoming clear that argument starts as soon as children communicate (even in the pre-verbal phases), but it is also becoming evident that as a communicative principle – linked closely, as it is, with the development of dialogue – argumentation plays as important a part as narrative. With increased understanding about pre-writing and the role of dialogue writing in the development of children, the place of spoken and written argument seems set to move to a position alongside narrative and commentary in the early linguistic development of the child.

Not only the expression of opinion[9] will be developed by an increased emphasis on argument in these years, but a sense of what it means to argue well. There is no reason why children in the infant and junior years should not be introduced to sources of argument and to simple methods of research and the weighing of evidence. More access to books, magazines, television programmes and material in other media that incorporate argumentative texts will help in the development of these skills.

Dialogic writing

We saw earlier in the book how it was possible to set up a dialogue in writing between a ladybird and a group of nursery-age children. The in-role dimension of this writing engagement was crucial in motivating children to take up pens, pencils and felt-tips and compose letters to the ladybird. What the in-role approach allowed was a dialogue based on an equal footing; the asking and answering of questions in writing; and, most importantly, the exchange of letters between teacher and children. I am in no doubt that this method, whether in role or person to person (out of role), can be very effective in taking children into the 'zone of proximal development' in a natural and engaging way, not only at nursery level but at all levels of eduction. We also saw an example of an exchange of letters in role between a teacher and a Year 9 pupil.

This kind of writing – perhaps because it offers an immediate audience and the promise of response, perhaps because of its proximity to thinking processes, perhaps because of its closeness to speech exchanges – is an exciting addition to the repertoire of written forms at any age.

The essay is dead. Long live the essay

The essay as a form for use in school and university contexts has come in for criticism in the course of this book, for a number of reasons. It has been seen to have fossilized as a form; to be imposed upon students as the only way of expressing what they know about a subject. It confuses exposition with argument, suggests a rigid way of approaching expression on a topic (the 'for-and-against' model),[10] and limits the personal dimension by insisting on formalities of impersonality. Its very broad definition is itself a problem: it has become the default genre for writing in the humanities, a ritualized form with little connection to expression or thought. It has lost its association with experimentation and discursiveness. It is used as the principal extended written form for assessment.

At the same time explorations of the historical roots of the essay in Renaissance discourse, and a widening of the repertoire of discourse forms that stand alongside or contribute to the development of the essay, have revitalized the essay form. This has happened because (1) we can now see the essay in clearer light, freed from the shackles of its use in educational contexts, as a form in which personal expression can entertain ideas; (2) there has been an increase in interest in 'non-fictional forms' particularly in North America; and (3) the wider range of discursive forms like the review and dialogue-writing have a closer connection to personal expression, to talk and to thought processes, and they bring that energy to the essay form.

Links with critical thinking

Our research at Hull has suggested that students often take an 'unthinking' approach to a written assignment in that they do not spend enough time on the intermediate stage of composing that is called 'planning'. This sounds a long-winded way of expressing a dissatisfaction with planning, but the point is that thought and planning are not synonymous. Many of the plans we have seen in the course of our work are ritualized and superficial: they are either too sketchy or too much like what the subsequent piece of writing is going to become. They are not, on the whole, places where thoughts can be tried out, shaped and reshaped. Techniques such as brainstorming, the placing of ideas in hierarchies or other patterns suggestive of categorizing and then compositional sequence are rare.

The recommendation, therefore, is that methods of planning be reviewed and expanded – particularly as regards the location of sources for argument, the arrangement of elements of the argument on the page, and the *re*arrangement of such elements. Kaufer and Geisler's suggestion that we should think of sources not as 'evidence' to prove a point, but as reference points against which we might define the course of our arguments, links closely to the concern with renewed and liberating approaches to the structure and composition of written argument.[11]

Argument as a mode of communication

I have tried to argue the case for seeing argument not as a genre but as a *mode* of communication alongside narrative, description and dialogue (and possibly other categories too). As a mode, it operates at a level between those of functions and genres (or text-types), embracing a large range of speech acts and acting as a generating station for composition. In educational contexts, this is a useful level to define because it mediates between function and form and affords considerable flexibility in the way a communication may be made.

A caveat with regard to this formulation is that these categories are not watertight. On the contrary, the blends and mixes between the modes are part of the liveliness of language. Freeing argument from its traditional place in opposition to narrative or as merely an abstraction from narrative allows argument to be seen as an expressive mode as well as the principal mode for communication in the rational paradigm. The psychological importance of argument has been underestimated because of the conventional associations.

On the nature and function of evidence

This book has tried to argue two major points with regard to the question of evidence. The first is that there are various types of evidence and in the school and university context we need to look at these types carefully in order to weigh up how students find, arrange and deploy them. Simply sending students to libraries to find evidence is not enough: there are skills involved in searching for, selecting and using evidence.

The second is that the Aristotelian model of 'statement and proof' may not be the one that informs most writing. Indeed, when it comes to the processes of composing argument, the notion of sources in reference to which the arguer moves is probably closer to the truth. Accepting such a view leads us to see argument differently from the conventional view of operation at an abstract plane supported by evidence at the concrete plane and of argument as adversarial. Instead, we can see that argument can also be conceived of 'horizontally' as having much in common with narrative; and as a journey, dance and construction as well as a battle.

The importance of listening

It follows from the previous paragraphs that if our conception of argument is to move beyond that of the adversarial 'for-and-against' model in which the aim of the argument is to defeat the other side, then we should put more emphasis on listening to the views of others and building upon them. In particular, the metaphors of dance and construction help us to see argument as collaborative and often (ultimately) consensual.

If difference is to be explored and defined (and part of the function of argument is to do just that) it can be carried out within a frame of consideration and mutual agreement (as in 'Let's agree to differ'). Indeed, the very function of argument is to provide an arena within which disputes may take place without the need for a breakdown in communication or a *real* division. When the point is reached at which verbal argument is no longer possible, the result is either separation or war (or both). Argument has an important function in keeping people talking about an issue in an effort to resolve it peacefully.

It will be obvious that from such a perspective, listening to others' points of view in order to build on them or counter them fairly is a crucial element in argumentation. The function of listening is often to clarify ('Are you saying that...?').

Argument in the curriculum

Argument is under-represented in the curriculum, especially in language arts/English programmes. Curriculum planners need to take account of this problem and to find ways in which argument can be introduced to children and students, even at the earliest stages of schooling. I do not believe that the interests of children and students are best served by decontextualized thinking skills courses or textbooks which teach argument skills. Argument is best learnt in specific contexts and through forms which take pupils beyond the confines of the classroom into communities of learning – the school, the local community, the country, the world – in which argument has a real role to play.

In such communities – and classrooms can become such communities too – writing becomes less of a ritualized monologic act and more of a dialogic act in which responses are expected. The responses received in turn inform further utterances. This socialization of school writing creates a communication pattern which is internalized by pupils/students as a way of thinking: ideas that are tried out in collaboration become internalized as thought. Differences are considered and writing becomes not only an act that is intent on improving itself, but a way of understanding other people and their views.

Curriculum planning to enhance argumentation – and, indeed, other modes of composition – might take the form of setting up situations in which such communication would ensue, as well as thinking in terms of linguistic forms (Australian genre theory inspired curricula) or themes and topics (British conventional practice in the 1980s and early 1990s). I stress *as well as* rather than *instead of* as I believe curriculum planning needs to be multi-layered, working at different language levels. One thing is clear: the production of language in classrooms can no longer be seen in terms of churning out inert *product*.

Assessment

The preceding comments on the curriculum have implications for assessment. If language is to be seen no longer in terms of a product that can be assessed but as a means to ends, as part of an ongoing dialogue, how can it be assessed? This is the most difficult question to answer, and one which we are only beginning to come to terms with. A first principle must be that the examination format, just as it is unsuitable for the assessment of speech competence, is equally unsuitable for the assessment of written argument.

Such a position is heresy, because ironically it is the essay – the bastion of argumentation in schools and universities' humanities courses – that has provided the keystone of assessment forms in examinations, and that pre-eminence has had an impact on curricula. Moving away from the examination format has a double effect: it allows for a different process approach to writing and at the same time it opens up a wider range of forms of writing to the student. Far from being obliterated by this move, the essay survives and re-emerges as a more clearly seen, more specific and more useful form, standing alongside other forms such as the review, the story, the letter, the written dialogue and the symposium as means for the expression of knowledge.

NOTES

1 Take the television reviews of the *Observer*'s John Naughton, for example. In a review of Kiri Te Kanawa's 'birthday concert', in which she sang from *The Sound of Music* (Naughton, 1994) he began with two coruscating paragraphs on Reagan: 'The 1983 G7 Economic Summit was hosted by the United States at Williamsburg. On the afternoon before it opened, James Baker, then White House Chief of Staff, delivered a briefing book to the President, one Ronald Reagan. The following morning, Baker called at the President's residence to find the file opened where he had left it. Uncharacteristically, he asked his boss why he hadn't done his homework. "Well, Jim," said Hopalong calmly, "*The Sound of Music* was on last night." I cite this merely as a corroboration of Naughton's First Law of Mental Deterioration which states that an enthusiasm for *The Sound of Music* is invariably a prelude to senility...' The *function* of such criticism is ultimately to uphold the quality of presidents, divas and television programmes, as well as to amuse.

2 I am not claiming that the metaphors discussed here are exclusive to argument, nor that they are the only metaphors used to denote argument. In Chapter 1 I referred to the metaphor cluster around geometrical terminology: notions of angles, lines, points and measurement. This is a fruitful cluster to consider, and has close links with metaphors of dance.

3 I am grateful to Martin Brooks and Sally Mitchell for some of the perceptions in the second half of this section.

4 That these arenas 'in which classical rhetoric was practised were open only to free male citizens' is one of the ironies of Athenian democracy (Matsen *et al.*, 1990, p. vii).

5 To return to Kress's point about the fundamental difference between narrative and argument: it may be generally true to say that narrative tends to produce closure and argument to produce openness and difference. This is to focus on their textual characteristics. But it is possible to have narratives that produce openness and difference if they operate or are deployed in a context which does not share the same cultural values as the narrative; equally, it is possible to have arguments that produce closure if the power relations between the participants are such that true dialogue is not possible.

6 Maybin concludes her 1991 article on children's informal talk and the construction of meaning as follows: 'The plural and provisional nature of meaning and the complex interplay between contexts in children's talk makes it a rich source for learning. To investigate this further, we need a model of language which acknowledges the collaborative production of dialogue, and the centrality of context to its meaning. The model of language which is currently influential in educational policy and practice is strongly focused on ideas about individual speakers and their purposes and capabilities. It is this model which has propagated the idea of certain children being "impoverished" in their use of language. I would suggest however that it is the model itself which is impoverished, in its inability to address the richness and complexity of dialogues between children' (p. 48).

7 Meno, a character in a dialogue by Plato, prompts Socrates to expound his theory of

knowledge as recollection of what is already known before birth. Socrates uses Meno's slave to prove his theory, leading the slave through a series of questions to the solution of a geometrical problem. The historical Meno was a Thessalian general whose treacherous conduct is related by Xenophon.

8 One advantage of the 'faulty path' definition, however, is that it helps in the characterization of ironic argument. The satiric essay, like Swift's *A Modest Proposal*, 'establishes a single faulty path and carefully masquerades it as a main path' (Kaufer and Geisler, 1991, p. 117).

9 See Mitchell (1993e) which gives an account of a research visit to a high school in Denmark undertaken in November 1993 for the purposes of identifying methods in the teaching of argument. The general impression formed was of an education system that encouraged the development of personal views and opinions, as opposed to one which put emphasis on a more academic approach to argument ('for and against', the essay, a balancing of views). In other words the Danish approach was more advocative, more geared toward the development of self-esteem and the *expression* of opinion; a more individualistic model than the British one.

10 See Lamb (1991) for a critique of the essay from a feminist perspective.

11 See also Flower *et al.* (1994).

Coda

Q: You end the book with a series of recommendations on the learning and teaching of argument, and yet you don't specify a teaching programme that might be adopted by education systems wishing to institute a national curriculum, and wishing to provide for the teaching and learning of argument.

A: That is because I do not wish to force the development of argument into a straitjacket of 'attainment levels' linked to the age of children and young adults. Throughout this book I have tried to move away from such a constraint, preferring to look at the range of structures and activities that will help students to argue more effectively, and also looking at the situations and contexts in which such development might occur. One of the points made is that, given the right pedagogical approach, spoken and written argument can be fostered and developed at any age. I have thus hoped to provide a foundation from which curricula and syllabuses might be built.

Q: The model of language learning in which you argue for the teaching and learning of argument is essentially one based on a contemporary conception of rhetoric, and yet you don't explore fully the connection between argument and rhetoric.

A: True. There is long and rich tradition of exploring this connection, running back as far as Isocrates. It would require another book to do justice to that question.

Q: Other lacunae are the cultural ideologies informing notions of argument and the question of gender and argumentation...

A: Yes. These are areas I would like to explore further. There is already work going on in Canada as far as the cultural framing of argument goes. What is assumed to be 'the way to argue' in one culture may well not be taken for granted in another culture, and such differences can lead to misunderstanding when the two cultures come into contact. With regard to gender and argumentation, research is in its very early stages. There were suggestions in the small-scale study in Beverley that there might be differences between the sexes in attitudes to arrangement and rearrangement in the composition of written argument; this suggestion requires further research. I think we can, however, reject the connection between dialogic and narrative forms of writing as argument on the one hand, and feminist compositional practice on the other. Changes in discoursal practice in institutions (e.g. the move away from the essay) are part of a large-scale diversification of discourse practices which is going on alongside developments in gender relations in school and university teaching courses. To associate monologic discourse with patriarchal systems is too neat, too obvious.

Q: This bring me on to another area of the learning of argument that has not been fully addressed in this book: the relationship between argument and power. Surely you cannot claim to have explored the state of argument without considering questions of power relations?

A: Agreed. I have attempted to explore argument within education institutions in relation to argument in domestic and (some) public forums. The nature of argument changes according to the power relations of those engaged in it. What are required at this point are case studies of argument in particular contexts, showing how argument is deployed in situations where the participants are of an equal or unequal standing. My aim in this book has been to provide a foundation for such studies.

Q: You seem to admit much that is yet to be done in the field, and much that is missing from this book.

A: Inevitably. In the field of argument and argumentation, more obviously than in any other field, there must always be the possibility of alternative angles, new directions, the right of reply. That is how argument operates.

Appendix 1: Methodologies of the Three Research Projects

This book draws on three research projects: in chronological order, they are my own doctoral research into narrative and argumentative structures in the writing of Year 8 students (the 'doctoral research'), undertaken between 1987 and 1992; 'Improving the Quality of Argument 5–16', a two-year action-research project which ran from 1991 to 1993 (the 'Esmée Fairbairn project'); and 'The Teaching and Learning of Argument in Sixth Forms and Higher Education' (the 'Leverhulme project') which ran from 1991 to 1994. The methodologies used in each project are described below.

THE DOCTORAL RESEARCH

The main empirical study took place in the spring and summer terms of 1989 in three comprehensive schools in Beverley, England. A sample of 150 Year 8 students, 36.5 per cent of the total number of Year 8 students in Beverley during the academic year 1988–89, was taken, consisting of 79 girls and 71 boys. The research instrument included the composition of a narrative using a set of photographs, with optional planning and a note made of the possibility of changing the order of episodes; the composition of an argument, with free choice of topic, a compulsory plan and a note made of the possibility of changing the order of the points; a questionnaire administered to all 150 students; and semi-structured interviews with three students from each of the six classes involved in the study (18 students, or a 12.5 per cent sub-sample).

The research and a fuller account of the methodology are written up in Andrews (1992a).

THE ESMÉE FAIRBAIRN PROJECT

This was an action-research project involving the University of Hull and 20 schools (10 primary, 10 secondary) in Humberside and Lincolnshire. The approach taken in the project was one of practitioner research. Within the overall aims of the project, teachers identified their own objectives, worked out their own detailed plans and devised ways of assessing improvement. In this work they were supported by the two directors of the project who in turn recorded progress. In this way it was intended to change and develop practice within schools rather than merely provide results from an applied research project.

The project ran from March 1991 to May 1993, supported by the Esmée Fairbairn Charitable Trust. Two reports emerged from the project: Andrews and Costello (1992) and Andrews, Clarke and Costello (1993).

THE LEVERHULME PROJECT

This project ran from May 1991 to July 1994 at the University of Hull. Funding from the Leverhulme Trust enable the appointment of a research fellow, Sally Mitchell. The methodology employed during the project was initially one of grounded theory (see Glaser and Strauss, 1968), developing into an ethnographic and qualitative study with some quantitative input. The research was strategic, intended to generate new knowledge in argumentation in various disciplines in order to enable specific applications to be identified.

The results of the project are reported in Mitchell (1992b, 1994b) and in a forthcoming book.

Appendix 2: Questionnaire on Argument at Sixth-form Level

```
FOR OFFICIAL USE ONLY
```

Leverhulme Argument Project Questionnaire

NAME: _____

Please tick as appropriate:

I am a student at Wheeler College ☐   Chantry School ☐

I am a member of the Lower Sixth Form ☐   Upper Sixth Form ☐

I am Male ☐   I am Female ☐

When you write an essay setting out a point of view or looking at several points of view and deciding which you agree with, you are usually conducting an **argument**. You also engage in **argument** when you discuss an issue or topic with others, or when you try to explain your ideas or why you think something is right or wrong. **Argument** is more than just a row, although, of course this is part of its meaning.

We want to find out what you think about **argument**, and how relevant **argument** is in each of the different subjects you are studying.

This questionnaire is **confidential.**

Please write the names of your three main subjects **indicating whether they are A or AS level** above the columns and answer the questions by ringing a number on the scale of 1–5 where 1 is high and 5 is low.

For example if the question asks 'How important is the ability to argue in your subject?' then 1 = very important, 2 = important, 3 = moderately, 4 = hardly important, 5 = not at all important.

	Subject 1 .... A/AS	Subject 2 .... A/AS	Subject 3 .... A/AS
1. Which of these forms of argument is used in your subject? (1 = very often 5 = never)			
a) making points related to previous points	1 2 3 4 5	1 2 3 4 5	1 2 3 4 5
b) raising questions related to previous points	1 2 3 4 5	1 2 3 4 5	1 2 3 4 5
c) supplying evidence as proof	1 2 3 4 5	1 2 3 4 5	1 2 3 4 5
d) persuading someone of your point of view	1 2 3 4 5	1 2 3 4 5	1 2 3 4 5
e) seeing both sides of an issue or question	1 2 3 4 5	1 2 3 4 5	1 2 3 4 5
f) weighing up the arguments of others	1 2 3 4 5	1 2 3 4 5	1 2 3 4 5
2. How important are the following aspects to success in your subjects? (1 = very 5 = not at all)			
a) reasoning	1 2 3 4 5	1 2 3 4 5	1 2 3 4 5
b) knowledge of facts	1 2 3 4 5	1 2 3 4 5	1 2 3 4 5
c) the **way** you say things	1 2 3 4 5	1 2 3 4 5	1 2 3 4 5
d) memory	1 2 3 4 5	1 2 3 4 5	1 2 3 4 5
e) making logical connections	1 2 3 4 5	1 2 3 4 5	1 2 3 4 5
f) sensitivity	1 2 3 4 5	1 2 3 4 5	1 2 3 4 5
g) decision making	1 2 3 4 5	1 2 3 4 5	1 2 3 4 5
3. How important is participation in spoken argument to success in your subjects? (1 = very 5 = not at all)	1 2 3 4 5	1 2 3 4 5	1 2 3 4 5
4. To what extent does classroom discussion help you to write (essays or other written forms)? (1 = greatly 5 = not at all)	1 2 3 4 5	1 2 3 4 5	1 2 3 4 5
5. Spoken argument takes place on television, radio, in school and in society generally. To what extent do you think the following forms help to shape your ability in argument? (1 = greatly 5 = not at all)			
a) interviews	1 2 3 4 5	1 2 3 4 5	1 2 3 4 5
b) roundtable discussions	1 2 3 4 5	1 2 3 4 5	1 2 3 4 5
c) formal debates	1 2 3 4 5	1 2 3 4 5	1 2 3 4 5

d)	question and answer sessions	1 2 3 4 5	1 2 3 4 5	1 2 3 4 5
e)	speeches	1 2 3 4 5	1 2 3 4 5	1 2 3 4 5
f)	documentaries arguing a particular case	1 2 3 4 5	1 2 3 4 5	1 2 3 4 5
g)	the news	1 2 3 4 5	1 2 3 4 5	1 2 3 4 5

6. Which of these written forms do you actively use in
   your studies? (1 = very often 5 = never)

a)	comprehension/stimulus responses	1 2 3 4 5	1 2 3 4 5	1 2 3 4 5
b)	notes to yourself	1 2 3 4 5	1 2 3 4 5	1 2 3 4 5
c)	narratives	1 2 3 4 5	1 2 3 4 5	1 2 3 4 5
d)	summaries	1 2 3 4 5	1 2 3 4 5	1 2 3 4 5
e)	diary/log	1 2 3 4 5	1 2 3 4 5	1 2 3 4 5
f)	scientific report	1 2 3 4 5	1 2 3 4 5	1 2 3 4 5
g)	problem-solving exercises	1 2 3 4 5	1 2 3 4 5	1 2 3 4 5
h)	essays	1 2 3 4 5	1 2 3 4 5	1 2 3 4 5
i)	other, please specify _____	1 2 3 4 5	1 2 3 4 5	1 2 3 4 5

7. Do you write essays in your subject?
   (1 = very often 5 = never)   1 2 3 4 5   1 2 3 4 5   1 2 3 4 5

8. How well do the following definitions describe the essays
   you are asked to write? (1 = very 5 = not at all)

a)	the presentation of a line of reasoning	1 2 3 4 5	1 2 3 4 5	1 2 3 4 5
b)	an exploration of my personal opinion	1 2 3 4 5	1 2 3 4 5	1 2 3 4 5
c)	a way of demonstrating what I have learnt	1 2 3 4 5	1 2 3 4 5	1 2 3 4 5
d)	a discussion of more than one point of view	1 2 3 4 5	1 2 3 4 5	1 2 3 4 5
e)	a way of working out what I think	1 2 3 4 5	1 2 3 4 5	1 2 3 4 5

9. How essential are the following features to a good essay?
   (1 = very 5 = not at all)

a)	structure	1 2 3 4 5	1 2 3 4 5	1 2 3 4 5
b)	clarity of expression	1 2 3 4 5	1 2 3 4 5	1 2 3 4 5
c)	knowledge of the subject	1 2 3 4 5	1 2 3 4 5	1 2 3 4 5
d)	logical development	1 2 3 4 5	1 2 3 4 5	1 2 3 4 5
e)	data/examples/illustrative material	1 2 3 4 5	1 2 3 4 5	1 2 3 4 5
f)	strong conclusions	1 2 3 4 5	1 2 3 4 5	1 2 3 4 5
g)	originality	1 2 3 4 5	1 2 3 4 5	1 2 3 4 5

10. How happy are you with the definition of argument used
    in this questionnaire? (1 = very 5 = not at all)   1 2 3 4 5   1 2 3 4 5   1 2 3 4 5

11. Please use the remaining space to record your own ideas
    about what argument is and how and where it is used.

Thank you for completing this questionnaire!

References and Further Reading

Abbs, Peter (ed.) (1993) *Aspects of Education.* **49** (special issue on Socratic eduction). Journal of the Institute of Education, University of Hull.

Abrahamson, Priscilla A. (1993) Between a rock and a soft spot: reviewing college preparatory writing. *English Journal* **82** (6), October 1993, 14–20.

Adams, Katharine H. (1984) Forms of discourse: what their originators intended. *Teaching English in the Two-Year College* **11** (2), December.

Ahlberg, Janet and Ahlberg, Allan (1977) *Burglar Bill.* London: Heinemann.

Anderson, Chris (ed.) (1989) *Literary Nonfiction.* Carbondale: Southern Illinois University Press.

Andrews, Richard (1987) *Language(s) Across the Curriculum.* Report for Island School. Hong Kong: English Schools Foundation.

Andrews, Richard (ed.) (1989) *Narrative and Argument.* Milton Keynes: Open University Press

Andrews, Richard (ed.) (1990) *English in Education* **24** (1) (special issue on narrative and argument). Spring.

Andrews, Richard (1991a) *Poetry* (Macmillan English Modules). London: Macmillan.

Andrews, Richard (1991b) *The Problem with Poetry.* Buckingham: Open University Press.

Andrews, Richard (1992a) An exploration of structural relationships in narrative and argumentative structures in writing, with particular reference to the work of Year 8 students. Unpublished Ph.D thesis, University of Hull.

Andrews, Richard (ed.) (1992b) *Rebirth of Rhetoric: Essays in Language, Culture and Education.* London: Routledge.

Andrews, Richard (1993) Argument in schools: the value of a generic approach. *Cambridge Journal of Education* **23** (3), 277–85.

Andrews, Richard and Costello, Patrick (1992) *Improving the Quality of Argument 7–16: Interim Report.* Hull: University of Hull, School of Education, Centre for Studies in Rhetoric.

Andrews, Richard and Mitchell, Sally (forthcoming) The development of argument in English and politics in 16–18-year-old students. In *Literacy Learning: Secondary Thoughts.*

Andrews, Richard, Costello, Patrick and Mitchell, Sally (1992) Philosophers of the classroom. *The Times Educational Supplement*, 3 January, p. 6.

Andrews, Richard, Clarke, Stephen and Costello, Patrick (1993) *Improving the Quality of Argument, 5–16: Final Report.* Hull: University of Hull, School of Education, Centre for Studies in Rhetoric.

Anthony, Phyllis J. (1986) Examining children's written narratives: the relationship between writing ability and logical thinking during the period between concrete and formal operations. Unpublished D.Ed., Rutgers, State University of New Jersey.

Applebee, Arthur (1978) *The Child's Concept of Story.* Chicago: University of Chicago Press.

Aristotle (1926) *The 'Art' of Rhetoric* (trans. John Henry Freese). London: Heinemann (Loeb Classical Library).

Bain, Alexander (1866) *English Composition and Rhetoric: A Manual.* London: Longmans & Co.

Bakhtin, Mikhail (1981) *The Dialogic Imagination.* Austin: University of Texas Press.

Bakhtin, Mikhail (1986) *Speech Genres and Other Late Essays*, trans. Vern W. McGee, ed. Caryl Emerson and Michael Holquist. Austin: University of Texas Press.

Barnes, D. (1976) *From Communication to Curriculum.* London: Penguin.

Barnes, Douglas (1988) The politics of oracy. In M. Maclure, T. Phillips and A. Wilkinson (eds) *Oracy Matters.* Milton Keynes: Open University Press.

Barnes, D. and Todd, F. (1977) *Communication and Learning in Small Groups.* Cambridge: Cambridge University Press.

Barnes, D. and Barnes, D. with Clarke, S. (1984) *Versions of English.* London: Heinemann.

Barnes, D. Britton, J. and Torbe, M. (1990) *Language, the Learner and the School* 4th edn. Portsmouth NH: Boynton/Cook. First published 1969.

Barrs, Myra (1987) Mapping the world. *English in Education* **21** (1), Spring, 10ff.

Barthes, Roland (1966) *Introduction to the Structural Analysis of Narratives.* Birmingham: University of Birmingham, Centre for Contemporary Cultural Studies.

Barthes, Roland (1988) *The Semiotic Challenge.* Oxford: Basil Blackwell.

Bazerman, Charles (1988) *Shaping Written Knowledge.* Madison: University of Wisconsin Press.

Bean, Mary and Wagstaff, Paul (1991) *Practical Approaches to Writing in the Primary School.* York: Longman.

Beard, Roger (1984) *Children's Writing in the Primary School.* London: Hodder & Stoughton.

Bearison, David J. and Gass, Stephen T. (1979) Hypothetical and practical reasoning: children's persuasive appeals in different social contexts. *Child Development* **50**, September, 901–3.

Béchervaise, Neil E. (1990) *Issues and Persuasion.* South Melbourne: Thomas Nelson.

Béchervaise, Neil E. and Trethowan, Julie (1993) *Issues, Persuasion and the Press.* South Melbourne: Thomas Nelson.

Benoit, Pamela (1983) Extended arguments in children's discourse. *Journal of the American Forensic Association* **20** (2), 72–89.

Bereiter, C. and Scardamalia, M. (1987) *The Psychology of Written Composition.* Hillsdale, NJ: Lawrence Erlbaum Associates.

Berrill, Deborah (1990) What exposition has to do with argument. *English in Education* **24** (1), 77–92.

Berrill, Deborah (1991) Metaphors of literacy: argument is war – but should it be? Unpublished paper, International Convention on Language and Literacy, University of East Anglia, April.

Berrill, Deborah (1992) Issues of audience: egocentrism revisited. In Andrews (1992a).

Bettelheim, B. (1976) *The Uses of Enchantment: the Meaning and Importance of Fairy Tales.* London: Thames & Hudson.

Billig, Michael (1987) *Arguing and Thinking: a Rhetorical Approach to Social Psychology.* Cambridge: Cambridge University Press and Paris: Editions de la Maison des Sciences de l'Homme.

Brent, Doug (1992) *Reading as Rhetorical Invention: Knowledge, Persuasion and the Teaching of Research-based Writing.* Urbana, Illinois: National Council of Teachers of English.

Bridwell-Bowles, Lillian (1992) Discourse and diversity: experimental writing within the academy. *College Composition and Communication* **43** (2), October, 349–68.

Britton, J. (1970) *Language and Learning.* Harmondsworth: Penguin.

Britton, James (1987) Vygotsky's contribution to pedagogical theory. *English in Education* **21** (3), Autumn, 22–6.

Britton, J., Burgess, A., Martin, N. and McLeod, A. (1975) *The Development of Writing Abilities, (11–18).* London: Macmillan.

Brown, John and Jackson, David (1984) *Varieties of Writing.* London: Macmillan.

Brown, John, Clarke, Stephen, Medway, Peter, Stibbs, Andrew with Andrews, Richard (1990) *Developing English for TVEI.* Leeds: University of Leeds/The Training Agency.

Bruner, Jerome (1985) Vygotsky: a historical and conceptual perspective. In J.V. Wetsch (ed.) *Culture, Communication and Cognition.* Oxford: Oxford University Press.

Bruner, Jerome and Haste, Helen (1987) *Making Sense.* London: Methuen.

Burnett, Rebecca E. and Foster, Elizabeth (1993) 'The *role's* the thing': the power of persona in Shakespeare. *English Journal* **82** (6), 69–73.

Burtis, P.J. Bereiter, Carl, Scardamalia, Marlene and Tetroe, Jacqueline (1983) The development of planning in writing. In B. Kroll and G. Wells (eds) *Explorations in the Development of Writing*. New York: John Wiley.

Burwood, Stephen (1993) *Essay Writing: An Introduction*. Hull: University of Hull, Department of Philosophy.

Calcutt, David (1993) *Review of Press Self-Regulation*. London: HMSO.

Cambourne, B. and Brown, H. (1989) Learning to control different written registers. In Andrews (1989).

Campbell, G. (1776) *The Philosophy of Rhetoric*, 2 vols. London.

Case, Robbie (1985) *Intellectual Development: Birth to Adulthood*. New York: Academic Press.

Chang, G.L. and Wells, G. (1988) The literate potential of collaborative talk. In M. MacLure, *et al.* (eds) *Oracy Matters*. Milton Keynes: Open University Press.

CHP [Cambridge Advanced Level History Project] (1992) Pilot Scheme Syllabus. University of Cambridge Local Examinations Syndicate.

Cicero (1893 ed.) *De Oratore*, ed. A.S. Wilkins. Oxford: Clarendon Press.

Cicero (1954 ed.) *Ad Herennium*, trans. Harry Caplan. London: Heinemann (Loeb Classical Library).

Clark, Ruth Ann (1985) Training fourth graders in compromising and persuasive strategies. *Communication Education* **34** (4), October, 331–42.

Clarke, Stephen (1984) An area of neglect. *English in Education* **18** (2), Summer, 67–72.

Clarke, Stephen (1993) Evaluation of the project. In R. Andrews, S. Clarke and P. Costello, *Improving the Quality of Argument, 5–16*. Hull: University of Hull, School of Education, Centre for Studies in Rhetoric.

Clarke, Stephen and Sinker, John (1989) Rediscovery of the Diverse. In Andrews (1989).

Clarke, Stephen and Sinker, John (1992) *Arguments*. Cambridge: Cambridge University Press.

Cockcroft, Robert and Cockcroft, Susan M. (1992) *Persuading People*. London: Macmillan.

Cole, Tamasin and Cressey, James (1988) *Fourteen Rats and a Rat-Catcher*. London: Black.

Conniff, Caroline (1992) *Developing the Argument*. Croydon: Davidson Professional Centre.

Cook, Jonathon, Forrestal, Peter and Reid, Jo-Anne (1989) *Small Group Learning in the Classroom*. Perth, WA: Chalkface Press and London: The English and Media Centre.

Cook-Gumperz, J. and Green, Judith L. (1984) A sense of story: influences on children's storytelling ability. In D. Tannen (ed.) *Coherence in Spoken and Written Discourse*. Norwood, NJ: Ablex.

Cooper, Sheila and Patton, Rosemary (1993) *Ergo: Thinking Critically and Writing Logically*. New York: HarperCollins.

Corbett, Edward P.J. (1965) *Classical Rhetoric for the Modern Student*. New York: Oxford University Press.

Costello, P.J.M. (1988) Primary school philosophy: open to discussion? *Links* **14** (1), 11–14.

Costello, P.J.M. (1989) When reason sleeps: arguments for the introduction of philosophy into primary schools. *Irish Educational Studies* **8** (1), 146–59.

Cowie, Helen (1984) *The Development of Children's Imaginative Writing*. London: Croom Helm.

Cowie, Helen (1985) An approach to the evaluation of children's imaginative writing. Unpublished Ph.D thesis, University of London.

Cromwell, H. (1950) The relative effect on audience attitude of the first versus the second argumentative speech of a series. *Speech Monographs* **17**, 105–22.

Crowhurst, Marion (1987) Cohesion in argument and narration at three grade levels. *Research in the Teaching of English* **21** (2), May, 185–201.

D'Angelo, Frank (1975) *A Conceptual Theory of Rhetoric*. Cambridge, MA: Winthrop.

Daniels, Harry (ed.) (1993) *Charting the Agenda: Educational Activity after Vygotsky*. London: Routledge.

Dearing, Ron (1994) *The National Curriculum and its Assessment: Final Report* (The Dearing Report). London: School Curriculum and Assessment Authority.

De Bono, Edward (1991) *I Am Right, You Are Wrong*. London: Penguin.

Delia, J. G., Kline, S. L. and Burleson, B. R. (1979) The development of persuasive communication strategies. *Communication Monographs* **46** (4), November, 241–56.

DES [Department of Education and Science] (1975) *A Language for Life* (The Bullock Report). London: HMSO.

DES (1978) *Primary Education in England: A Survey by HMI Inspectors of Schools*. London: HMSO.

DES (1981) *Mathematics Counts* (The Cockcroft Report). London: HMSO.

DES (1988) *Discipline in Schools* (The Elton Report). London: HMSO.

DES (1988a) *Report of the Committee of Inquiry into the Teaching of English Language* (The Kingman Report). London: HMSO

DES (1989) *English 5 to 16* (The Cox Report). London: HMSO.

DES/Welsh Office (1987) *The National Curriculum 5–16: a Consultation Document*. Department of Education and Science/Welsh Office.

DES/Welsh Office (1990) *English in the National Curriculum No. 2*. London: HMSO.

DfE [Department for Education] and Welsh Office (1993) *English for Ages 5 to 16 (1993): Proposals of the Secretary of State for Education and the Secretary of State for Wales*. London: Department for Education and the Welsh Office.

Dixon, John (1989) If it's narrative, why do nothing but generalize? In Andrews (1989).

Dixon, John (1994a) Categories to frame an English curriculum? *English in Education* **28** (1), Spring, 3–8.

Dixon, John (1994b) Writing in response to each other. In Freedman and Medway (1994).

Dixon, John and Freedman, Aviva (1988) *Levels of Abstracting: Invitations to a Dialogue*. Ottawa: Carleton University (Carleton Papers in Applied Language Studies, Occasional Paper 1).

Dixon, John and Stratta, Leslie (1981) *Criteria for Writing in English*. Discussion Booklet 1: A Report on the 1980 CEE Cross-Moderation Exercise. Southampton: Southern Regional Examination Board.

Dixon, John and Stratta, Leslie (1982a) *Teaching and Assessing Argument*. Discussion Booklet 2: A Report on the 1981 CEE English Cross-Moderation Exercise. Southampton: Southern Regional Examination Board.

Dixon, John and Stratta, Leslie (1982b) *Recommendations for Future Examining*. Discussion Booklet 5: CEE Cross-Moderation Exercise, Southern Regional Examination Board.

Dixon, John and Stratta, Leslie (1982c) Argument: what does it mean to teachers of English? *English in Education* **16** (1), Spring, 41–54.

Dixon, John and Stratta, Leslie (1986a) Argument and the teaching of English: a critical analysis. In A. Wilkinson (ed.) *The Writing of Writing*. Milton Keynes: Open University Press.

Dixon, John and Stratta, Leslie (1986b) *Writing Narrative – and Beyond*. Sheffield: National Association for the Teaching of English.

Donaldson, Margaret (1978) *Children's Minds*. London: Fontana.

Dyke, Stuart (1991) Developing the argumentative language of young learners. Paper presented to International Convention of Language and Literacy, UEA, April.

Eagleton, Terry (1983) *Literary Theory*. Oxford: Basil Blackwell.

Edwards, D. and Mercer, N. (1987) *Common Knowledge*. London: Methuen.

Eliot, V. (ed.) (1971) *T.S. Eliot, The Waste Land: A Facsimile and Transcript of the Original Drafts Including the Annotations of Ezra Pound*. London: Faber & Faber.

Erikson, Frederick (1984) Rhetoric, anecdote and rhapsody: coherence strategies in a conversation among Black American adolescents. In D. Tannen, (ed.) (1984) *Coherence in Spoken and Written Discourse*. Norwood N.J.: Ablex.

Evans, P.D. (1992) *Some Thoughts on Assessment*. Hull: Andrew Marvell School.

Fairbairn, Gavin J. and Winch, Christopher (1991) *Reading, Writing and Reasoning: A Guide for Students*. Buckingham: Open University Press.

Farrell, J.G. (1973) *The Siege of Krishnapur*. London: Weidenfeld & Nicolson.

Fisher, R. (1990) *Teaching Children to Think*. Oxford: Basil Blackwell.

Fisher, W. (1987) *Human Communication as Narration: Towards a Philosophy of Reason, Value and Action*. Columbia: University of South Carolina Press.

Flower, L., Wallace., D.P., Norris, L. and Burnett, R.E. (1994) *Making Thinking Visible: Writing, Collaborative Planning and Classroom Inquiry.* Urbana: National Council of Teachers of English.

Fox, Carol (1989) Divine dialogues. In Andrews (1989).

Fox, Carol (1990) The genesis of argument in narrative discourse. *English in Education* 24 (1), Spring, 23–31.

Fox, Carol (1993) *At the Very Edge of the Forest: the Influence of Literature on Storytelling by Children.* London: Cassell.

Freedman, Aviva and Medway, Peter (1994) *Teaching and Learning Genre.* Portsmouth, NH: Heinemann/Boynton-Cook.

Freedman, Aviva and Pringle, Ian (1984) Why students can't write arguments. *English in Education* 18 (2) Summer, 73–84.

Freedman, Aviva and Pringle, Ian (1989) Conflicts for developing argument. In Andrews (1989).

Frowe, Ian (1989) Arguing. In Andrews (1989).

Frye, Northrop (1957) *Anatomy of Criticism.* Princeton, NJ: Princeton University Press.

Gibson, Howard and Andrews, Richard (1993) A critique of the chronological/non-chronological distinction in the National Curriculum for English. *Educational Review* 45 (3), November, 239–49.

Gillespie, Joanne S. (1993) Buddy book journals: responding to literature. *English Journal* 82 (6), October 64–8.

Glaser, B. and Strauss, A.L. (1968) *The Discovery of Grounded Theory.* London: Weidenfeld & Nicolson.

Goodman, Nelson (1981) Twisted tales; or story, study and symphony. In Mitchell (1981).

Goodwyn, Andrew (1992) English teachers and the Cox models. *English in Education* 26 (3), Autumn, 4–10.

Gorman, T.P., White, J., Brooks, G., MacLure, M. and Kispal, A. (1988) *Language Performances in Schools: Review of APU Language Monitoring 1979–1983.* London: HMSO.

Graves, Donald (1982) *Writing: Children and Teachers at Work.* Oxford: Heinemann.

Griffiths, Sian (1993) Essays under siege. *The Times Higher Educational Supplement* 30 July, 4.

Grimshaw, Jane (1990) *Argument Structure.* Cambridge MA: MIT Press.

Gross, John (ed.) (1991) *The Oxford book of Essays.* Oxford: Oxford University Press.

Gubb, Jenny (1987) Discursive writing – a small-scale observation study. in J. Gubb *et al.* (1987) *The Study of Written Composition in England and Wales.* Windsor: NFER/Nelson.

Habermas, Jürgen (1984) *The Theory of Communicative Action: Vol. 1 Reason and the Rationalization of Society,* trans. Thomas McCarthy. London: Heinemann.

Habermas, Jürgen (1987) *The Philosophical Discourse of Modernity,* trans. Frederick Lawrence. Cambridge: Polity Press in association with Basil Blackwell.

Hackman, Sue (1987) *Responding in Writing: The Use of Exploratory Writing in the Literature Classroom.* Sheffield: National Association for the Teaching of English.

Hall, Nigel (ed.) (1989) *Writing with Reason: The Emergence of Authorship in Young Children.* London: Hodder & Stoughton.

Halliday, M.A.K. and Hasan, R. (1976) *Cohesion in English.* London: Longman.

Halligan, D. (1988) Is there a task in this class? In M. MacLure, T. Phillips and A. Wilkinson (eds) *Oracy Matters.* Milton Keynes: Open University Press.

Hardy, Barbara (1977) Narrative as a primary act of mind. In M. Meek, G. Barton and A. Warlow (eds) *The Cool Web.* London: Bodley Head.

Haworth, Avril (1992) Towards a collaborative model of learning. *English in Education* 26 (3), Autumn, 40–9.

Hesse, Douglas Dean (1986) The story in the essay. Unpublished Ph.D thesis, University of Iowa at Iowa City.

Hesse, Douglas Dean (1989a) Persuading as storying: essays, narrative, rhetoric and the college writing course. In Andrews (1989).

Hesse, Douglas Dean (1989b) Stories in essays, essays as stories. In C. Anderson (ed.) *Literary Nonfiction.* Carbondale: Southern Illinois University Press.

Hesse, Douglas Dean (1992) Aristotle's poetics and rhetoric: narrative as rhetoric's fourth mode. In Andrews (1992b).

Holloway, John (1979) *Narrative and Structure: Exploratory Essays*. Cambridge: Cambridge University Press.

Hountalas, Bill and Craigen, Jim (1991) *Argumentative Discourse: Oral Argument Component*. Ontario: Durham Board of Education.

House, Jeff (1993) The first shall be last: writing the essay backwards. *English Journal* **82** (6), October, 26–8.

Hovland, Carl (ed.) (1957) *The Order of Presentation in Persuasion*. New Haven: Yale University Press.

Howatson, M.C. (ed.) (1989) *The Oxford Companion to Classical Literature*. Oxford: Oxford University Press.

Jenkins, John P. and Summers, Vivian (1982) *Approaches to Essay Writing*. Leeds: Edward Arnold.

Johnson, Barbara (1987) *A World of Difference*. Baltimore: Johns Hopkins University Press.

Johnson, Sophie (1980) *The Stuff of Argument*. West Melbourne: Thomas Nelson.

Jones, Terry (1988) *Attacks of Opinion*. London: Penguin.

Kaufer, David S. and Geisler, Cheryl (1991) A scheme for representing written argument. *Journal of Advanced Composition* **11** (Winter), 107–22.

Kazin, Alfred (1961) The essay as a modern form. In *The Open Form: Essays for Our Time*. New York: Harcourt, vii–xi.

Kinneavy, James (1971) *A Theory of Discourse*. Englewood Cliffs, NJ: Prentice-Hall.

Kinneavy, James (1983) A pluralistic synthesis of four contemporary models for teaching composition. In A. Freedman, I. Pringle and J. Yalden (eds) *Learning to Write: First Language, Second Language*. London: Longman.

Kinneavy, James, McCleary, W. and Nakadate, N. (1985) *Writing in the Liberal Arts Tradition: A Rhetoric with Readings*. New York: Harper & Row.

Klaus, Carl H. (1989) Essayists on the essay. In Anderson (1989).

Knoblauch, C.H. and Brannon, Lil (1984) *Rhetorical Traditions and the Teaching of Writing*. Upper Montclair, NJ: Boynton/Cook.

Kraft, Robert G. (1975) The death of argument. *College English* **36** (5), January, 548–51.

Kress, Gunther (1989) Texture and meaning. In Andrews (1989).

Kuhn, Deanna (1991) *The Skills of Argument*. Cambridge: Cambridge University Press.

Labov, William and Waletsky, Joshua (1967) Narrative analysis: oral versions of personal experience. In J. Helm (ed.) *Essays on the Verbal and Visual Arts*. Seattle: University of Washington Press.

Lakoff, George and Johnson, Mark (1980) *Metaphors We Live By*. Chicago: Chicago University Press.

Lalljee, B., Stickland, R., Slater, A., Bliss, J. and Munroe, V. (1991) *Developing Argument and Reasoning in the Classroom*. Oxfordshire-Buckinghamshire Oracy Project.

Lamb, Catherine E. (1991) Beyond argument in feminist composition. *College Composiiton and Communication* **42** (1), February, 11–24.

Lancaster, L. and Malcolm, A. (1992) *Developing Argument*. Shrewsbury: Shropshire Primary English Advisory Team.

Lawrence, D.H. (1948) *Sons and Lovers*. London: Penguin. First published 1913.

Leith, Dick and Myerson, George (1989) *The Power of Address: Explorations in Rhetoric*. London: Routledge.

Levine, S. (1983) The child-as-philosopher: a critique of the presuppositions of Piagetian theory and an alternative approach to children's cognitive capacities. *Thinking: The Journal of Philosophy for children* **5** (1), 1–9.

Lewis, William F. (1987) Telling America's story: narrative form and the Reagan presidency. *Quarterly Journal of Speech* **73** (August), 280–302.

Liberal Democrats (1993) *Facing up to the Future: Enduring Values in a Changing World*. London: Liberal Democrat Publications.

Light, P., Sheldon, S. and Woodhead, M. (1991) *Learning to Think*. London: Routledge.

Lightfoot, Martin and Martin, Nancy (eds) (1988) *The Word for Teaching is Learning*. Oxford: Heinemann.

Lingard, Joan (1989) *The Twelfth Day of July*. London: Penguin.

Lipman, M. (1982) Philosophy for children. *Thinking: The Journal of Philosophy for Children* **1** (3 and 4), 35–44.

Lipman, M. (1983) *Lisa*, 2nd edn. New Jersey: The First Mountain Foundation.

Lipman, M. (1985) *Harry Stottlemeier's Discovery*. New Jersey: The First Mountain Foundation.

Lipman, M. (1987) Ethical reasoning and the craft of moral practice. *Journal of Moral Education* **16** (2), 139–47.

Lipman, M. (1988) *Philosophy Goes to School*. Philadelphia: Temple University Press.

Lipman, M. (1991) *Thinking in Education*. Cambridge: Cambridge University Press.

Lipman, M. and Sharp, A.M. (1978) *Growing up with Philosophy*. Philadelphia: Temple University Press.

Lipman, M. and Sharp, A.M. (1979) Some educational presuppositions of philosophy for children. *Thinking: The Journal of Philosophy for Children* **1** (2), 47–50.

Lipman, M., Sharp, A.M. and Oscanyan, F.S. (1980) *Philosophy in the Classroom*, 2nd edn. Philadelphia: Temple University Press.

Littlefair, Alison (1991) *Reading All Types of Writing*. Buckingham: Open University Press.

Lodge, Jane (1992) *The Development, Assessment and Recording of Speaking and Listening Capability: an Interim Report on the Project at Andrew Marvell School*. Hull: Andrew Marvell School.

Lukacs, Georg (1978) On the nature and form of the essay. In *Soul and Form*, trans. Anna Benstock. Cambridge, MA: MIT Press, 1–18.

Lund, F.H. (1925) The psychology of belief: the law of primacy in persuasion. *Journal of Abnormal Social Psychology* **20**, 183–91.

MacIntyre, A. (1967) *A Short History of Ethics*. London: Routledge & Kegan Paul.

McKeough, Anne (1986) Developmental stages in the narrative compositions of school-aged children. Unpublished Ph.D thesis, University of Toronto.

Mallett, Margaret (1992) *Making Facts Matter: Reading Non-Fiction 5–11*. London: Paul Chapman.

Mallett, Margaret and Newsome, Bernard (1977) *Talking, Writing and Learning 8–13*. London: Evans/Methuen Educational for The Schools Council.

Mann, Eileen (1993) From the chalk-face: thoughts of a reflective practitioner. *Curriculum* **14** (1), 14–22.

Martens, E. (1982) Children's philosophy – or: is motivation for doing philosophy a pseudo-problem? *Thinking: The Journal of Philosophy for Children* **4** (1), 33–6.

Martin, J.R. (1985) *Factual Writing: Exploring and Challenging Social Reality*. Oxford: Oxford University Press.

Matsen, P., Rollinson, P. and Sousa, M. (1990) *Readings from Classical Rhetoric*. Carbondale: Southern Illinois University Press.

Matthews, G.B. (1980) *Philosophy and the Young Child*. Cambridge, MA: Harvard University Press.

Matthews, G.B. (1984) *Dialogues with Children*. Cambridge, MA: Harvard University Press.

Maybin, Janet (1991) Children's informal talk and the construction of meaning. *English in Education* **25** (2), Summer, 34–49.

Medway, Peter (1981) *Finding a Language*. London: Writers and Readers Co-operative.

Medway, Peter (1986) What gets written about. In A. Wilkinson (ed.) *The Writing of Writing*. Milton Keynes: Open University Press.

Meno Thinking Skills Service (1993) *The Meno Thinking Skills Service 1993–1994: An Introduction* and accompanying material. Cambridge: University of Cambridge Local Examinations Syndicate.

Miller, Carolyn (1984) Genre as social action. *Quarterly Journal of Speech* **70**, 151–67.

Milner, Joseph O. (1983) Writing stages: a developmental hierarchy. Paper presented at the 73rd Annual Meeting of the National Council of Teachers of English. Denver, Colorado, 18–23 November.

Mitchell, Sally (1992a) *Questions and Schooling* (Centre for Studies in Rhetoric Occasional Paper 1). Hull: University of Hull, Centre for Studies in Rhetoric.

Mitchell, Sally (1992b) *The Teaching and Learning of Argument in Sixth Forms and Higher Education: Interim Report*. Hull: University of Hull, Centre for Studies in Rhetoric.

Mitchell, Sally (1993a) The aesthetic and the academic: are they at odds in English Literature at A level? *English in Education* **27** (1), Spring, 19–28.

Mitchell, Sally (1993b) The teaching and learning of argument in sixth forms and higher education – a Leverhulme Trust project: report on the second year, 1992/93. Hull: University of Hull, unpublished report.

Mitchell, Sally (1993c) Not so much a 'trying out' as a 'handing in' – a challenge to the academic essay. *CueNews* (Newsletter of the Council for University English) **5** (2), Summer, 7–8.

Mitchell, Sally (1993d) Argument: ways of thinking about it and doing it. Hull: University of Hull, School of Education, unpublished paper.

Mitchell, Sally (1993e) *Report on a Visit to Paderup High School (Gymnasium), Randers, Denmark, 22–26 November 1993, for the Purpose of Observing Practice in English Classes, Particularly with Regard to Argument.* Hull: University of Hull, School of Education.

Mitchell, Sally (1994a) Room for argument in English literature at A level and beyond? Paper given at Etude (English Teachers in University Departments of Education) conference, University of Leeds, 8 January and published in *Etude Newsletter* **2** February.

Mitchell, Sally (1994b) *The Teaching and Learning of Argument in Sixth Forms and Higher Education: Final Report.* Hull: University of Hull, School of Education, Centre for Studies in Rhetoric.

Mitchell, Sally (1994c) A level and beyond: a case study. *English in Education* **28** (2), Summer.

Mitchell, Sally and Andrews, Richard (1994) Learning to operate in advanced level history. In A. Freedman and P. Medway (eds) *Teaching and Learning Genre.* Portsmouth, NH: Heinemann/Boynton-Cook.

Mitchell, Sally and Kenyon, Dave (1993) *Proposed Study Skills Induction Module on Notemaking, Argument Construction and Essay Writing.* Hull: University of Hull, School of Education and University of Humberside, Department of Communication Studies.

Mitchell, Sally and Reid, Mark (unpublished) 'on becoming a judicious amateur: the negotiation of genre in the A level English language essay'.

Mitchell, W.J.T. (ed.) (1981) *On Narrative.* Chicago: Chicago University Press.

Moffett, James (1968) *Teaching the Universe of Discourse.* Boston: Houghton Mifflin.

Moffett, James (1981) *Active Voice*, Vol. 1. Upper Montclair, NJ: Boynton/Cook.

Moffett, James (1986) *Active Voice*, Vol. 4. Upper Montclair, NJ: Boynton/Cook.

Moger, Ros and Richmond, John (eds) (1985) *Say What You Think: Argument and Discussion Writing by London School Students.* London: English and Media Centre.

Monk, Jenny (n.d.) *The Language of Argument in the Writing of Young Children.* (Linc paper 3). Slough: NFER/Centre for Research in Language and Communication.

Morris, Charles (1946) *Language, Signs and Behavior.* New York: Prentice-Hall.

Myerson, George (1992) *The Argumentative Imagination: Wordsworth, Dryden, Religious Dialogues.* Manchester: Manchester University Press.

Nadeau, Ray (1952) The *Progymnasmata* of Aphthonius. *Speech Monographs* **19**, 264–85.

Nash, Walter (1980) *Designs in Prose.* Harlow: Longman.

National Curriculum Council (1990) *Education for Citizenship* (Curriculum Guidance 8). York: NCC.

Naughton, Bill (1969) *Late Night on Watling Street.* Harlow: Longman.

Naughton, John (1994) Potent cheap music. *The Observer* 20 March, Review Section, 28.

New York City Board of Education (1981) *Global History 1: A Curriculum Guide. Second Semester Theme III.* New York: Board of Education.

Norman, Kate (1992) *Thinking Voices: The Work of the National Oracy Project.* London: Hodder & Stoughton.

Phillips, Terry (1985) Beyond lip-service: discourse development after the age of nine. In G. Wells and J. Nicholls, *Language and Learning: An Interactional Perspective.* Brighton: Falmer Press.

Phillips, Terry (1992) Why? The neglected question in planning for small group discussion. In Norman (1992).

Piaget, J. (1926) *The Language and Thought of the Child*, trans. M. Gabian. London: Routledge & Kegan Paul.

Piaget, J. (1929) *The Child's Conception of the World.* London: Kegan Paul, Trench, Trübner.

Piaget, J. (1977) Logique génetique et sociologie. In *Études Sociologiques*. Paris: Libraire Droc.

Pirie, David B. (1990) *How to Write Critical Essays*. London: Routledge.

Plath, Sylvia (1978) *Letters Home*, ed. Aurelia Schober Plath. London: Faber & Faber.

Plath, Sylvia (1981) *Collected Poems*, ed. Ted Hughes. London: Faber & Faber.

Plato (1974) *The Republic*, 2nd edn (revised). Harmondsworth: Penguin.

Ponsot, Marie and Deen, Rosemary (1982) *Beat Not the Poor Desk*. Montclair, NJ: Boynton/Cook.

Pratchett, Terry (1987) *Equal Rites*. London: Corgi.

Pringle, I. and Freedman, A. (1979) *The Carleton Writing Project, Part 1*. Ottawa: Carleton University.

Pringle, I. and Freedman, A. (1980) *The Carleton Writing Project, Part 2*. Ottawa: Carleton University.

Pringle, I. and Freedman, A. (1985) *A Comparative Study of Writing Abilities in Two Modes at the Grade 5, 8 and 12 Levels*. Toronto: Ministry of Education.

Protherough, Robert (1985) *Developing Response to Fiction*. Milton Keynes: Open University Press.

Protherough, Robert (1993) *Journal Index: English in Education from Spring 1964 to Autumn 1992*. Sheffield: National Association for the Teaching of English.

Reid, Gloria (1991) Agree with me: the argumentative function in children's writing. Unpublished M.Ed dissertation, University of Hull.

Reid, Ian (ed.) (1987) *The Place of Genre in Learning: Current Debates*. Geelong, Victoria: Deakin University Press.

Reid, Ian (1992) *Narrative Exchanges*. London: Routledge.

Reissman, Rose C. (1993) Give the gift of family literacy – student-designed gift books. *English Journal* **82** (6), October, 74–6.

Richardson, Paul (1991) Language as personal resource and as social construct. *Educational Review* **43** (2), 171–90.

Ricoeur, Paul (1970) *Freud and Philosophy: An Essay on Interpretation*. New Haven: Yale University Press.

Rogoff, Barbara (1990) *Apprenticeship in Thinking*. New York: Oxford University Press.

Rosen, Harold (1984) *Stories and Meanings*. Sheffield: National Association for the Teaching of English.

Sargeant, Jan (1993) Gender and power: the meta-ethics of teaching argument in schools. *Curriculum* **14** (1), 6–13.

SCAA (1994) *English in the National Curriculum: Draft Proposals*. London: School Curriculum and Assessment Authority.

SCAA (forthcoming) *The National Curriculum Orders*. London: School Curriculum and Assessment Authority.

Scholes, Robert (1985) *Textual Power: Literary Theory and the Teaching of English*. New Haven: Yale University Press.

Selfe, Cynthia L. (1989). Redefining literacy: the multilingual grammars of computers. In Gail E. Hawisher and Cynthia L. Selfe. *Critical Perspectives on Computers and Composition Instruction*. New York: Teachers College Press.

Sheeran, Yanina and Barnes, Douglas (1991) *School Writing*. Buckingham: Open University Press.

Sheridan, Daniel (1993) Writing in response to literature: the paper of many parts. *English Journal* **82** (6), October, 58–63.

Sitler, Helen Collins (1993) What college writing instructors expect and why you should join the resistance. *English Journal* **82** (6), October, 21–5.

Snyder, Ilana (1991) Writing with word processors: the computer's impact on writing quality, composing processes and classroom interactions. In D. Philips (ed.) *Best of Set: Writing Research Information for Teachers*. New Zealand: Australian Council for Educational Research and New Zealand Council for Education Research.

Snyder, Ilana (1992) Writing with wordprocessors: an effective way to develop students' argumentative writing skills. *English in Education* **26** (2), Summer, 35–45.

Snyder, Ilana (1993) The impact of computers on students' writing: a comparative study of the effects of pens and word processors on writing context, process and product. *Australian Journal of Education* 37 (1), 5–25.

Stein, Nancy L. and Glenn, Christine G. (1979) An analysis of story comprehension in elementary school children. In Roy O. Freedle (ed.) *New Directions in Discourse Processing*. Norwood, NJ: Ablex.

Steinbeck, John (1965) *Of Mice and Men*. London: Heinemann.

Stratta, Leslie and Dixon, John (1992) Genre theory: what does it offer to the teaching of English in the National Curriculum? *English in Education* 26 (2), Summer, 16–27.

Styles, Morag (ed.) (1989) *Collaboration and Writing*. Milton Keynes: Open University Press.

Summerfield, Geoffrey (1968) *Voices 1–3*. Harmondsworth: Penguin.

Swales, John (1990) *Genre Analysis*. Cambridge: Cambridge University Press.

Swift, Graham (1983) *Waterland*. London: Heinemann.

Tan, Amy *The Joy Luck Club*. London: Heinemann.

Taylor, Laurie (1993) Column in *The Times Higher Educational Supplement*, 6 August, 28.

Van Dijk, Teun A. (1981) Episodes as units of discourse analysis. In D. Tannen (ed.) *Analyzing Discourse: Text and Talk* (Georgetown University Round Table on Languages and Linguistics 1981). Washington, DC: Georgetown University Press.

Vickers, Brian (1988) *In Defence of Rhetoric*. Oxford: The Clarendon Press.

Vlad, Roman (1960) *Stravinsky*. Oxford: Oxford University Press.

Vygotsky, L. (1978) *Mind in Society*. Cambridge, MA: Harvard University Press.

Vygotsky, L. (1986) *Language and Thought*. Cambridge, MA: Harvard University Press.

Vygotsky, L. (1991) Genesis of the higher mental functions. In P. Light, S. Sheldon and M. Woodhead (eds) *Learning to Think*. London: Routledge.

Walton, Douglas (1989) *Informal Logic: A Handbook for Critical Argumentation*. Cambridge: Cambridge University Press.

Warnock, M. (1988) *A Common Policy for Education*. Oxford: Oxford University Press.

Whalley, M.J. (1987) Unexamined lives: the case for philosophy in schools. *British Journal of Educational Studies* 35 (3), 260–80.

White, Janet (1987) Children's argumentative writing: a reappraisal of difficulties. Paper presented at AILA congress, 16–20 August, Sydney, Australia.

Wilkinson, Andrew (1986a) Argument as a primary act of mind. *Educational Review* 38 (2), 127–38.

Wilkinson, Andrew (1986b) *The Writing of Writing*. Milton Keynes: Open University Press.

Wilkinson, Andrew (1989) Our first great conversationalists. *English in Education* 23 (2), Summer, 12–24.

Wilkinson, Andrew (1990) Argument as a primary act of mind. *English in Education* 24 (1), Spring, 10–22.

Wilkinson, A., Barnsley, G., Hanna, P. and Swan, M. (1980) *Assessing Language Development*. Oxford: Oxford University Press.

Winterowd, W. Ross (1975) *Contemporary Rhetoric: A Conceptual Background with Readings*. New York: Harcourt, Brace Jovanovich.

Womack, Peter (1993) What are essays for? *English in Education* 27 (2), Summer, 42–59.

Name Index

Adams, K.H.   70
Adamson, J.   160
Ahlberg, J. and A.   90
Aphthonius   30
Applebee, A.   24, 36, 157
Aristotle   12, 30, 56, 75, 76, 102

Bacon, F.   11, 31, 60
Bain, A.   72
Bakhtin, M.M.   22, 57, 60, 76, 158
Barnes, D.   23, 54, 127, 146, 164
Barrs, M.   125
Barthes, R.   39, 75
Bazerman, C.   23
Bean, M.   48
Béchervaise, N.   30
Benoit, P.   47
Bereiter, C.   46
Berrill, D.   20, 146, 148, 159
Billig, M.   62, 150, 165
de Bono, E.   45
Brannon, L.   31
Britton, J.   5, 65, 67, 68, 76, 77, 164
Brown, H.   33, 51
Brown, J.   93, 147, 154
Bruner, J.   19, 66
Burnett, D. 84–5
Burtis, P.   46

Burwood, S.   45, 140–41

Cambourne, B.   3, 33, 51
Carter, R.   100
Case, R.   19
Chaucer, G.   4, 9
Cicero   12, 30, 50, 56
Clark, R.   47, 98
Clarke, S.   4, 23, 24, 100, 112, 117, 150, 175
Cook, J.   164
Corbett, E.   50, 57
Costello, P.   45, 159, 175
Cowie, H.   24
Craigen, J.   57–8
Cromwell, H.   76
Crowhurst, M.   49

Dalton, D.   90
D'Angelo, F.   70–71, 76, 77, 139
Dearing, R.   23
Delia, J.   47
Dixon, J.   22, 27, 37–9, 63–4, 68
Donaldson, M.   19, 68, 158
Dyke, S.   48

Subject Index